The Big Picture Man

REFLECTIONS ON THE LIFE AND THOUGHT OF ALFRED LOUIS KROEBER

Scott L. Rolston

iUniverse, Inc.

New York   Bloomington

Contents

Preface ix

SCRAPS FROM THE GREAT FEAST OF LANGUAGES 1

Part One
Kroeber's Stake in American Historical Linguistics 3

Overview: 3
Some Components of Kroeber's Scientific Worldview: 12
The Matter of Evolution: 17
The Boasian Context of Kroeber's Linguistics: 23
Kroeber's Professional Emphasis upon Linguistics: 26
Kroeber as an Ethnographer: 32
The Indo-European Option and Franz Boas' Reaction: 34
Turf Alarms: 49

Part Two
A Narrative of Cooperation and Friction 55

Overview: 55
A Cooperative Phase: 58
The Orthography Committee: 61
Kroeber's Genetic Epiphany and the
    Unspoken Question of Priority: 64
The Long Retreat: 87
Kroeber Exits: 100
An Aborted Return: 110
The 1934 Linguistic Train Wreck: 122

KROEBER, WHITE, AND BIDNEY:
TRIANGULATING THE SUPERORGANIC 133

List of Abbreviations 157

References Cited 158

Notes 173

Index 201

Preface

These two essays, the first long and the second quite short, reflect the life and thought of Alfred Louis Kroeber, one of the founders of American Anthropology as it came to be practiced in the twentieth century. Kroeber died in 1960, fifty years ago, and I intend this as a timely tribute to a man of high intellect who wrestled with some great questions in ways that are instructive of how our times and contexts limit our vision. A third, forthcoming essay will deal with what I regard as the most striking instance of this in Kroeber's life, having to do with the concept of emergent complex systems.

In this little book I intend to focus chiefly on how he dealt with evolution, one of the foundational scientific questions of his day, with considerable impact upon his chosen fields of study; chiefly ethnology and linguistics. In the matter of cultural evolution we may see Kroeber missing opportunities to lead the field at least twice – though with good reasons for failing to seize the moment (that very phrase enjoins the kind of precipitous, almost instinctive leap of faith that ran entirely against the grain of his character). Not least of those reasons was that the whole question was inimical to the ethos and political commitment of his tribe, a rather diverse group of anthropologists called with imperfect coherence "Boasians", that is, people educated by Franz Boas or his students along with those who aligned themselves with his vision of the ethnological endeavor in the Americas. For as long as Boas lived that vision was resolutely opposed to the notion of cultural evolution as it existed in the early twentieth century, a prejudice that died hard even afterward, when newer and different evolutionary models were suggested.

Therefore, although focused on different periods of Kroeber's life, these two essays have in common the central importance of evolution in the development of culture theory in the United States. Given the general attitude among Boasian ethnologists toward evolutionary thinking about cultural phenomena, the first crucial question; whether and to what degree cultural evolution, if the idea was to be suffered at all, might support analogies with biological evolution, was highly contentious. Those with use for such analogies have often been hard put to make them cogently, over and above the obvious and generally agreed point that the mechanisms must be different. That much was already appreciated in the nineteenth century, as the different evolutionary visions of Herbert Spencer and Charles Darwin were limned and compared, and the persistent recurrence of "Lamarckian" notions of biological heredity befogged the issue. Thereafter the foundations for any such analogy had to be laid in the shifting theoretical sands of evolutionary theory in the life sciences throughout the first half of the twentieth century, when the "New Synthesis" that eventually offered a common field for discussion was just being hammered out. Perhaps inevitably, the term "evolutionism" was often meant to encompass, or at least was accused of encompassing, rather too much. Certainly that was a Boasian sentiment, and because it was later maintained by some that they were simply prejudiced against one of the greatest of modern conceptual advances, it is important to tease out exactly what it was about the term "evolution" to which Boasians objected. When we do so, we begin to see their point.

Early on the point of contention was all that unpacked from the broad designator "nineteenth century cultural evolutionism", or "classical evolutionism", a spectrum of ideas which, on the whole, descended more from the work of Herbert Spencer than from that of Charles Darwin or Alfred Russell Wallace.[1] Thereafter evolutionary thinking in American anthropology was notable mostly for its absence from professional discourse during what I am calling the "Boasian Ascendancy", especially the inter-war years of the twentieth century, when Boas and his students and allies pushed through a genuine paradigmatic shift in American ethnology. During that time they came to dominate many, and eventually most, academic programs (though not some other important anthropological venues, notably several great museums). Still later, in the late nineteen-forties and nineteen-fifties, new kinds of evolutionary thinking were rather rapidly introduced into American anthropology, where they found a more congenial home among archaeologists than among ethnographers and culture theorists. But evolution had been an underlying assumption of historical linguistics right along, with Boas' program for "rescue" study of dying Native American languages, the parent program that spawned the work of the main characters in this study, being a notable exception.

Kroeber's long career spanned the whole period outlined above, from the turn of the twentieth century to 1960. He was an ambivalent evolutionist throughout that time, advancing upon the topic only to retreat from it, coming to clear positions of support for it only twice, once very early and once again very late in his life. Yet evolution was the most fundamental underlying issue affecting the way he envisioned the rise and career of cultures and civilizations, and it was the *sotto voce* assumption that underlay the great efforts made by him and several colleagues, chiefly Edward Sapir, as they approached a revision of the map of New World languages. To this enterprise, to which Sapir's contribution was more noteworthy than Kroeber's, they brought the evolutionary model and some of the methods already used with great success in establishing the Old World Indo-European family of languages. However, they operated with that evolutionary model of languages without making it explicit.

Kroeber worked with a genuine intellectual dilemma, illustrated by his lifelong devotion to grand sweeping theoretical questions of the kind that the Boasian school generally discouraged. Yet his professional context and his personal loyalties lay almost entirely within Boasian anthropology. In and of itself this bred a measure of circumspection, but his intellectual dilemma was exacerbated by a more political one. It is sometimes difficult to recapture the attractive and repulsive forces generated by Franz Boas' imposing personality, as well as the problems attendant upon the Germanic character of his closest disciples in an era of two world wars. I do not want to over-emphasize these but I want to give them their due, for the Boasian "particularistic" approaches in anthropology and linguistics dominated the academic field for a time, but within a broader world political context in which Germanic affiliations were sometimes disparaged and suspect. Boas was a scion of the Germanic scholarly and scientific tradition, and was not shy about touting its superiority or his devotion the German vision of science. Kroeber, though a native-born American, was the product of a Germanic education within the German diaspora in the United States, and he felt the dilemmas of German cultural identity in the early twentieth century keenly.

Boasian Historical Particularism achieved a foothold in American academic anthropology during the first decade of the twentieth century, and by about 1919 it may be said to have triumphed. Boas' leadership certainly met with further challenges, first of all the political fallout from his pro-German leanings during the Great War and his opposition to the entry of the United States into that conflict. Thereafter he faced an internal professional challenge in the linguistic field from Edward Sapir, his former student. Before the end of World War Two Boas was dead, and by the early post-war era the expanding nature of academic anthropology, as well as the circumstances of the world crisis, had already diffused and refracted Boasian tenets through a wide array of research methodologies and toward a wider range of research goals. Boas' own version of Historical Particularism was not so much displaced as it was transcended. But while he lived Kroeber was tender of his feelings, was reluctant to oppose the older man openly, and suffered on the occasions when he did so.

I should make several disclaimers. First and foremost, these essays are my accounts of Kroeber, and are not intended to be adequate accounts of either Boas or Sapir. They figure large here, but their lives and works have been depicted by others whose qualifications to do so exceed mine. I came to be interested in Kroeber through research into his work as an archaeologist, and I am currently most interested in his prescient thinking about Culture and Civilization (both singular and capitalized here because that is how he approached both concepts, as entities). In short, he conceived of them in terms that after his death the late twentieth century came to call "emergent, self organizing systems" and "levels of organization" in the natural world, though he never acquired the tools and vocabulary needed to articulate this adequately.

Similarly, although the longer of these two essays has the linguistics programs of Boas and several of his students as its backdrop, and while I hope it is adequate as a sketch of what they did together, it is not intended as an authoritative or comprehensive account of the linguistic enterprise in the New World. That story would require a linguist as well as an historian to author it, and would fill volumes. Instead I will relate my view of the relationships among Kroeber, Boas, and Sapir, particularly the personal dynamic that I found to have operated between the latter two, first outlined by Victor Golla (1984). To accomplish this I will describe some aspects of the linguistic programs they founded and furthered, and will give an account of how some salient aspects of their work played out, but a comprehensive treatment of even those smaller bodies of work must await further efforts by scholars chiefly interested in Sapir. There were important factors at work, such as the concept of "drift" in Sapir's model of language evolution, and his and Kroeber's views regarding culture and language areas, which, if fully described and integrated into this piece, would double its length without helping to elucidate their personal relationship. Such topics receive gestures and acknowledgement here, not in-depth treatment.

I should also address several possible objections at the outset. The first is that I have put too much emphasis on evolutionary thinking as the underlying issue during the development of historical linguistics. The second is that the professional dynamic among Boas, Kroeber and Sapir outweighed the personal factors. The third is that several others were active in this work and my account slights them. To the first objection, already voiced by one person who read the draft, I simply assert that in my view evolution was indeed the most encompassing, pervasive, and causal intellectual question in the life and human sciences after the mid-nineteenth century. As such it was the tectonic issue that underlay most of the tensions within American anthropology and linguistics in the early twentieth century. Evolution was also the main component assumption of the Old World linguistic enterprise that produced the successful Indo-European model of languages grouped into families, and in unspoken fashion it came to be the semi-visible Cheshire elephant in the corner of the Boasian ethnological program, especially his linguistic work.

However, I also wish to qualify the picture of Boas as an opponent of evolutionism, a picture that is generally accurate but lacking in nuance. I am certainly not in agreement with the extreme indictment of Boas as an anti-evolutionist put forward by Leslie White (1945, 1963), after Boas' death. For all his sometimes fiery character Boas is a sympathetic character even in this, an issue in which I believe he was wrong. His opposition to evolutionism should be seen in its context. He saw a need to defeat the version of "classical" evolutionary thinking which had descended to the anthropology of his day from the thought of Spencer, Tylor, and Morgan, among others. While it may have been the case that those ideas were already on the wane when Boas emerged vindicated from a politically motivated brush with his critics in the American Anthropological Association during 1919-20 (many of those same critics not coincidentally being representatives of what classical evolutionism had become in the early twentieth century), this would not have been clear to him at the time. Indeed it was one of the greatest tragedies of a tragic century that racism as an internationally acceptable political platform still had at least one more violent generation to run. For a time Boas did seek to exclude the dangerous and convoluted topic of evolution from academic anthropology, which he and his students came to dominate in the United States. Such a prohibition could not have worked for long, and would not have worked even for as long as it did had not wider political events lent it some additional support by showing how some of the social and racial assumptions that ran parallel to it as it came out of the nineteenth century could have terrible consequences in the world. But even as the dust settled and the smoke cleared in 1945, moves were already afoot to reconsider what the term "evolution" might mean in social and cultural contexts, once shorn of the racial components and assumptions that had tainted it.

To the second point I can only suggest that reading the correspondence between Kroeber and Sapir with an eye to tonality (if such a metaphorical construction is permissible) supports my view of their relationship. Kroeber began his career with a primary focus on languages and with every intention of excelling in that field, but gradually withdrew as Sapir's manifest superiority became clearer and more pervasive. There is nothing in the letters Kroeber wrote to Sapir before about 1915 to suggest that he intended his research and fieldwork time to be divided evenly with any other anthropological enterprise. Even ethnography, of which he did a great deal and Sapir did some, took a back seat to language work from time to time during those years. The dynamic that worked between them is interesting, a small and personal story, but that dynamic also provided the force that shifted Kroeber farther a-field.

Nonetheless, this is not intended as a gossipy account of how two strong intellects dealt with large questions and with each other. Its importance lies in its evolutionary context (which I gave above as point one). In the end, Kroeber yielded the field and went elsewhere to work, and when he did so his interests changed as well. Of course, Sapir's interests, too, changed over the years. The pre-1920 Sapir was focused on language classification, and if his later interest in culture and personality detracted from the time he could spend on pure linguistics, we should also remember that Bloomfield (1926, 1933) had already begun to revolutionize the field by the late 1920s, and in an inward direction rather than the more embracing cross-disciplinary approach Sapir had gradually come to favor. Finally, by the mid-nineteen thirties, when his most serious clash with Boas occurred, Sapir was already sick with the heart condition that would eventually kill him. [2]

To the third criticism I must plead guilty. A clutch of prominent field workers labored for years in the Boasian rescue program for American Indian languages, and while some of them are mentioned herein, none of them, not even Sapir, are given anything remotely like their due. In Sapir's case that is not simply because of time limits and space constrictions, but because his work has spawned an industry among historians. Volumes of his notes and correspondence, as well as analyses of his work are gradually appearing thanks to the work of Konrad Koerner, J.T. Irvine, Richard Handler, Regna Darnell and many others.

I wish to thank the staff of the Bancroft Library at Berkeley, the American Historical Society in Philadelphia, and the National Anthropological Archives in Washington D.C. for their help and hospitality over the several years during which I hunted and gathered in their holdings, as well as for their kind permissions to quote from what I found there. I also thank Regna Darnell for her painstaking critique of the draft of the first essay. At her suggestion I am soft-peddling the term "Boasian Ascendancy", which she does not like. I cannot expunge it entirely because it remains in my view meaningful, referring to the success experienced by Boas and his students in taking the high ground in academic anthropology during the years between the wars, particularly in cultural anthropology, encompassing general ethnology, linguistics, folklore studies and the relationship between culture and personality. Since I have not taken all of Professor Darnell's penetrating suggestions, she is not responsible for the errors that doubtless remain. I also wish to thank George Stocking for his encouragement when my research and writing entered the doldrums, and for his many attempts to improve my mind over the years when he suffered me as a student.

The second, shorter essay, entitled Kroeber, White, and Bidney: Triangulating the Superorganic, appeared previously in the *History of Anthropology Newsletter* (XXX: 2), in December, 2003.

SLR
Bangkok
June 6, 2010

Scraps from the Great Feast of Languages

Alfred Louis Kroeber's Withdrawal from American Historical Linguistics

Part One
Kroeber's Stake in American
Historical Linguistics

"I am always sorry when any language is lost, because languages are the pedigrees of nations."

Samuel Johnson

"It is difficult to decide whether translators are heroes or fools. They must surely know that the Afrikaans for Hamlet, I am thy father's ghost, sounds like Omlette, ek es de papa spook."

Beatrix Potter

"We called him Tortoise because he taught us"

Lewis Carroll

Overview:

Alfred Kroeber wants a new biography. For all he wrote and all that has been written about him he remains difficult to know, not just because he was careful not to expose himself unnecessarily, but also because after his death accounts of him beatified – even canonized him for a time. If canonized he was, he did not become the patron saint of anything, having declined two salient opportunities to take the lead in theoretical shifts in American anthropology; both of them concerned with evolution. The first was with regard to the genetic or evolutionary view of languages, an issue that forms part of the backdrop for my topic here. The second was the post-World War Two re-introduction of cultural evolutionary thinking. In recent years Kroeber's personality and professional behavior been given more critical attention (Buckley, 1996; Brightman, 2004), but in several early biographical sketches the term "Olympian" was supposed to sum him. That was too precious, though given his habits of reading in classical history and literature, and of using psychoanalytical terms rather casually, he might have seen humor in it. As a description of his preferred perspective though, it was perfect, for Kroeber was American Cultural Anthropology's big-picture man.

Lengthy treatments of Kroeber's career include his widow's affectionate farewell portrait (T. Kroeber, 1970), an ungrateful exorcism (Harris, 1968: ch.12), and two ambivalent sketches by the most temperamental and theoretically influential of his students (Steward, 1961, 1973). Additional biographical details are to be found in a range of sources (Alsberg, 1936; Beals, 1968; Hymes, 1961; Rowe, 1962; Willey, 1988, as well as several recent titles in the *History of Anthropology* series). Most of the earlier accounts had the soft polity of eulogies, but some gave valuable assessments of Kroeber's contributions to several branches of anthropology; Beals for ethnology, Hymes for linguistics, and both Rowe and Willey for general archaeology. His measure as a theorist was taken by Bidney (1953, pt. 4) and Hatch (1973). Driver's (1962) account focused on his thinking about culture areas. Carmichael (1998) described his archaeological fieldwork in Peru. Buckley (1996) examined his philosophical connection to Franz Boas and some ethical dimensions of his ethnography. Darnell (1990a and b, 1998) also examined him as Boas' fellow traveler – an important subject in view of their ambivalent relationship. Thereafter (2001) she traced his notion of the Superorganic as a divergent theoretical branch within the Boasian Ascendancy, emphasizing the many continuities with earlier anthropology.

Anyone who writes about Kroeber the man gets little help from him. On several occasions he said of himself that he was not a public person, and Steward (1973) noted that he left no lengthy account of his own career and almost no autobiographical materials. Public opinion pained him and he had little use for what he once called, in an unguarded moment, "the common ruck" of humanity. He probably would have found repulsive any suggestion that the public had claims on him. His life is well documented, if not always well interpreted, and for a man with so little regard for public opinion he took good care of his *persona*. He would not play to the public, but he played to posterity by writing letters for the record (in high contrast to Steward's mercurial and scatological epistolary style). He clearly wanted his correspondence to be fodder for historians one day, particularly his many exchanges with Edward Sapir (Hymes, 1961), and so it was (Golla, 1984).

Rather than being disputed or refuted, after his death Kroeber simply went out of fashion. During the 1970s and 80s he faded, first into bibliographic and then card catalogue immortality, and afterward there sometimes seemed to be a measure of embarrassment about his former stature, as if he had never really deserved his lofty reputation. That is a sentiment anyone who examines his work closely is unlikely to share. Harris' (1968) account of him, and perhaps Steward's (1973), helped to create that negative image. It has also become part of the stock description of Kroeber that he was viscerally given to compromise, which is true but scarcely an indictment. For a start, compromise is meant to be to be a political virtue, and anthropology has always been a peculiarly political discipline. That negative tint is sometimes enhanced in contrast with Boas, to whom compromise came harder.

Kroeber and Sapir are the main protagonists in this story but Boas was ever the third man. Few anthropologists who have held the attention of historians had small conceit of themselves, and Boas, Kroeber and Sapir were dominant characters in a small arena – confident of their worth and jealous of their positions atop a new and fast-growing field in theoretical flux. Boas' life has been amply documented and variously interpreted, so herein it serves as only another backdrop. [3] Sapir gets rather more direct attention, but only in dimensions in which he interacted with Kroeber or came into conflict with Boas. These are considerations of space, not comparative worth.

My sketch of Kroeber must range widely, but the primary field of competition and cooperation between him and Sapir was American historical linguistics – a stage from which Kroeber eventually made a somewhat disgruntled exit. Evolutionary thinking underlay the historical question of the relations among languages, while other versions of evolutionary thinking also animated those who opposed the growth of Boasian ethnology, and I believe that evolutionary issues sparked some of the triangular dynamic among the three men. However, this essay is not about linguistics *qua* linguistics, but about evolution as an impinging issue in Kroeber's professional life, about the interpersonal dynamics he and Sapir displayed, and about how those dynamics eventually resulted in Kroeber's withdrawal from the field. In professional comparison we must ultimately share Kroeber's own stated view – that he could not attain the stature in linguistics that Sapir seemed to achieve so effortlessly. What he might not have been prepared to admit was the degree to which Boas remained a powerful damping force in his life as long as the older man lived, particularly with regard to cultural evolution.

Sapir necessarily appears two-dimensional here. I can only sketch him briefly in the contexts of language and culture, and cannot pretend to give a professional account of his linguistic science. His personality emerges from his letters. [4] As Boas' stellar linguistics student, Sapir mastered the New World Powellian and Boasian language program in which he was trained at Columbia, while superimposing upon it components of an Old World, Indo-European one in which the assumption that languages evolved in a manner that left readable patterns was central. Because my purpose is to depict Kroeber rather than Sapir, I place some events that have been described before in a somewhat different light, and slight others.[5] For example, I merely gesture toward the emergence of phonemics – a large, technical and divisive topic on which Sapir is now at the mercy of posterity, with divergent, even contradictory interpretations of his sense of phonemic meaning (Silverstein, 1986: 70-82).

Eric Hobsbawm (1964: 337) wrote of historical linguistics that it was 'the first science which regarded evolution as its very core.' That seems right. Evolution was an all but inescapable underlying issue in the Boasian uses of historical linguistics, even if it was seldom the central topic of conversation among those who worked in the Boasian paradigm. Possibly more open discussion of it might have cleared the air somewhat, but this would have been difficult to achieve any time before the New Synthesis in evolutionary thought, a set of developments that belonged to the following generation. Sapir and Kroeber avoided the worst pitfalls of the evolutionary theory of their day; they recognized historical linguistic residues, not structures that placed languages in any cultural hierarchy or developmental sequence. Boas, fearing and loathing precisely such hierarchies and sequences, and seeing that they usually emerged from comparative studies, opposed this necessarily comparative procedure. For example, Anderson (1990) pointed out that Sapir's concept of typology used the core features of a language as stable indicators of relationships – what a paleontologist might have called homology. This was evolutionary, specifically paleontological thinking, but not of the kind of staged, teleological, and orthogenic evolution to which Boas most objected. As a Boasian, Sapir would have had little use for stages of ascent toward anything (such as inflection), even though his concept of "drift" in languages incorporated a measure of directionality (Sapir, 1921a: 160-65, Eggan, 1986: 3). This was historical perception rather than prescription, and he was charting descent and consanguinity, not ascent. To accomplish this he was obliged to "walk back" the effects of drift over the course of centuries, seeking deep structures that would tell about heritage. [6]

Sapir necessarily described languages almost entirely in prose rather than in formal analytical terms, something for which non-linguists may be grateful. His contributions were later overshadowed by Leonard Bloomfield (1933), who worked with a more viable shorthand analytical system (a calculus of the greatest methodological importance; witness the advances in mathematics that followed the devising of many mathematical symbols during the sixteenth century). Nonetheless, Sapir has been often and unabashedly described as a "genius", most notably by Kroeber (1922 and 1959, the latter first printed in Koerner, 1984). The criteria for that should be rigorous and not very abstract. Sapir's admirers might point to his study of the Wiyot and Yurok Languages in California (1913, 1915a), or to his account of Na Dene (1915b), or *Sound patterns in language* (1925), in which he furthered the idea that the phoneme has *emic* psychological as well as more strictly *etic* analytical reality – though all these hypotheses have had detractors, as well (Silverstein [1986] maintained that the *emic* experience of languages was ever Sapir's chief object). Darnell (1986) highlighted the decade between 1915 and 1925, which encompassed many of the events depicted herein, as a period of frenetic intellectual activity for Sapir; masterful and exhausting linguistic work punctuated by periods of depression, doubt, and therapeutic experiments in art.

Sapir's manifest gift for languages can be sampled without delving into his individual linguistic studies for it is evident in the way he used his own to explain the character of Language. The ability to synthesize many complex lines of evidence and present the synthesis through compact and persuasive reasoning is a kind of applied genius, and Sapir's facility in this makes him a joy to read. *Language* (1921a), or his contributions under the same title to the 1928 edition of the *Encyclopedia Britannica* and the 1933 edition of *Encyclopedia of the Social Sciences,* wherein his polemic points were conveyed with remarkable subtlety, showcase this remarkable ability. So does *A Bird's Eye View of American Languages North of Mexico* (1921b), in which he annunciated the broadest conception of the genetic approach with application to the New World. In admirably compact style he wrote wide-ranging implications into most paragraphs – often into single sentences. [7] The effect was deceptive simplicity. If his language was transparent, the meaning he conveyed was complex indeed. To the retrospective eye it is remarkable how skillfully he rehearsed his readers into acquiescence in the evolution of languages at a time when the word "evolution" was not often uttered among Boasians. Kroeber acknowledged this quality of Sapir's writing several times over the years as he gradually withdrew from linguistics.

In 1984, the centenary of Sapir's birth, Victor Golla published the correspondence between Kroeber and Sapir, most of it dating to the second decade of the twentieth century, when together they constituted the cutting edge of Native American linguistics. Thereafter Golla distilled from that correspondence a perceptive linguist's account of their efforts to work out the first genetic linguistic model of New World Prehistory (Golla, 1986). He noted that they had stopped collaborating before Sapir's first convincing demonstration of the genetic relations of New World languages (Sapir, 1921b) a break that was more gradual than we may suppose and deserves more attention than it has received. While Kroeber's loss of place to Sapir was implicit in Golla's edited collection, which chronicled both sides, the primary focus was necessarily on Sapir with Kroeber playing second fiddle. For the history of linguistics this was the optimal perspective, but it scanted Kroeber's motivations and career worries, and could not emphasize the role played by Boas at the apex of a triangular dynamic. Remarking that the thread of their relationship, as visible in their correspondence, was severed in 1915, Golla (1986: 31) concluded that that "...for reasons as much personal as intellectual, Kroeber drew back from the relationship with Sapir, and from [linguistic] historical work generally." I wish to examine those personal and professional reasons because the story merits re-telling from what we can reconstruct of Kroeber's perspective.

In brief, I wish to show that a decade of competitive collaboration between Kroeber and Sapir led to Kroeber's abandonment of linguistics, once he was certain that he could no longer inhabit the first rank. [8] After an initial period during which he was the senior man, and they were cooperating in applying a controversial genetic theory of languages to the New World, Sapir's radiant abilities gradually up-staged Kroeber and led him to seek a field in which he could continue to shine as brightly. Their close collaboration, already waning during 1914, effectively ended in 1915-16 when Kroeber went on a sabbatical *cum hegira*. After several more years of less energetic effort (and a continued, though less frequent correspondence with Sapir, who was also suffering from depression, and whose efforts flagged occasionally but never ceased during this long stretch of sustained effort), Kroeber abandoned linguistics almost completely as the 1920s began, making no further methodological or theoretical contributions, doing little additional fieldwork, and never hiring a linguist into his Berkeley Department. He served a term as President of the Linguistic Society of America in 1940, after Sapir had died, but his late interest in lexicostatistics had more to do with arithmetic methods for tracking cultural evolution than with languages. Throughout his life, however, he maintained the pace of his ethnological writing, though he also turned to archaeology and thereafter to some pioneering if ultimately unsatisfactory uses of statistics in culture history. His excursion into archaeology, important as it was for archaeologists, lasted only a few years. In the meantime, and again in the nineteen-thirties, several untoward events ensured that his estrangement from linguistics would be permanent.

In tracing the course of Kroeber's abandonment of linguistics I will observe some of the same events recorded by Golla, Darnell and others, but from Kroeber's side. Although the point is not crucial to my overall argument, it is reasonably clear that by 1903 Kroeber and Dixon already foresaw the strength and elegance of a genetic, evolutionary mode of linguistic explanation. They gingerly elaborated this, without making overt claims, over the course of more than a decade-and-a-half (Dixon and Kroeber 1903, 1913a and b, 1919; see also Darnell, 1990a: 110-11).[9] Though they were leery of overtly evolutionary explanatory frameworks, there could have been no other baseline hypothesis coherent and powerful enough to justify their Penutian group of language families, or to lead Kroeber (1910a) to link the Costanoan and Maiduan languages into a family. Although a few other linguists (especially J. P. Harrington, and J. R. Swanton) were also lending their hands to this lumping effort, Kroeber and Dixon were entitled to a measure of priority. Furthermore, their work helped to convince Sapir.

By 1915 Kroeber knew that he was obliged to yield the field to Sapir. Indeed, he probably knew this by the close of 1913, the year Golla (1984: 25) called the *annus mirabilis* of North American linguistics, but he still had some cards to play, particularly with regard to his work on the Penutian super-family. There was another factor, as well. For both of them the late teens of the century was an unsettled, discouraging time, following the death of Henriette Rothschild Kroeber, Alfred's first wife, and Florence Sapir's mental illness. They both considered dropping linguistics, and anthropology generally, and turning to other things – psychoanalysis for Kroeber, poetry and music for Sapir (Handler, 1986). Ever practical, Kroeber wanted another profession, while Sapir considered a field even less remunerative than anthropology. Though he dabbled in art and psychoanalysis, Sapir did not make any serious move. But Kroeber drifted more widely, never to completely return, his decaying orbit around linguistics boosted outward by a series of events that made it ever clearer that their places in the tiny firmament of American linguistics had reversed. In each important professional encounter Kroeber's *persona* was diminished and Sapir's enlarged. This role reversal began with Kroeber's *Noun Incorporation in American*

Languages (1910c), a challenge met triumphantly by Sapir (1911), in both European and American journals. He thereby upstaged Kroeber's linguistic debut before a German audience, at that point in his career the professional audience that mattered most to him, after the Boasian circle. Ironically, it was Kroeber who later prodded Sapir to write a general theoretical work on language. The result was *Language: An Introduction to the Study of Speech* (1921a), Sapir's only full-length book and the most influential work in the field before Bloomfield (1933). Although aimed at students and the intelligent lay public, and not a technical work, *Language* set the seal on Sapir's ascent and Kroeber's eclipse.

We are obliged to reconstruct much of Kroeber's side of this story, but the source materials for such a reconstruction have been trimmed. Few truly personal items remain in his papers, which were culled perhaps three times, leaving evident scars of excision. Several people had motives and opportunities to tidy the record. Steward (1973: 18) noted that Kroeber relished gossip, and his elliptically romantic correspondence with Berna Pinner during the early 1920s, some of which he conducted under a playful *nom de plume*, confirms this. It seems likely that he protected himself by being the first to winnow his own papers. Theodora Kroeber, his second wife and biographer, used his correspondence before turning it over to the Bancroft Library at Berkeley, and may have removed items she deemed too personal or sensitive for public view. The near total lack of correspondence with Steward suggests that he too may have removed letters while researching his biography (Steward's letters were occasionally of the sort that embarrass the writer on re-reading).

Despite a handful of surviving examples of Kroeber's most personal writings, on the whole what remains offers us a too-dignified picture. His two main biographers (T. Kroeber, 1970, Steward, 1971) both called him "seamless", which might be taken to mean that he had few inner feelings or outward signs of self-doubt or contradiction. However, by "seamless" his second wife probably meant "consistent and coherent", while Steward may have simply meant "impervious". His wife had the best claim to knowing his inner feelings, and as she had anthropological credentials of her own, her account is the best starting point. Other, shorter biographical pieces contain similar sentiments, variously expressed, but I cannot concur. Kroeber was coherent and polished, but not seamless. He was too sensitive to be so featureless and often too timid to be so sure. Rather he was intellectually able to encompass and subsume contradictions, and to rise above them by means of his preferred high and broad cultural historical perspective.

Some Components of Kroeber's Scientific Worldview:

Although a "Boasian" of the first rank, Kroeber did not hold with all of the tenets of Boasian anthropology as they gradually emerged. In fact, he was at odds some of them, and it is therefore striking how little strong criticism he was subjected to during his lifetime. The credit he amassed for his strong critique of William Rivers' kinship ideas (Rivers, 1907; Kroeber, 1909), framed wholly in Boasian terms, seems to have protected him throughout a subsequent decade of accumulating heresies. The salient exception to this was the negative reaction many of his colleagues (especially Robert Lowie, Edward Sapir and, at one remove, Franz Boas) displayed to his notion of "Superorganic" Culture (Kroeber 1917), which they regarded as a reification. His Superorganic Culture concept was of considerable theoretical and philosophical importance as an early instance of thinking about emergent and self-organizing levels of organization in the natural world, yet it was a concept that he seldom defended, sometimes regretted, and once even renounced in Galilean fashion (Kroeber, 1952: 22-23), but never really surrendered. In fact, much of his thought was incoherent without the Superorganic. During his middle years he usually just allowed for this meta-structural product of his youthful thinking rather than invoking it outright, but in the 1930s and early 1940s he returned to it more overtly, configured as stages in the development of civilizations and other super-individual and even super-cultural trends and forces. Having twice caught a lineament of it in motion and transfixed it in his studies of women's fashions (Kroeber, 1919a; Kroeber and Richardson, 1940a), he then sought to document an aspect of it even more dramatically through a massive exercise in data casting, and was disappointed when his laboriously compiled *Configurations of Culture Growth* (1944) failed to do this. [10] The book's failure was significant, for his method had failed to support theory, and induction had failed even to produce telltale patterns.

This counter-instance for the primacy of empirical procedures came quite late in Kroeber's career, and he subsequently returned to the "larger questions" that Robert Lowie, his long-time Berkeley colleague, had always believed to be his greatest interest. Lowie, who probably knew him best on a professional plane, wrote a sketch of him for his *festschrift*, and mused on his tendency to fasten upon the great riddles of anthropology (Lowie, 1936). In his view, Kroeber was given to questions that could neither be coherently asked nor productively answered, such as relations of race or psychology to culture. These choices said as much about Lowie as a Boasian as about Kroeber (the relations among race, language and culture being Boas' own chief professional preoccupations), but the general description of his predilections was accurate, and indicated the degree to which Kroeber's thinking ran against the grain of some Boasian tenets. For example, after Boas was dead he pushed the limits of Old World diffusion patterns in *The Ancient Oikoumene as an Historic Culture Aggregate* (Kroeber, 1946a), maintaining that a whole range of culture traits and complexes of traits had diffused to every corner of Europe, Asia, and much of Africa, like the molecules of a gas spreading to an even distribution throughout connected rooms. Apparently he had always felt that way, though he was not always so open about it, perhaps in part because hyper-diffusionists had long made odd and controversial claims about the influences of the ancient Near East upon New World cultures. Only the great oceans were left as barriers to diffusion in his nearly hyper-diffusionary model, and he even probed those. For example, in sketching the culture history of the Philippines (Kroeber, 1919b), he called for ethnographic work in the Oceanic cultures and consideration of the Pacific as a conduit of cultural influences rather than a barrier. He thus took diffusion, a crucial Boasian mechanism for culture change, and envisioned long distance circuits for transmission of whole and coherent trait complexes that Boas could scarcely have endorsed. Yet Boas might have seized upon one important point on which Kroeber was inconsistent. The diffusion of whole trait complexes surely paralleled the diffusion of complex language structures – that is of grammar – something Boas correctly believed possible, but which Kroeber and Sapir denied, evidently to allow for a core of deep homologies stable enough to show linguistic phylogeny. [11]

The differences between Kroeber and his fellow Boasians stemmed from an overall world-view more than from methodology, and were not trivial. He avoided unnecessary conflicts through a broad commitment to the historicist philosophical substrate of the Boasian School, and to a resolutely empirical approach to data as required by Boasian methods. He usually avoided openly schismatic positions, but this could not have been easy, for he was inclined to focus on larger phenomena than individual cultures afforded, and he compared and connected cultures into larger wholes – a concomitant of his preferred vantage point overlooking great distances and long stretches of time. Rather than focusing on the systems that compose cultures, he was among those inclined to "...see as 'real' systems that we ourselves are parts of" (Eldredge 1999: 26). His abiding interest in great civilizations and his eclectic approach gradually crowded out his early, Columbia-instilled commitment to cultural things within a given culture for their own sakes. Instead he preferred to treat whole civilizations comparatively, as large-scale instances of the culture concept at work – an approach and subject matter out of tune with the Boasian ethos. The Boasian program certainly emphasized cultures as wholes, but put no emphasis on them as parts of greater wholes – the perspective Kroeber customarily inhabited – and it is difficult to imagine a Boasian teaching or research program focused on civilization *per se*, which, as Stocking (1987: 9-45) observed, had long been a highly problematic notion. Throughout his life Kroeber remained by temperament a historian of the great and long patterns of civilizations, a commentator on style, and an aesthete. Yet even as he was leaving linguistics behind, he finished a massive, empirical, resolutely a-theoretical, and almost entirely non-linguistic Boasian dissertation (Kroeber, 1925 – finished by the end of 1917 but delayed in publication).

Kroeber may have preferred to think about higher-level, emergent cultural phenomena, but he did not slight the lower levels. Indeed he reveled in manipulating raw data. We may therefore wish to pause in the face of assertions that he regarded languages as parts of cultures as opposed to being their matrix (the latter a perspective that Sapir may have bequeathed to Benjamin Whorf). If we wish to accept those assertions it must be with the qualification that his world-view encompassed and tolerated some contradictions and tensions. Styles, patterns, and growth curves were observational devices that he used to set off whole civilizations, with the result that some of his work reads more like cultural criticism than anthropology. As in the relationship between paleontological units of taxonomy and paleo-species, these devices were distinct from the process they parsed and illustrated, a categorical point he may not have fully appreciated.

Yet Kroeber definitely believed these wide vistas should be firmly based on data, and it was a nearly life-long ambition for him to find them to be so. As Hymes (1961) noted, he used the same basic procedure in linguistics, ethnology, and archaeology – trait casting and search for patterns, coupled with an aesthetic component for pattern recognition in wide space and deep time. [12] Although Indo-European Linguistics formed little if any part of his training, in this broad sense he was close to the ways in which Indo-Europeanists reconstructed the evolutionary history of languages in the Old World. Just as in bio-geography, absence of traits was nearly as significant as their presence. His approach to culture history was similar, as he once described it in a nearly statistical, but still somewhat Boasian context:

> "This method, whatever its field, rests upon the recognition of isolable and definable features or traits, [referred to] as elements, whose presence or absence can be determined for a number of populational groups, or territorial entities, such as races, tribes, cultures, castes, or, in the present study, languages." (Kroeber, 1937a).

This was a trait-totting credo, and Kroeber, who measured such a large and vaporous notion as "civilization" by stacking up the traits he thought necessary to it, worked happily at either end of the spectrum of cultural entification. He liked nothing better than to trace the history of an individual motif, a trait, an invention, or complex of inventions, as in his treatments of the alphabet, systems of counting, and "the flying gallop" (Kroeber, 1948a: ch.11). However, his strongest affinity was with the large patterns and long trends of macro-Culture, and he did not see micro-changes as evolutionarily significant (we may prefer to read "evolutionarily interesting" here, but he seems to have meant significant). This prejudice was apparent almost from the beginning of his career, when he misjudged the cultural evolutionary findings of his archaeologist student, N. Nelson in the San Francisco Bay shell mounds (Nelson, 1909, 1910, Gifford, 1916). The Superorganic (Kroeber 1917) was an emergent level of cultural organization and an entity greater than the sum of its parts, the emergence of which summed cultural evolution and matched closely what was later called "general evolution". It is scarcely surprising that he usually eschewed defining close mechanisms for cultural processes. Indeed, for such a broad and sweeping process as he conceived significant cultural evolution to be, they would have been all but impossible to derive from the data to hand.

Kroeber was also an almost inaudibly professed materialist, unable to accept all the implications of a fully materialist doctrine (ALKP: ALK-Leslie White, 9/11/45). He needed emergent levels of cultural phenomena as manifestations of superorganic Culture, but this was also a dimension of ever-increasing abstraction. He believed the world to be hierarchically nested and steadily evolving to produce distinct and independently operating levels of organization, in effect "emergent" evolution. However, on evolution itself he remained deliberately obscure, and we must piece his views together from scattered evidence. [13] The Superorganic and materialism were not antithetical, but neither were they wholly congenial. Asked about a ghost in the machine he denied it, of course, but he was quite prepared to appeal to the *gheist* of a civilization. In retrospect he seems more like a dabbler in materialism than a truly convinced and systematic materialist.

Kroeber's work exhibited a supra-individual character which he made explicit on several occasions (Kroeber, 1915a, 1917, 1919a, 1940a and b), so it is unsurprising that he had trouble deciding what to do with individual people. As an inheritor of an historicist ethos he disliked the synchronic views of social science and aimed to keep American anthropology clear of them – so much so that he came into conflict with Steward and others during and after World War Two, as they sought to re-fashion the AAA along social scientific, politically active, and applied lines (Steward: 1971: 21-22; ALKP: ALK-Strong, 12/31/45, WDSP: Steward-Strong, 10/2/40;

WDS-Steward, 10/25/40; 10/17/45). His broad, distant view of cultures and civilizations admitted of no viable approach to the humanity that populated them, other than behaviorism, which he likewise disdained. He was therefore usually disposed to simply ignore individuals, which seems odd given his years of work in psychoanalysis. If nothing else, his deep exposure to Freud meant that he believed *qualia* mattered. But when he came to discuss them as data it was only in their pan-cultural collectivity that he found a use for them, as when he launched the late-career data casting project that resulted in *Configurations of Culture Growth* (1944). [14] In that book, exceptional individuals, in their aggregates at least, found places as parts of a half-articulated mechanism for cultural evolution. He described the curves of occurrence of genius in time and space in order to show higher level historical patterns at work ("lower level mechanisms" seems more accurate in this context, but "patterns" as active, causal phenomena, rather than passive residues, did heavy lifting in Kroeber's philosophy, and the term is more in keeping with his preferred perspective). The *vera causa* he offered can be summed as something akin to Darwin's saplings and trees analogy for the proliferation and geographic distribution of species – genius thrives upon genius and in concentrations begets more of it. One would have expected a "seamless" materialist to have chosen something less mindful.

The Matter of Evolution:

Of those within the early inner circle of Boasians, Kroeber showed the greatest ambivalence about being there (Buckley, 1996). His Boasian credentials have been rightly configured as a commitment to historicist principles, but a focus on his historicism fails to entirely capture the parallel dimension – evolutionism – in which he differed so significantly from the rest of the Boasian camp. It is difficult to see in retrospect why deep-time evolutionary patterns were not discerned in American linguistic data (by Americans, that is) earlier than they were, but it is pretty clear why they were not trumpeted in Boasian professional venues. Neither Kroeber nor Sapir bandied the term "evolution" because it was under interdict, and to do so would have exacerbated their already growing theoretical estrangement from their mentor. To be sure, Kroeber claimed to share Boas' mistrust of evolution in the nineteenth century Spencerian mode, and his celebrated kinship debate with William Rivers (Kroeber, 1909) was an attack on Morganian evolutionary thinking undertaken on behalf of the Boasian program (Stocking, 1976: 6). In 1916, three years after he and Dixon had given an essentially evolutionary and genetic account of California languages, he wrote to Sapir of kinship systems there in terms that treated evolutionism and Boasian ethnology not merely as different frames of reference, but as antithetical:

> "There do not seem to be any distinctive types of social organization corresponding with the culture areas. I infer therefore that [it] is the cultural color or setting or attitude of mind that has chiefly shaped the kinship systems. I think this finding will commend itself as reasonable to anyone who is an Ethnologist and not an Evolutionist" (ALKP: ALK-Sapir, 9/5/16).

The phrasing was loose, but the general idea showed an interesting structural affinity with Darwin's argument that it is ecological relationships and competition among species that circumscribe their distributions in habitats. Nonetheless, the "evolutionists" to whom he referred negatively were certainly Spencerian, not Darwinian, though evidently it was during that same approximate time frame Kroeber himself began to acquire a more Spencerian notion of cultural evolution (Kroeber, 1915a; 1917). He did not, at first, confound these perspectives. He was well versed in natural history and his primary source for evolutionary thought appears to have been Darwin himself, whom he read with approval and understanding during the early decades of the twentieth century, when Darwinian evolution was rather out of favor. According to his wife, he also read widely in biology, paleontology and evolutionary theory (T. Kroeber, 1970: 257-66). He once even produced an article on Galapagos *flora* (Kroeber, 1916a), but none of this is to imply that he was a thoroughgoing Darwinian where cultural phenomena were concerned, for even after his death for some years it remained possible to be a believer in biological evolution, but hold culture apart from its sphere of operation. Certainly Kroeber never offered a biologically analogous image of cultural evolution, however much his observations regarding cultures sometimes paralleled those of Darwin on species. Ironically, it was Boas who did that with his focus on undirected and direction-less culture change in the short term and at close range – something analogous to gene pool oriented population thinking in evolutionary biology. [15]

The kind of evolutionary thinking against which Boas tilted was Spencerian, generally subsumed under the title "19 Century Cultural Evolution." It was different from Darwinian evolution in the organic world, but because the crucial differences were not clearly and explicitly elucidated before about the third decade of the twentieth century we must be circumspect about claiming that we know with certainty what writers before that time meant by the term. While most culture theorists were cognizant of the diverging/converging nature of the "tree of culture", it would not always have been as obvious that someone propounding a cultural-evolutionary scheme for such a fundamental cultural phenomenon as language was going to make and hold to that distinction. Indeed, in Kroeber's case, at least, a critical observer (such as Boas) would have been justified in skepticism. Over time, perhaps in part due to the emergent character of the Superorganic concept, Kroeber's sense of cultural evolution elided by insensible degrees into a more Spencerian mode with which it actually was more in keeping. Most of his nearly life-long ambivalence regarding evolution probably proceeded from this dichotomy – torn between imposing but non-cooperating versions of what it was.

In fact, Kroeber's thought contained some components that were antithetical to a truly Darwinian view. Although he often linked cultures into larger groupings, unlike Darwin he was trying to separate spheres, not conflate them. He framed the question in Darwinian terms but answered it in his preferred terms of central tendency. [16] His Superorganic was an emergent self-organizing system, tethered to the material natural world, but also floating above it as a higher level of organization. As his focus was on larger patterns, broad sweeping trends and emergent levels of organization. The purpose to which he put evolutionary thought was elucidation of culture history on a large scale and in the long term – in effect, the natural history of civilizations. His uses of culture change therefore paralleled paleontological uses of evolution "above the species level", a view of macro-evolution that did not find its justification until later. At almost any time before about mid-century they were apt to be confused with the kind of teleology Tielhard de Chardin was touting. However, even the early German literature on evolution and paleontology, completely accessible to Kroeber, had a strong big-pattern bias and exuded a vapor of *geist* and emergence, gradually moving toward macro-evolution as more than the sum of all its bits of micro-evolution; a plane of evolutionary motion in its own right. The still-nascent components of this vision of emergent evolution, later synthesized by Rensch (1947/1960), were bound to appeal to Kroeber, reflexively mirroring as they did the pattern he had posited for Superorganic Culture.

Kroeber saw a match between his studies of civilizations and paleontological studies of paleo-taxa, and said as much (Kroeber, 1943, 1948a, 1953, 1958). He made his nearly visceral focus upon larger patterns clear in an early description of California culture areas into which cultures fit in relations analogous to those of genera and species:

> "A biology recognizing only species is a scientific impossibility, but a biology dealing with nothing lower than genera would be equally impossible" (Kroeber, 1908: 296).

The point was they took different kinds of observing. The assumptions and conceptual tools requisite to any coherent method, be it glottochronology, Indo-European style comparison, a focus on whole linguistic texts, or (in Kroeber's case) stacking culture traits to illustrate their comparative mass, all imposed certain legitimate objects, foci, and other parameters of perception upon the researchers who used them (just as instruments affect scientific research in the natural sciences). Kroeber's methods in culture history were adapted from taxonomic work, bio-geography, and examination of a fossil record. However close he remained to Boas in his devotion to rescue ethnology, a methodology that employed the conceptual instruments of an historical view of the life sciences was bound to appear evolutionary to someone with Boas' convictions. For example, on Northwest Coast cultures Kroeber wrote:

"...Essentially Northwest Coast culture shares with American culture only basic universal elements presumably derived from Asia [i.e. at a very remote time in the past]; that it lacks regularly the generic American elements that were developed on American soil and became diffused; and that what is specific in it is either a direct outgrowth on the spot from the relatively undifferentiated primitive American culture or the result of later Old World influences." (Kroeber, 1923: 7-8; brackets mine)

If Kroeber regarded micro-change as unimportant in the grand scheme of cultural evolution, definable mechanisms for macro-change were necessary as the base line on which the evolutionary melody was played. He eventually attempted to elucidate one in his *Stimulus Diffusion* (1940b), but the role of diffusion in culture change, analogous to genetic recombination for changes in the content of a gene pool, must have seemed insignificant for describing – still less for explaining – the broader developments he believed were most important, such as the emergence of great civilizations from simple cultures, urban life, feudalism, industrialization, and other grand trends of human history (concurrently the preferred questions of the "New History", one of several instances of such "new" disciplinary overlapping). Nor could diffusion explain the great movements of civilizations, such as the fall of Rome, the rise of Imperial China, or the spread of Islam. This was a gap – even a mismatch between his methods and his goal, which he tried to bridge in his fashion studies (Kroeber, 1919a, 1940a) and *Configurations of Culture Growth* (1944).

If Kroeber did not confuse organic and cultural evolution, he occasionally showed some uncertainty about the differences between them. The flyleaf of the second edition of his *Anthropology* was conspicuously adorned with Lowie's interconnected, Lamarckian "tree of culture", an illustration of culture change that emphasized limitless potential for variation, with no barriers but technical ones to the constant recombination of traits. No such image (wholly distinct from Darwin's ever-branching organic world), was present in the first edition of *Anthropology*, but the language in that early effort was clearly aimed at Boas' antagonists, proponents of nineteenth century cultural evolutionism and its surviving descendents. Mixture and convergence were the rule, occurring by certain yet unnamed principles. Anthropological science had been damaged by:

> "...[the] vague idea of evolution, the organic aspect of which Darwin gave such substance that the whole group of evolutionistic ideas has luxuriated rankly ever since" (Kroeber, 1923: 7-8).

It is noteworthy that he believed organic evolution to be a subset of the general idea, and not a wholly different kind of process, but he nonetheless wanted to highlight their differences. To illustrate the difference between culture change and organic evolution, and incidentally to show the power and sweep of convergence, he turned to the powerful imagery of flight:

> "Thus a comparison of the acquisition of the power of flight respectively by birds in their organic development out of the ancestral reptilian stem some millions of years ago, and by men as a result of cultural progress in the field of invention during the past generation, reveals at once the profound differences of process that inhere in the ambiguous concept of 'evolution.' "

These were telling examples. In an era when the middle-aged remembered believing it impossible, heroic powered flight was potent public currency, and the little shaman *Archaeopteryx*, dancing in German stone, was delicately perfect. To Kroeber the fossil was an object of bemusement. He seldom emphasized "things between", but kept a sense of them at hand, as in his work in seriation (Kroeber, 1916b and c), and when discussing the boundaries of civilizations during the 1950s (Kroeber, 1963). His preferred focus was on means and modes – data representations of entities in the record, clusters of data, collections of traits, and nexes of styles, rather than variance. He referred to *Archaeopteryx* in other writings as well, nonplussed and perhaps a little alarmed by such a perfectly transitory state. At once logically necessary and visually improbable, such a link was not visible to the unaided empiricism of taxonomy or bio-geography. And it would have fallen like Icarus between Kroeber's stacked towers of traits.

The Boasian Context of Kroeber's Linguistics:

Stocking (1960, 1968a and b, 1974a, b, and c, 1977, 1979, 1992, 1996) elucidated the parameters and character of the Boasian Ascendancy. Darnell (1998) emphasized continuities between the Boasians and their predecessors, specifically the Bureau of American Ethnology's late nineteenth century language program, which produced J.W. Powell's (1891) map of North American languages and ultimately Franz Boas' plan for linguistic research. Before the turn of the twentieth century, Boas had frequent recourse to Powell's book (Stocking, 1974a: 455-58), and thereafter maintained several key components of the BAE program. However, as Stocking pointed out, greater weight is due what Boas' language program eventually became than how it began, and emphasis should be given to his evolving attitudes and goals. His commitment to language classification was particularly short-lived, effectively ending with his essay *Classification of the Languages of the North Pacific Coast* (1893), written for the World's Fair Congress of Anthropology in Chicago. Nonetheless, if Boas made a revolution in American anthropology, and if revolutions essay to coin or to suppress some vocabulary, none can depose altogether the grammar of the old regime. The seventy-nine-page Introduction to his *Handbook* (1911) was Boas' manifesto – an account of the linguistic enterprise as he conceived it and of the ethos of his version of ethnology. Like Sapir's *Language* a decade later, it was also a polemic addressed to the intelligent non-linguist, beginning with an account of early classifications of race, language, and culture and ending with a list of the North American language families that was quite similar to Powell's.

We may consider, then, the degree to which Kroeber and Sapir, who occasionally wrote to each other gleefully of the impending destruction of the Powell system (as well as others who worked to link languages before about 1920), were parties to Boas' program of substantial revision, or whether their work constituted an entirely different approach. Given the distribution of native languages in the region, the primary mission of West-Coast anthropology as a Boasian outpost was linguistics, with many important distribution questions to be answered. Forty-nine of fifty-five North American language families were located west of the Mississippi and in the Arctic, while only six were in the East. By far the greatest concentration was in California (twenty by Boas' count – somewhat fewer than the twenty-two of fifty-two families in Powell's mapping). Also, American language diversity suggested that they had either recently migrated in or had differentiated and diverged with astonishing speed. Their right-skewed geographic distribution also seemed to reflect successive waves of migration from Asia, something Ales Hrdlicka's brittle orthodoxy in physical anthropology made about contemporary with Bishop Ussher's creation. Some saw California as a kind of *cul-de-sac* for peoples with little reason to migrate farther a-field. Like fish behind a weir, successive groups with their very different languages migrated into a mild climate, with comparatively easy if low-level subsistence circumstances and with either more hostile or more populated habitats around them. [17]

The scientific question was not the only impetus to work in California. The "Boas Plan" for recording Native American languages was intended to ameliorate a situation that by the last decade of the nineteenth century had become dire. Native American cultures seemed to be expiring, with some languages spoken only by small and rapidly dwindling groups. Therefore even the very early field campaigns were conceived as rescue work and priorities were as often set by worries about looming extinction as by research interests. A rapid reconnaissance and language sketch option necessarily existed in Boas' program – indeed he trained some field workers to operate chiefly toward these summary accounts. But the preferred method was text-collection, emphasizing oral histories, myths, folk tales, and genealogies, a procedure that accomplished several things at once. It compiled narratives, large and complex yet coherent bodies of cultural information that otherwise might slip away unrecorded, thereby achieving a primary goal of ethnography while simultaneously helping to prevent the cultural amnesia that appeared to be taking hold among Native Americans. These bulky texts, onerous to editors and carnivorous of publishing budgets, were also in effect an attempt to create a written corpus of American languages that might represent, as written Chinese does, mutually unintelligible languages. It transcribed these narratives into grammatically, syntactically, and lexically illustrative texts that could be expanded or corrected in collaboration with further informants. This exercise served to give the ethnographer the "feel" of the language while providing a target for continued peer review. Indeed, this gave ethnographic research some elements of an experimental approach by making it replicable. The crucial boundary condition was the degree to which sound recording was objectively accurate and uniform – a troublesome point. Early on, Boas (1889) had been at pains to warn about the vagaries of hearing and recording (his orthography committee within the American Anthropological Association included both Kroeber and Sapir). The textual method made a collective object, a specimen, of a corpus of data (Stocking, 1977: 5).

Boas was not linguist enough to produce a wholly new system, and was almost never inclined to classify. Also, his plan of research gradually took on a more relativist cast as his doubts about the viability of searching out genetic connections among languages grew. The thrust of his editorship of the *Handbook of American Indian Languages* accordingly came to resemble that of his general anthropological program, a campaign to dissociate race, language, and culture and to promote "diffusionist linguistics" (Stocking, 1974c: 474-81). When Dixon, Kroeber and others began linking languages in California they too used Powell's classification as a foundation. In retrospect however, Kroeber looked upon the Powell system as an obstacle that had to be overcome to allow the genetic approach to succeed (Hymes, 1961: 8; Kroeber, 1952).

The classification of far western languages, worked out among Kroeber, Dixon and Sapir, was not based on lexical criteria alone (the hallmark of Powell's BAE system), but also took account of structural characteristics such as pronoun incorporation, syntax, tones, and morpho-phonemics. It was the status they accorded such structures that distinguished them from Boas' method. Hymes (1961) called the result imperfect, but good for its day, and a solid heuristic for subsequent work. [18] This effort grew out of the Boas "plan" and built upon it, but also operated with a fundamentally different view of language change. Did languages change constantly by accumulating diffused traits and processing them into new meaning, or were they anchored in their past by the innate conservatism of certain (mostly grammatical) structures? Both processes could apply, of course, but only comfortably so long as the question of evolution went begging. Kroeber's sometime allegiance to both views may have kept him from taking a clearer position as friction developed between Boas and Sapir. By 1919-1920, with many other contentious issues affecting Boas' supporters, and despite his own decade of energetic work to shrink the number of language families recognized for North America, Kroeber again became unaccountably cautious as he moved away from linguistics. Meanwhile, Sapir had grown more impatient as his stock of evidence for wider and deeper linguistic consanguinity grew.

Kroeber's Professional Emphasis upon Linguistics:

Kroeber was more interested in linguistics than any other sub-field of anthropology, but at different times he worked in three of the four that pertain in the New World. Only in physical anthropology, a field with which Boasians (except Boas) usually had little to do was his contribution almost negligible.[19] Of the remaining three, ethnology was a steady professional interest and archaeology a brief but fruitful mid-career digression. Linguistics, however, was the centerpiece fieldwork enterprise of early twentieth century American cultural anthropology, and if Kroeber quickly went his own way theoretically, he began as a key participant in the effort to record endangered native tongues, and remained ever keen that this rescue work should be put forward.[20] Late in life he still believed that language work was anthropology's royal road and the better part of ethnology – a sentiment he made clear in his (posthumous) *Forward* to Hymes' *Language in Culture and Society* (1964).[21] Observable social and material traits and trait complexes formed a lesser part of the available evidence, while the fragments recovered by archaeology were by far the least part.

As a fully bilingual child Kroeber had been pre-adapted to language study. To this foundation was added a liberal-humanist education in the New York immigrant version of the German tradition, emphasizing early and sustained exposure to languages, ancient and modern. As an old man he recalled his pleasure as a boy when the patterns and structures observable in languages dawned on him (Darnell, 1990a: 10; Kroeber, 1964 *op. post*; T. Kroeber,

1970: 46-47). This talent for discerning patterns in data (necessary but presumably not sufficient for a career in linguistics) was a readily identifiable thread running throughout his life's work (Kroeber, 1952: 169-174; 1953). His undergraduate and early graduate work at Columbia University, devoted largely to the English Language and literature, was therefore an elaboration of a well-established learning process and an effective background for the more formal training that began in 1896 in the context of Boas' linguistics seminars, where the basic exercise was distilling grammar from Chinook texts. His first fieldwork was conducted as part of Boas' program for recording Native American languages and cultures, wherein fieldwork for selected students was also the chief activity supporting the program's core project, the *Handbook of American Indian Languages* (Boas, 1911, 1922).

If Kroeber's Boasian sense of the need for rescue ethnography and language collection survived for many years, his willingness to participate in Boas' *Handbook of American Indian Languages* did not. He evaded several opportunities to contribute, beginning in 1903, soon after he arrived in California, and this remained a sore point between them for years (Stocking, 1968b; 1974a: 461). Kroeber had three reasons for not cooperating; one tactical, one strategic, and one vindictive. First, he quite unrealistically wanted control of all anthropological work carried out in California, a hubristic notion that would not have occurred to him, or to anyone, a generation later. Once established at the University of California, he increasingly viewed himself as the state anthropologist, with the chair of the Berkeley Department as his seat of office. Enlistment in the *Handbook* effort would, *de facto*, give Boas considerable say about how linguistic research was conducted in the state (as will be seen, he briefly acquired that say anyway, a quarter of a century later, as the result of a funding event). Secondly, as Darnell (1998) suggested and as I wish to emphasize in this essay, he had come to a view of languages that ran counter to Boas' conception of them, and must have been apprehensive about collaboration, knowing they would clash on the most fundamental and general question about languages, the meaning of their relationships. Lastly, Kroeber was still miffed that before he had gone to California for the second time Boas had seen fit to tell the Berkeley Department's founding committee and F.W. Putnam and that he was not yet professionally ready for the job there.

Although Kroeber was wary of evolutionary discussions, Hymes (1961: 15-19) noted that one of his last contributions to the history of linguistics was to "place Indo-European relationships in the context of general science", meaning evolutionary science (Kroeber, 1960b). In that essay, written for a 1959 Darwin Centennial venue devoted to the topic "Evolution after Darwin", he tried to synthesize "evolution, history, and culture". But that was a late, indeed eleventh hour effort. Usually he had been vague on the subject of evolution, and still could be. A few months before his death he replied to a request from a European admirer to enumerate his interests and evaluate his influence on the field. In two sentences he gestured toward his wide range of interests, giving linguistics first mention in a list of ascending generality and breadth, while carefully maintaining the distinction between cultural and social phenomena (a distinction sometimes often lost upon Old World interlocutors). Even at that late date the effect was evidently calculated to encompass cultural evolution without naming it:

> "I am most interested in linguistics, ethnology, culture history, and [the] growth of civilizations. I might say this is patterned culture, in contrast to social groups." (ALKP: ALK-Poeder, 6/30/60).

Just why Kroeber abandoned linguistics work therefore seems a question worth pursuing. A chronological plotting of his publications by subject shows a near-total cessation of his linguistic output during his middle years. Linguistic titles cluster bi-modally in the first twenty and the last four years of his career, with the late work consisting mostly of retrospective treatments owed to half-forgotten materials, and enthusiastic support for lexico-statistics as a method. Between were a mere seven short descriptive pieces on old data and several reviews, scattered over more than thirty-five years during which he published some three hundred and thirty other titles. Almost all his linguistic work antedated 1920, and most of it was done before 1915. Linguistics, Kroeber's primary intellectual focus and chief interest when he began his work in California, represented just twelve percent of his total published output (Hymes put it at sixteen percent). In her biographical portrait, his second wife, who did not know him until he had entered his brief archaeological phase, did not even give linguistics a separate heading, suggesting that he did not emphasize it in retrospective discussions with her.

Steward (1973: 14-33) maintained that Kroeber believed linguistics and archaeology to be sub-set disciplines within ethnology, and that for him the study of languages was the means to a broader ethnological end, but he too would have had that from Kroeber during the nineteen-twenties, after he had quit the field. This sub-set status for linguistics also accords with the structure of the broad view of ethnology Kroeber offered in his textbook *Anthropology* (1923, 1948a), which Steward hyperbolically called "the most important book ever written in …anthropology". But when Kroeber was writing it he was increasingly alarmed by divisive, even secessionist tendencies among some linguists (including Sapir), for he did indeed want American anthropology to keep its four-fold bundle of cultural anthropology, physical anthropology, archaeology, and linguistics. Nonetheless, his devotion to that division of the field into four did not commit him to any particular view of their relative importance.

A cursory examination of his bibliography, and the secondary literature prior to 1984, then, might lead one to believe that Kroeber cared no more about linguistics than he did about archaeology, but that was not the case. Having begun his anthropological career with the study of languages before Sapir arrived to foment conflict with Boas, for more than a decade after his arrival in California Kroeber not only held himself to be a linguist, but to be the arbiter and curator of linguistics there (Darnell, 2001). Even after he had ceased to be active in language work he continued to weigh in on linguistic matters and serve in other capacities. He was among the several influential anthropologists who, in 1924, called for the establishment of a professional linguistics association for New World languages (the Linguistic Society of America), and (much later) even served a term as its president. By the time his long mid-life linguistic hiatus ended, after both Sapir and Boas were dead, times had changed. By then Leonard Bloomfield dominated a much wider and more sophisticated professional field, to which

Kroeber could scarcely hope to contribute much that would be original or important.

Both Hymes (1961) and Steward (1973) suggested that Kroeber abandoned linguistics because he had finished his work; that he was not interested in languages for their own sakes, but as a means toward addressing larger ethnological questions. Kroeber himself implied as much on several late occasions, but that does not fully explain either the timing or the degree of his disenchantment, and it rings of retrospective face-saving. As late as 1912-13 he still intended to keep linguistics as the core of his anthropology program, as his extensive study of California's north coastal languages and phonetic constituents of California languages showed (Kroeber, 1911a and b). Yet this project never came to full fruition. Instead he soon thereafter found himself upstaged as Sapir raced ahead to link languages into evolutionary genetic relationships on a continental scale. In the 1920s Kroeber did not believe the opportunities for rescue fieldwork were exhausted, for he continued to promote some language studies, though he undertook none and hired no linguists in the Berkeley Department. In effect he wanted to have his cake and eat it, but his position astride California anthropology was untenable due to his neglect of the fast-expanding linguistics field and the increasing number of students wanting to work in the most puzzling linguistic region in America.

Hymes characterized Kroeber's linguistic work as having been chiefly in the service of ethnology, though his genetic view of language diversity and a theoretical attitude that may have grated on Boas were also subtly evident in Hymes' account:

> "Kroeber's empirical work was never data-gathering for its own sake. There was always in mind an immediate question or larger frame of reference. ... One of the questions of the day concerned the so-called 'intermediates', consonants variously perceived as voiced and voiceless by fieldworkers. ...Kroeber suspected a specific phonetic cause in the sounds themselves, voiceless onset of otherwise voiced stops...
>
> The California linguistic fieldwork had indeed an overall problem orientation from its beginning. ...Nearly half the stocks ...were represented in

one state. Explaining this extreme diversity was …
the 'fundamental problem of California linguistics'
(Kroeber, 1903). When similarity in grammatical
structure was glimpsed between a number of languages
whose vocabularies seemed unrelated, there seemed an
obvious bearing on the problem of diversity." (Hymes,
1961: 9-10)

This was what led Kroeber and Dixon to launch their survey
of California Indian grammars in 1902, and to offer their first
theoretical formulation of the problem in 1903.

Hymes went on to offer an account of linguistic work in
California in which we see Kroeber's language work in a wider
context. He suggested that the necessarily synchronic view of trait
distributions led naturally to a diffusionist prejudice that Kroeber
and Sapir may have had some initial difficulty in transcending
(particularly true of Kroeber, whose knowledge of Old World
linguistics was second-hand, and whose devotion to diffusion as a
mechanism exceeded even that of Boas). Kroeber's role in furthering
the genetic view of languages is apparent in Hymes account, though
Kroeber did not own to it at the time. Hymes recounted the general
belief among anthropologists that time depth was not yet available
in archaeology, that historical linguistics therefore seemed the better
bet, and he highlighted Kroeber's role in a first "areal classification of
a set of New World languages according to grammatical type" "…a
remarkably original step in the study of New World languages". It is
clear that Kroeber was heavily involved in the shift to an emphasis
upon genetic linguistic relationships by about 1910, and the
impressive list of connections made among languages over the next
several years featured his name at most important points. Whatever
else may be said of this accelerating body of rather non-Boasian
linguistic work, Kroeber played an active, foundational role in it.

Hymes (1961: 24) also observed that Kroeber's linguistic talents
were not exceptional, remarking that his chief contributions lay in his
fieldwork and example, not his impact on methods or on particular
students. Calling Kroeber a "self-taught pioneer" (by implication
the wholly self-taught Boas, his teacher, was not a qualified linguist
either), he asserted that Kroeber was "…shy of the technical core
of philology or linguistics, which contained methods whose rigor

he admired, but with which he did not feel wholly conversant, or free". Considering Kroeber's many contributions before and during the years when he collaborated with Sapir, and his lesser but real claim to a measure of priority in a genetic conception of New World languages (bearing in mind the undeveloped state of the linguistics at the time – a perusal of G. Gibb's 1863 piece entitled *Instructions for Research Relative to the Ethnology and Philology of America* suffices to show how low the base line was in the late nineteenth century), we may wish to believe that Hymes short-changed him, but evidently he did not. Kroeber wanted to be more of a linguist than he was, and took it hard that he did not measure up to Sapir. Nevertheless, he was enough of a linguist to know when he was outclassed, and struck out smartly into another sub-field of anthropology.

Kroeber as an Ethnographer:

After work on Boas' Northwest Coast texts, some armchair exposure to Eskimo linguistics (Kroeber, 1899 a and b; 1900), and a summer of *tour de horizon* ethnographic fieldwork among the Arapaho, Gros Ventres, and Assiniboine, Kroeber defended an admirably brief twenty-eight-page dissertation on Arapaho decorative symbolism and was awarded his Ph.D. in 1901. He had begun his long California career already, in 1900, with museum-related work for the California Academy of Sciences, but that arrangement could not sustain him professionally, and he returned to New York at the end of his one-year contract. His speedy permanent remove to California in August 1901, and his association with the Anthropology Department of the University of California at Berkeley, and its research museum, at the distance of a continent made him independent. Despite early alarms about control of the department, which led him at least twice to look eastward in search of another position, Berkeley remained his home for the whole of his pre-retirement professional life. He left most of the museum's administrative details to his assistant, Edward W. Gifford, who made a career of them, but kept rather close overall administrative control. This position also gave him nearly exclusive access to one of the best collections of pre-Columbian Peruvian artifacts in North America, which was later a great advantage in making his reputation in archaeology.

As an ethnologist Kroeber was eclectic, studying with varying degrees of intensity no fewer than thirty-three native peoples in California, most of them during the first decade of the twentieth century (Hymes, 1961: 1-5). This was a remarkable achievement in Boasian-style ethnography, though he modified Boas' preferred methods. To highlight his intellectual energy, several of Kroeber's biographers related that once, while waiting for a train, he spotted an Indian and "took a vocabulary" in the short time available (Hymes, 1961; T. Kroeber, 1973; Steward, 1961, 1973). From the Native American standpoint this probably did seem relentless – perhaps even larcenous, but it was unremarkable behavior in anyone with a sense of time and opportunity. What the incident most exemplified, and what his notebooks confirm, was his devotion to linguistic work. Looking back on this time, he once wrote to George Stocking that he had not found time to actively participate in the founding of the American Anthropological Association in 1902 because he was too busy recording Yurok religion and the Yuki language (ALKP: ALK-Stocking, 3/1/60). As Steward (1973: 8) pointed out, the Yurok (a culturally distinctive group in the northernmost peri-coastal reaches of the state, in the Lower Klamath River Valley), and the Mohave (a Yuman group in the Mohave Valley in the Colorado River basin), posed special ethnographic problems, and Kroeber worked on these groups at different times throughout his life. In his last years he was still trying to catch up with publishing Yurok and Mohave materials, calling them his "greatest unfinished ethnographic work" (ALKP: ALK-P. Fejos, 2/19/53, 1/21/57).

The two groups were opposites in many respects, subsisting in utterly different environments and exhibiting extreme cultural differences. In addition they were usefully situated at either end of the state (the Yurok close to the coast and the Oregon border, the Mohave in the desert southeast), and thereby might serve as boundary markers of Kroeber's anthropological territory.[22] He also undertook comprehensive linguistic and ethnographic efforts among the Yuki (small clan groups in comparatively high mountain habitats in the Northwest Coastal Range), and the Yokuts (a widespread tribal people in the central San Joaquin Valley and the foothills of the Sierra Madre Range). These four groups ensured him a good sample across the range of human life-ways in the state, but the scale of field work necessary even to outline them adequately was huge, and the range of other cultures in the state was mind-boggling.

Kroeber therefore undertook less intensive linguistic "reconnaissance work" in many other cultures of California and adjacent areas, and reluctantly looked around for help.

The Indo-European Option and Franz Boas' Reaction:

Most nineteenth century historical linguists working in the Old World assumed languages to have evolved in some sense of that variously used term, and that assumption drew much in its train. By mid-century proto-linguists, nearly all of them philologists, had achieved a consensus that patterned language change was all but ubiquitous, a fact that was only later seen to parallel findings regarding species change in the life sciences. However, the long-term, worldwide patterns in language change were unlike those of organic evolution, and instead rather similar to the ones later proposed for cultural evolution, that is both diverging and converging.

Divided and troubled as the topic of evolution was among the several life sciences, and as uncongenial as it was in Boasian anthropological circles, there was little premium to be gleaned by any Boasian from flaunting it. Nonetheless, Kroeber did hold and use an evolutionary view of both culture and language, having begun his career with one, however tardy he was in again acknowledging it explicitly once the furor of his initial foray into the realm of strongly emergent evolutionary ideas with his Superorganic died down. Only after World War Two did American anthropology return to the issue of cultural evolution, and even then Kroeber's endorsements were few and less than resounding. Near the end of his life he at last stated a strong belief in an evolutionary view clearly (*op. post.*, in Hymes 1964: 654-66), but as he had never championed it very robustly during the decades when it was most controversial, he could scarcely claim the garlands. [23]

The Indo-European approach to languages, an evolutionary historical methodology that began with the work of Sir William Jones (1746-94) in the Eighteenth Century, and was elaborated by Franz Bopp (1791-1867) and Rasmus Rask (1787-1832), aimed to reconstruct past languages within in their familial groupings. By the middle of the nineteenth century the method rendered an enormously persuasive model of language evolution, to which

August Schleicher (1821-68) offered an organismic analogy, Jakob Grimm (1785-1863) the rule of law, and Karl Verner (1846-96) the vindicating explanations of its apparent counter-instances. Although the founder of this idea was British, it quickly became primarily a Germanic and Scandinavian science. Grimm's "laws" (he never called them such) eventually helped to reconstruct Indo-European as an *Ur* language for Eurasia, with a telltale lexicon suggestive of what technological, economical, social and religious traditions existed in prehistory. Later, a Neo-Grammarian movement within this Old World paradigm (likewise dominated by German scholars) used the comparative method with rather more confidence in reconstructing prehistoric languages, citing as they did so certain "laws" of language evolution, based upon uniformities in the data. Over the middle decades of the nineteenth century the Indo-European demonstration that languages came in families and had diverged from each other over time became strong, indeed incontrovertible evidence of evolutionary consanguinity. This was comparable to the insight Darwin had offered by retrospectively inspiring Linnaeus' branched (but not branching) tree of organic nature with evolutionary motion. What was more it was accomplished by means of a comparative method similar to that employed in nineteenth century evolutionary anthropology – the primary target of the early Boasian Ascendancy.

Talk of "laws" may have been premature, but the findings of the Indo-Europeanists were strongly confirmed. There was no more reason for linguists to await the discovery of a viable mechanism for language evolution before charting its patterns than there was for paleontologists to do so with regard to biological evolution, and they did not wait (Kroeber, 1964, *op. post.*). A French linguist, Michel Breal, tried to measure rates of semantic change in individual words, to little avail. His greatest problem was the all-pervasive effect of lexical diffusion, which made boundary conditions too difficult to establish or control (Boas later elevated this difficulty to the status of a negating principle). Breal's failure was informative, for it led to the half-true insight that words diffuse readily, phonology and syntax diffuse only with great difficulty, and other grammatical structure or morphology diffuse almost never or not at all. This assumption eventually found a role in twentieth century American linguistics, wherein it remained muted, but underlay most of what Kroeber,

Sapir, R.B. Dixon, J.P. Harrington, P. Radin, and others did as they linked and lumped languages into family groups. However, lexical borrowing was assumed to be all but unconstrained, particularly when accompanied by diffused artifacts, foodstuffs, practices, beliefs, motifs, or technologies.

The Indo-European model, which seemed both satisfactorily empirical and theoretically supported, also offered a staged progression of sounds – a kind of trajectory of voiced through unvoiced to fricative stops, such that the sounds uttered changed over time in a patterned manner. The order of mouthing positions and the phonetic roles remained static as the sounds passed through them in a sequence, keeping more-or-less steady in their mutual relations. A similar pattern was discerned for velar to palatal stops, and these too were taken to be the (somewhat) visible lineaments of diverging language lineages. In other words, a static physical substrate disposed itself into anatomical positions which were in turn informed by a finite set of phonemic possibilities. The sounds in each language were developed through this (nearly mind-body-like) joint structure, in an odd reflexive way akin to the ways peoples were held by nineteenth century cultural evolutionary theory to pass through stages of cultural evolution. For those with the breadth of scope to encompass it, the world as represented by race, language, and culture must have seemed to be of a piece. Situational logic such as this must have made nineteenth century evolutionary theory seem insidiously formidable to Boas, even well into the twentieth century.

Believing that both grammar and vocabulary could diffuse, Boas was keen to demonstrate that pervasive diffusion was the main agent of language change, thereby swamping all meaningful traces of phylogeny. In his view, the role of diffusion was so great (with even elements of syntax and morphology diffusing) that what had almost always pertained was a swarm of influences, not a process of branching differentiation. If such deep traits could move among different language families, then the notion of a reconstruction of the evolutionary tree of languages was necessarily nonsensical.[24] Neither Kroeber nor Sapir discounted the effects of borrowing in language change, but Boas emphasized diffusion as the primary factor, just as in culture change generally. We can observe Kroeber still struggling with some of the implications of this very late in his life (in Hymes, 1964). The assumption of the fixity of grammar has not stood the test of time. Linguists have come to accept that grammar does indeed diffuse, chiefly through the mechanism of bilingualism, albeit much more slowly than vocabulary. Thus, in the early twentieth century the several positions taken by Kroeber, Sapir, and Boas as they ranged themselves around the question of genetic relations among languages, were about equidistant from a growing body of evidence that, viewed from different angles and in the context of the time, may have been seen as supporting them all in turn.

Throughout the nineteenth century the Linneaen task of collecting, comparing, and classifying occupied historical linguists in the Old World, and their successes suggested that something similar might be accomplished in the New – that comparative historical linguistics might help to reconstruct the life-ways, mutual relations and past geographical distributions of prehistoric American peoples. The strongest qualification (Boas, Michelson, and others called it a disqualifier) was that nearly all the New World Languages were unwritten, while the fossil forms that Indo-European linguists sought were mostly manifested in concrete written symbols from which the *Ur* forms were extrapolated. Languages acquire greater stability when written, and having thereby emerged into history may indeed have thereafter changed at tempos more in accordance with the assumptions of Indo-Europeanists. However, the ancestral languages of the New World had to be approached by comparison and extrapolation from surviving common features to extinct ones. Such extrapolation from known extant forms to unknown ancestral ones was unsound and unscientific in the Boasian frame of reference.

Nonetheless, given the explanatory power of Indo-European linguistics, it is striking that Boas should have opposed its introduction into the study of New World languages for as long as he did. We may suppose that he opposed it for reasons that had as much to do with his dislike of confusions of race and culture, and his rejection of nineteenth century notions of cultural evolution, as with his beliefs about language. If Boas displayed a failure of vision on this issue, it was in refusing to accept that New World Languages did not constitute a special case for being unwritten, and that measures of their relatedness could be distilled from structures revealed in texts recorded with a more-or-less uniform orthography. The question of diffusion of grammar thereby acquired considerable importance. Where one stood regarding the degree to which grammar and morphology might diffuse almost defined where one stood on evolutionary genetic relations among languages. In turn, with language viewed as the hereditary material of culture, where one stood on language evolution could scarcely fail to have a strong effect upon one's stance on the question of general cultural evolution.

How fast unwritten languages may have changed in the deep past was anyone's guess, but for this question, too, a method of inquiry was eventually offered. Glottochronology, the first attempt at an objective measure of the tempo of linguistic evolution, was developed in Germany during the late nineteenth century and eventually given its strongest New World expression by Sapir's student, Morris Swadesh, who was inclined to regard Kroeber as a pioneer in the method (Hymes, 1961: 11). [25] Like numerical taxonomy and evolutionary rates judged from Mitochondrial DNA in the classifying branches of the life sciences, glottochronology assumed that language change was rather regular, and that time-distance could be inferred from degrees of lexical and occasionally grammatical differentiation (Campbell, 1998: 177-85). [26] This concept worked on Kroeber's imagination, not only answering research needs in linguistics, ethnology, and archaeology, but suiting his personality as well. This can already be glimpsed in Dixon and Kroeber (1919), wherein they tried to bring some simple mathematical tools to bear upon language change. In his 1923 *Handbook of the Indians of California* Kroeber did indeed seem to yearn for numeric tools such as glottochronology and lexico-statistics (p. 218), about which he was enthusiastic when they later appeared. His fascination with glottochronology and lexico-statistics was deep and lasting (Kroeber 1958; 1960). [27] Boas never condemned this, and his own arithmetic criteria for deciding the closeness of two dialects (though over much shorter distances) worked with some of the same basic pre-suppositions as glottochronology. [28]

If Kroeber's published opinions were seldom completely clear or consistent on the question of the genetic view of language, he had reasons for circumspection. For one thing (and it may have been the main thing) he had no wish to subvert the Boasian program. For another, he was probably genuinely uncertain about it for several years. Of course, it would have been rash for Kroeber and Dixon to abandon their received paradigm altogether without considerable, indeed overwhelming evidence in hand. At the very least, shifting to the genetic view entailed changes in methodology and doing much work over again, and this would have seemed dauntingly difficult, even with the Indo-European model to imitate. This timidity cost them, for what measure of priority he and Dixon deserved turned first of all upon their early general overview of California languages (Dixon and Kroeber, 1903), but in that article they approached an evolutionary view, only to dance gingerly away from it (pp. 2-3), insisting rather too loudly that they were committing no evolution and were dealing only with "...structural resemblances, not with definite genetic relationships; [that] ...we are establishing not families, but types of families. They then compared sixteen "stocks", rendering three language types in California: Central, Northwest, and Southwest, typified by Maidu, Yurok, and Chumash, respectively. In discussing traceable family relationships they barely kept to the letter of Boas' program, and not at all to its spirit. By protesting too much they merely called attention to the genetic character of the underlying question and to their veiled but evident perspective on it. Kroeber later fully accepted consanguinity among California language families, eventually linking Chontal, Seri, and Yuman in such a grouping (Kroeber, 1914), but for a time he also professed to believe, along with Boas, that grammar could diffuse frequently enough to be an agent in language change, a qualification that appeared to kick the methodological and theoretical props from under the genetic view by disqualifying its chief data base. As late as 1910 he described Maya-Tsimshian and Uto-Aztekan-Algonkan as, "...adjacent languages of unrelated origin and diverse vocabulary [which] have influenced each other in their methods of structure" (Kroeber, 1910b). Franz Boas, the looming and disapproving father figure, was the cause of this timid inconsistency.

Dixon and Kroeber's disclaimer certainly would not have deceived Boas, who as it happened, already knew something was afoot. Before publishing, Kroeber had written to inform him of their forthcoming article, noting numerous curious lexical similarities among the languages they were studying and even mentioning the possibility that they might be "related" – ambiguous but suggestive language (FBP: ALK-Boas, 4/24/03). Boas did not reject the idea outright (as he should have done if he truly believed that historical linguistics did not fit the American situation at all), but denigrated it gently as, "very interesting for outsiders", meaning either that it was speculative and therefore not scientific, or that it would be grist for the mill of evolutionists. He counseled them to "go on working a few years longer before you write such a general paper" (FBP: ALK-Boas, 4/24/03; FB-ALK, 5/1/03; Darnell, 1990a: 110-21). In fact, Kroeber had written to F.W. Hodge at the BAE eight months before, outlining their plan to publish a general paper on California languages that would be "altogether comparative" and aimed at establishing "a classification", including sketch maps "in the manner of Ripley's (1899) *Races of Europe*" (FBP: ALK-Hodge, 8/16/02). This hand-written letter survives in Boas' papers, to whom Hodge, a frequent and cordial correspondent, promptly sent it. Boas seems to have said nothing to Kroeber about this, so Kroeber was unsuspecting when he wrote to test the waters.

It is understandable that Kroeber was not prepared to flaunt this half-formed idea openly in 1903 (Dixon appears to have remained agnostic about it for several more years). It struck at the Boasian tenet that the non-genetic, free-ranging inheritance of ideational culture (and by definition of language, as well) precluded the possibility that cultural change was a process similar to organic evolution. Coming from his own student, fresh from his graduate program and with less than two years of experience on his own, this would certainly have given ammunition to his adversaries. Boasians had a better sense of themselves as a group than to do that. Of course, it probably would also have drawn a bolt from Columbia on high. But Kroeber's behavior suggests that he was straining at the Boasian leash on this question from the start, as did his eventual (private and unpublished) announcement of a virtually Pauline conversion to the genetic view (ALKP: ALK-Sapir, 1/3/13).

Thus Dixon and Kroeber, who were already reasonably sure of the genetic parallel in language evolution in 1903, lost their chance for priority through their timidity and lack of clarity. While their several joint publications over nearly two decades did much to achieve a preliminary mapping of Western language-based culture areas, they remained slow to commit themselves explicitly to the evolutionary view, which made Sapir's later, explicitly genetic approach to the problem appear all the more original. Darnell (1990: 110-13) suggested that Dixon and Kroeber were nonplussed by the evidence before them, and out of habit stuck to the Boasian tenet that similarities among languages resulted from borrowing. It seems unlikely that they were confused on such a fundamental point, though they did seem to look right through their data in the first two pages of their article, saying that despite all the structural similarities, the vocabularies were distinct, and that relationships strictly defined therefore "could not be alleged." If this was a sop to Boas' sensibilities, it got the thing backwards, as the vocabulary constituted the superficial set of traits and the grammar structures the deep homologies. Darnell (1998: 225) later suggested that Kroeber and Dixon did not turn to a genetic explanation until the possibility of "borrowing as a result of historical contacts failed to explain observed similarities." In other words, Boas was right until proven wrong, and diffusion remained their working assumption until they were forced away from it.

The practical professional considerations were not trivial, and the alarm that Sapir and Kroeber occasionally expressed at the prospect of angering Boas was genuine. Boas' students could not take his displeasure lightly, especially in the early years of academic anthropology, with new appointments often in the gift of his recommendation (Darnell, 1990a: 41-42). Dixon was well placed at Harvard, but Kroeber was far from settled on a career in California at that point, and very nearly lost out to archaeological interests in "his" department a few years later. At any time before he gained the chair of the Berkeley Department, and evidently for some time thereafter, New York remained the lodestone of his anthropology. Furthermore, he was already testing Boas' patience with his foot-dragging about contributing to the *Handbook*, while at the same time thinking about getting access to California language materials in the BAE, a deal he needed Boas to broker for him. [29] For Boas' part, because he wanted both of them to collaborate on the second volume of his *Handbook*, and wanted Kroeber to take a burdensome office in the AAA, he did not fly at Kroeber and Dixon over the matter and even held his peace when he had reason to believe that Kroeber had tried to mislead him.

By 1913, when Dixon and Kroeber's genetic views were more

clearly stated, they were still somewhat ahead of Sapir. By fits and starts, then, Kroeber had distanced himself from Boas on this key theoretical issue, though he remained careful to avoid controversy whenever possible. Several years later, when he was writing the most Boasian of his books, *The Handbook of California Indians* (written over many years, completed by mid-1917, but not published until 1925), he was still being circumspect, for it contained no language studies. Of course, to have made a book on California languages would have been a gratuitous slap at Boas, considering the content of his *Handbook* and Kroeber's foot-dragging about contributing to it, but there were several clues to Kroeber's view of languages in the book. For example, he called Yurok a "far-West offshoot of Algonquian", one of the dominant language families of Eastern North America (p. 98). That was merely suggestive. Thereafter (pp. 121-23) he put the Athabascan dialects in California into four "groups" that could only have been meant to imply an evolutionary divergence. In a discussion of Penutian, a language super-family he and Dixon discovered, he made of it a group of some 50 language "stocks" (p. 347), a common biological metaphor counterbalanced by his discussion of the dialect-binding factor of intermarriage (p. 493), a process of language hybridization. Most telling was a wholly Darwinian-looking branching chart (p. 227), a "family tree of Pomo dialects". These points are ambiguous but suggestive. Boas' hold on Kroeber was more powerful than Kroeber cared to admit.

What of Boas' own views and motivations? Accounts of historical linguistics in America that focus on Edward Sapir usually touch upon Boas' intractable attitude toward the genetic relations among languages, often depicting him as obdurate in the matter and letting it go at that. Boas could not simply maintain that languages were not related in something like a genetic sense, for it would have beggared belief that a set of principles might apply so handily to the languages of one hemisphere and not to those of the other. It would have been even more futile to take issue with the validity of European (mostly German) Indo-European linguistics in their Old World context, where it was a paradigm achieved. Instead, he recognized it as a science apart from his own and contented himself with a delaying action among his students (Boas, 1938: 1-6), keeping them away from such a slippery slope toward cultural-evolutionary thinking and keeping them focused on empirical work in a rescue mode. [30]

In retrospect, Boas' opposition to studying languages as products of evolutionary divergence seems myopic, but from his perspective it was tactically focused, theoretically defensible, and morally necessary. [31] If Boas was too dismissive of some persuasive evidence regarding language consanguinity, his over-arching philosophy of language, culture, and the methodology that could best explicate them, was consistent. The idea of genetic relations among American languages was a profound theoretical issue, pointing to equally profound differences between those who stood on one side or the other of Boas' revolution in American anthropology. As such it could also divide the Boasians themselves because it implied that some of his most cherished methodological ideas might not apply to languages, which were at the core of his program. To have this occur when that program was still embattled would have seemed particularly untoward, a gratuitous throwing of the match to the competing moiety within American Anthropology – to what Darnell (1998: xii) described as the other side of a fundamental divide, a physical anthropological, archaeological, natural science orientation as opposed to Boas' preferred linguistic, symbolic, and humanistic one. That other anthropological moiety was also the province of the many residues of what has been grouped as shorthand under the title "nineteenth century evolutionary thinking." It is perilous to attribute motives that were scarcely voiced, but circumstantial evidence counts. In 1919-1920 he suffered a brief professional setback when he was censured in the American Anthropological Association for his criticism of World War One espionage activities by American anthropologists in Mexico (Stocking 1968a). Even at that late date the struggle to eject Spencerian evolutionary schemes from American cultural anthropology would not yet have seemed won, though in fact the Boasians had already carried the day as more sophisticated versions of evolutionary theory emerged to be contrasted with mechanisms for culture change.

Later on Boas remained inflexible about cultural evolution not only because he was defending the field he had transformed from a resurgence of a scientific world-view he opposed, but probably also because he increasingly (and correctly) identified that world-view as naturally sympathetic to menacing political forces that emerged in the nineteen-twenties and thirties. The defeat of those forces by 1945 did much to finally discredit many evolutionary assumptions about human societies that had come down as parts of the heritage of nineteenth century evolutionary thought. But American academic anthropology became a Boasian stronghold well before the lamentable 1930s began. The totality of the post-World War Two collapse of the bundle of nineteenth century evolutionary ideas (for example, eugenics), an event which Boas himself did not live to see, plus the gradual realization of the limitations of his methods, conspired to telescope events and conceal from our retrospective gaze the degree to which Boasian anthropology had already triumphed by the early-nineteen twenties.

But the scientific picture needs greater resolution, for interpretation of the linguistic materials has not stood still, either. In privileged retrospect we may see now that neither the Penutian Super-Family proposed by Dixon and Kroeber, nor the Na-Dene Super-Family that was one of Sapir's most enduring legacies, have ever been proven taxonomically valid to the satisfaction of everyone (Hymes, 1961; Durr and Renner, 1995), though both survive as valid hypotheses, and are given pride of place in world language taxonomic maps. We are also to consider that although American historical linguistics has been the dominant paradigm for New World language work, it has not been the only successful one. Once the complexity of the field was apparent a student was almost obliged to either "go wide" or "go deep", to paraphrase Golla (2005), who labeled special cases of those two strategies "exogenous" and "endogenous". The former holds that New World languages in their bewildering variety show consanguinity with Old World stocks, and waves of prehistoric migration, account for their peculiar distributions. Deep time is not necessary for this, so when Dixon, Kroeber and Sapir postulated such connections, they were in comfortable conformity with the best archaeological evidence available at that time. The latter holds that New World Languages evolved *in situ*, through very deep time, from a single or a very few original stocks. All language groups presently found in the Americas are native "Amerind", (except Na Dene and Aleut), and the deep connections display only patterns of post-immigration diversification. While not necessarily entirely vindicated (both deep time presence and waves of migration could have been the case, and it was in this regard that Sapir's 1916 treatment of linguistics and archaeology in deep time was most useful and significant), this view gains support as the time depth of human presence in the New World is gradually extended by archaeology. Both of these strategies are at root historical and pose historical questions (Golla, 2005), and it was part of Sapir's genius that he could work at both, whereas the average student was hard put to master one.

As Durr and Renner (1995) pointed out, during the nineteen-twenties and thirties there also arose a presentist, structurally oriented reaction against the phylogenetic Indo-European method as it was applied to American Indian Linguistics. A mistrust of larger taxa took hold among some linguists, who suggested that historical questions were best ignored. The search for phylogeny was less useful than establishing relations based upon numeric treatment of characteristics to establish relative distances among present taxa. This paralleled cladistics in plant and animal taxonomy (a method Boas might have endorsed, had he lived to see it fully expressed).

Whatever their inner motives, as Kroeber gradually grew more persuaded by genetic relations among languages Boas became more conservative in the matter. In the Introduction to his *Handbook of American Indian Languages* (1911), Boas had acknowledged that the comparative historical studies of languages and cultures might have some place, but declined to say where that place was. A decade later he may have countenanced work highlighting "similarities" and "dissimilarities" in "the general historical problem" (Boas, 1920: 367-76), but remained opposed to linguistics based on an evolutionary principle. In *Evolution or Diffusion* (1924) he repeated his arguments as part of a discussion of the ubiquity of diffusion in the realm of culture. He wished to "set aside" questions of the origins of things and to concentrate on the mechanisms of universal admixture. Boas spoke of, "problems arising out of genetic relationships as either obvious or as impossibly difficult" (Voegelin, 1952: 439), and suggested that a great multiplicity of languages had existed almost from the beginning:

> "...So far as our historical evidence goes, there is no reason to believe that the number of distinct languages has at any time been less than it is now" (Boas, 1924)

In this uniformitarian stance on language there were no signs of a time in which the situation was less complex than it is now. Ultimate origins and relationships were lost in time and space by constant exchange of influences, all at short range. The original differentiation (whether one's theological leanings were toward a monogenetic or a polygenetic primordial source) was not only unrecoverable – it was immaterial to an understanding of diffusion. [32] Of course, Boas did not (and did not wish to) deny that languages changed, on their own through time as well as through borrowing. Nor did he deny that dialects became mutually unintelligible in time and space, another concomitant and tell-tale evolutionary pattern. Indeed, he once (quite late in life) even emphasized this (Boas, 1938: 134-36), acknowledging that dialects eventually became different languages (Sapir might have insisted that these analogies to speciation justified a genetic approach). That is, Boas appeared to relent on the issue somewhat eventually, though much too late to offer Kroeber or Sapir any comfort.

Like other aspects of culture, languages could as easily converge as diverge, and the swamping effects of borrowing made nonsense of attempts to chart them with divergence criteria. As has been seen, Boas' strongest expressions of this held that grammar diffused as readily as vocabulary (Boas, 1920, 1938). This, together with the problems inherent in studying non-written languages historically, constituted his chief technical justification for resisting the introduction of Indo-European methods into the New World. He saw cultures and languages as highly porous and open to diffusion, but also resilient, able and likely to turn imports to wholly new uses and meanings. Cultures could absorb, re-arrange, assimilate, and re-label virtually anything, material or ideational, that could diffuse. Meaning was the heart, very nearly the definition of culture, and because meaning change was all but ubiquitous in diffusion, it followed that cultures were incomparable. Their resilient porosity qualified them for individual treatment as unique combinations of traits and meaning, and what went for cultures also went for languages, which were their matrices. [33]

Sapir was not cited once in Boas' last general discussion of language, contained in his 1938 textbook *General Anthropology* (wherein he finally acknowledged some limited validity to genetic methods): "the problem of a genetic relationship between languages can be solved up to certain limits" (p. 136). However, he continued to maintain that grammar diffused as readily as vocabulary, and that the linguist's proper focus was on the language as it was lived and used, principally through fieldwork for text gathering and subsequent analysis. That preference reflected his focus on close processes rather than grand residues, without time consuming and futile searches for long trajectories in time and space. It also paralleled his insistence upon discussing culture change rather than cultural evolution. Thus, much as an ecologist is more apt to miss or dismiss the import of long-term fossil patterns in deep stratigraphy, he tended to dismiss those patterns when others found them. Here he and Kroeber inevitably parted company. Kroeber shared his disinclination to search for origins, but Boas was also discrediting back-azimuth and triangulation-type reasoning about culture history, methods which for Kroeber were indispensable. Clumps in the data, which Kroeber made such a great part of his life's work, seemed to him eminently comparable, even though they were also an occasion of sin.

Evolutionary schemes had occasionally rank-ordered languages, especially unwritten ones, according to their perceived distance from modern Western languages, in a kind of *scala natura*, yet another heritage concept from nineteenth century evolutionary thought. The parts of speech in the (presumably more complex) Western languages were sometimes taken as a standard by which other languages might be ranked as more or less advanced and therefore more or less conducive to complex thought. This presupposition eventually crumbled in the face of the exuberant complexity of the languages of even the most remote and technologically primitive societies, but in the teens of the twentieth century that complexity was not yet a canonical linguistic fact, and the home field advantage was still with those who claimed to wring a cultural premium from the Future Imperfect.

Rejecting the notion that the parts of speech in modern languages had less developed shadow counterparts in American Indian languages, Boas denied that there was a naturally optimal niche or role for such language components, for they were in no sense but a nominal one "natural", and were not any inter-lingual sense "optimal". It was therefore absurd to maintain that a lack of counterpart structures to parts of speech in modern European languages denoted a lack of sophistication. In his view, instead of being natural units of expression, the parts of speech were arbitrary lines of latitude and longitude being projected by linguists onto unfamiliar terrain. To assume the cross-cultural validity of parts of speech was to assume that logical accounts of verbal relations that had developed in their own right within and with self-reference to one language could be standards for judging wholly alien languages. The parts of speech, never mind the syntax in which they were used, were necessarily arbitrary. Indeed, it was not altogether clear that the English parts of speech were accurate depictions of what was happening in English. In the *Introduction* to his *Handbook* Boas argued that the sentence was the "natural unit" of meaningful expression (Boas, 1911), and that given the vagaries of sentence structure, even this vessel of meaning leaked.

Despite Boas' close focus, then, he assigned meaning to a level of language organization that was quite high and porous, carried by sentences and whole stories, well above the bits and bites of sound that cobbled its surface, which for Sapir (1933a) had psychological meaning. With his more particulate, bottom-up phonemic and morphemic approach, Sapir was probably not inclined to believe that he could not hear sounds aright, or even that parts of speech and their sequences were necessarily arbitrary. Moreover, for Sapir deep homologies helped to establish linguistic consanguinity. This made the modular and fragmenting data sets of linguistics amenable not only to fact collection, but to pattern recognition, both for the diffusing flow of "superficial" traits and the lineage-telling affinities of "deep" ones, the axes of phylogenetic investigation.

As in taxonomy, the utmost care had to be taken not to confound deep and superficial traits, homologies and analogies. Early on, Sapir showed some hesitation on this point with regard to a case of a possible convergent evolutionary trajectory in common between wholly different stocks:

> "…I don't know why Shoshonean linguistics has always been considered so simple. …The chief difference between Uncamphagre and Uintah Ute seems to lie in the fact that the former dialect has developed [certain constructs] …into long or doubled consonants …a peculiarity, curiously enough, that characterizes

Northern Yana as contrasted with Central Yana."
(ALKP: Sapir-ALK, 9/7/09)

On the best potential source of a solution he had no doubt. He had recourse to the work of German Indo-Europeanists and suggested that Kroeber do likewise (ALKP: Sapir-ALK, 12/12/09). At this early stage of their relationship Kroeber was already disposed to accept Sapir's advice in this manner, even though a first professional rift had opened between them the year before, as will be seen below. Meanwhile, Kroeber had begun one of his data-casting projects to elucidate degrees of language inter-relatedness by tabulating lexical borrowing throughout the greater California region. This would have been mostly a subtractive exercise given Kroeber and Sapir's convictions about the superficiality of most "cultural" (technological) vocabulary, and the more conservative nature of certain core vocabulary for such fundamental items as kin, body parts, and the like. Eventually it became the train of research that led to the discovery of the Hokan and Penutian language groups (Golla, 1984: 52).

Turf Alarms:

The first job of the Berkeley Anthropology Department, even before Kroeber arrived, was fieldwork, primarily archaeological collecting, but also ethnology, including linguistics. This was the intention of its founders and funders, foremost among them Pheobe Apperson Hearst, mother of the yellow peril newspaper magnate and the source of most of the departmental budget. After Kroeber arrived linguistic and ethnographic efforts received greater emphasis, but only over opposition. The University President and Regents were happy enough with the prospect of a research institute, but Kroeber wanted a department similar to that which Boas was constructing at Columbia, with students as well as a research program. To accomplish this he had to circumvent the absentee departmental chairman, F. W. Putnam, while also finding means to channel departmental resources away from archaeology and toward ethnography and linguistics. The former he accomplished easily, but the latter led to friction. Kroeber began teaching less than a year after he was hired, at first only one course every two semesters (ALKP: ALK-Advisory Committee, 11/8/02), but even this was more than his superiors had envisioned. In December 1901 Putnam, who believed that teaching would inhibit fieldwork and as an experienced administrator saw only folly in gainsaying those who wrote the checks, wrote angrily:

> "…It was distinctly understood that, for the present, there was to be no regular instruction at the University, in order that the time of all connected with the Department might be given to the accumulation of linguistic and archaeological and ethnological material." (ALKP: Putnam-ALK, 12/9/01)

He instructed Kroeber to talk the matter over with Berkeley's President Wheeler, apparently in the belief that Wheeler's position still corresponded to his own. This was a measure of how absent Putnam was, for student enrollments were growing quickly, and Kroeber had co-opted Wheeler with the promise of expanded undergraduate instruction. Five months later Putnam, an easy-going man, was sufficiently mollified to claim that he had only been piqued because he had not been consulted. He wrote approvingly of the work Kroeber and Dixon were doing on California languages (Dixon and Kroeber, 1903), as well as Kroeber's *A Preliminary Sketch of the Mohave Indians* (Kroeber, 1902), to which he wanted added a description of their distinctive facial tattoos. Reconciled to a teaching department, he merely admonished that he wanted:

> "…a few lines from you …as to what lectures or instruction you may have given during the past college year, as I wish to keep thoroughly posted on all that is taking place in the Department." (ALKP: Putnam-ALK, 5/8/02)

No one could have complained of the amount of fieldwork Kroeber did during his first three years in California, during which he was in the field for long stretches. In the most sustained ethnographic and linguistic field effort of his career he produced large components of a first comprehensive ethnographic and linguistic reconnaissance of the state. He was angling for the means to launch another such effort when Boas' graduate student, Edward Sapir, arrived in California to fill a temporary position in the linguistics program (Darnell, 1990a: 24-29). At Boas' suggestion, Sapir had begun corresponding with Kroeber in 1905, and they first met during the following year. By the summer of 1907, after some re-negotiating of terms when a potentially more permanent position at the University of Pennsylvania seemed to open up, Sapir was in the field, tasked by Kroeber with producing a grammar and basic dictionary of Yana, a distinctive but little-known Hokan language. Kroeber needed this study for his California survey. That is, it was meant to be part of a broad linguistic reconnaissance, and therefore reliant upon wider and necessarily more superficial recording than the preferred Boasian method of text-gathering. From the start Kroeber expected Sapir to conform to his research needs and urged a quick, sketchy approach. With a dissertation yet to defend before Boas, Sapir prudently stuck close to the textual method (ALKP: Sapir-ALK, 7/19/07), to which, as Darnell (1990b: 136-40) points out, he remained committed intellectually in any case. The Yana grammar and dictionary, emblematic of their relationship, was still unfinished when Sapir died in 1939. In later years both Kroeber and Sapir minimized this early disagreement, but in fact, to Kroeber's continual annoyed dismay, Sapir paid out parts of the Yana study in very small installments over the years.

We should not make too much of Kroeber's reluctance to use Boas' painstaking textual method. Stocking (1974a: 462) noted that: "despite his recalcitrance, [Kroeber] was clearly Boasian in his basic approach to American Indian Linguistics", and that attitude extended to what Boas saw as the optimal fieldwork and analytic tool. While there was a need to put Boas' preferred textual collection system on hold in California, this was a contingency and did not signify an abandonment of the method – still less any secession from the Boasian camp. Kroeber, too, collected texts, but with languages in danger of disappearing he saw no practical alternative to the survey approach used by the BAE in its first efforts to produce its linguistic map (Darnell (1998: 199-202; Lowie, 1936: xxi). Kroeber was still using texts to elucidate Mohave Culture many years later (Kroeber, 1948c). In fact, Boas himself sometimes wanted grammar and vocabulary served up in sketches to an approximate plan for his

Handbook, and had an early brush with Sapir on the issue (Darnell, 1990b), so Kroeber did not so much contradict Boas' method as simplify it in order to accomplish rescue-oriented reconnaissance.

In trying to garner more department resources for ethnography and linguistics, Kroeber quickly ran afoul of Charles Merriam, a geologist and archaeological enthusiast with a foot in several of the university's departments, as well as the Peruvianist archaeologist Max Uhle, who was more directly affiliated with both the Berkeley Museum and Anthropology Department. Both of them wished to use departmental resources to uncover the early cultures of California and to enhance collections – expensive objectives that would have left Kroeber without much funding. Pliny Earl Goddard, ethnologist, linguist and Kroeber's chief rival for leadership of the department once the awkward absentee arrangement with F.W. Putnam was terminated, was pulling in still another direction. He wanted a separate department of linguistics (Golla, 1984: 36), and managed to find common ground with the archeologists. Uhle got on quite well with German-speaking Kroeber, but none of them was above complaining about him to the University President and Regents.

The ensuing spat occasioned two ill-judged professional acts on Kroeber's part. The first was a nasty 10-page letter to Berkeley's President Wheeler about machinations against him, containing vitriolic attacks on Merriam and Goddard (ALKP: ALK-Wheeler, 3/2/09). Falling into the political hyperbole of the day, Kroeber called them "anarchists", insisting piously that he had only the best interests of the Department at heart and that he had no intentions of interfering with their work as they were interfering with his. Like Goddard, he threatened to resign, but unlike him, Kroeber had the advantage of fighting for the status quo – to sustain a general anthropology department rather than create a schism. More seriously, Kroeber allowed his heated frame of mind to cloud his scientific judgment, for he was thereafter unreasonably dismissive of the prehistory of California – something that helped to give him an overstated reputation for disdain of archaeology.[34]

This departmental turf fight became the context of a problem between Kroeber and Sapir, who wanted to stay on in California's language-rich environment. With Kroeber slow and perhaps unwilling to arrange something for him, the departmental squabble over resources presented Sapir with an opportunity. Evidently believing that the handwriting of brief tenure was on the wall for Kroeber, he appears to have rather half-heartedly thrown in his lot with Goddard, Merriam, and others who wanted to get rid of him. If this was in his mind, it was understandable, for someone would have to continue to do linguistic work and with Kroeber gone there was no reason why that person should not have been Sapir. Still lacking a degree, he was far too junior to have realistic designs on the departmental chair, and probably had no desire to occupy such a troublesome, time-consuming position. But a permanent job, which Kroeber was not offering, probably seemed possible. We may speculate whether Kroeber's reluctance to help Sapir stay at Berkeley was born chiefly of their methodological differences or of fear that such a talented person might eventually displace him. Whatever may have been the case initially, Sapir's ill-advised alliance with his adversaries would have clinched Kroeber's decision to send him packing. As Kroeber wrote to Putnam, and later to Berkeley's President Wheeler, unfaltering "loyalty to the department" (read "compliance with Kroeber's wishes"), was the most desirable quality in a job candidate (ALKP: ALK – Putnam, 2/19/08; ALK-Wheeler, 3/2/09).

Layers of misunderstanding surrounded this matter, with half-truths uttered and half-measures taken on both sides. At one point Kroeber did try to have the university take Sapir on in some additional temporary capacity in order to carry on with Yana fieldwork, but was constrained by regulations regarding what kind of work was to be pursued and by whom – a prosaic factor that the more ethereal Sapir seemed not to fully appreciate. [35] In fact though, Kroeber also negotiated to get Frank Speck into the position Sapir wanted so badly, and wrote to Putnam that Sapir was "not the man we want" (ALKP: ALK-Putnam, 5/15/08; 5/21/09; Golla, 1984: 23 and 38-39). It is unlikely that Sapir would have accepted any reduced-capacity position that might have been forthcoming, and external events made hiring him in any capacity that year impossible. An economic depression had set in across the country in 1907-08, and in its wake Hearst Family financial support for the Anthropology Department contracted so sharply for 1908-09 that fellowships were cancelled and hiring frozen. Whatever the relative weight of these several factors, Kroeber was not displeased to see the back of Sapir when he left to accept another temporary position in Philadelphia, and rejoiced at Goddard's departure to study with Boas and to work in the American Museum of Natural History in New York. [36] When he did have some funding available for a temporary position during 1909, he tuned Sapir down once again (Golla, 1984: 39). He briefly offered a rather sanitized recollection of those times, many years later:

> "…The staff of [the Department] was reduced to two, Goddard and myself. A year later, Goddard, depressed by the contract prospects at Berkeley, accepted a position at the American Museum of Natural History in New York." (Kroeber, 1960b)

On that late occasion Kroeber did not even mention Sapir (who after all had been only a temporary hire), and forgot or neglected to mention that he and Goddard had been at odds in an academic imbroglio in which Sapir had burned both ends against the middle. Despite this unhappy early chapter in their relationship, and the physical distance between them, Kroeber and Sapir were soon again drawn together by their central research interest, and embarked on a period of collaboration that peaked in 1913 and continued more sporadically for most the rest of the decade. The first part of this essay has set the stage for the second, which recounts their relationship during that time, and Kroeber's gradual withdrawal from linguistics to seek preeminence in other parts of anthropology.

Part Two
A Narrative of Cooperation
and Friction

Overview:

Kroeber and Sapir were mutually supportive in the interests of Boasian anthropology and Historical Particularism, its core methodology, and they worked together to establish the genetic view of languages in the New World. But alliances have tensions, in their case not only between them, but with Boas, with whom they had both theoretical and personal differences. In Sapir's case, much of the tension was born of his attempts to displace Boas as the leader of American linguistics, as well as the problem of genetic relations among American Languages (though Silverstein [1986] pointed out that Boas and Sapir remained rather close on the more philosophical plane where the essential nature of their scientific object was enshrined, and that the essential structure of Sapir's arguments always remained Boasian). Their gradually deteriorating relationship bracketed the time of Boas' wider political troubles and was acted out in several episodes – in effect a long contest for the primacy held by Boas by right of paternal possession, but which Sapir coveted. Kroeber was uncomfortably aware of Sapir's oedipal ambition, which complicated matters at a tense time when most

Boasians felt obliged to stand up and be counted; a time when, in Lowie's (1948) recollection, "every mother's son of us stood for the right."

In retrospect, the downturn in their relationship is signposted. In 1917 Sapir rejected a suggestion from Boas that he send him a preliminary copy of his Paiute Grammar (FBP: Sapir-Boas, 3/28/17), an event that may be taken as the end of their active cooperation and the beginning of a long process of estrangement. Because the core of their conflict contained theoretical matters as well as a turf scrap, their feud, if not inevitable (Darnell, 1990a: 16-29), was always in the cards. An evolutionary, genetic approach to languages was objectionable to Boas, but Sapir's bid to control funding, and his eventual espousal of a linguistic secession from ethnology, threatened the fragile unity of American anthropology. That last aspiration was the most serious, though it was not fought out until the 1930s, when Sapir came to believe that the field had to be divorced from American anthropology if it was to prosper. But well before that, by the beginning of the 1920s he already envisioned a new linguistic program for the Americas, with linguistic methods closer to Old World Indo-European work and a professional organization that could transcend its connection with the American Anthropological Association. Regarding methods he had Kroeber's support, but in secession he did not. To be sure, Kroeber once wrote to Sapir urging him to "shake off the anthropology stamp" (Golla, 1984: 362, ALK-Sapir, 1/17/21), but he was by then in despair of ever measuring up to him as a linguist. Kroeber saw no gain in divorcing linguistics from ethnology, even though he divorced himself from linguistics. The remainder of this essay is an account of episodes that, from Kroeber's perspective, constituted handwriting on the wall, and led to that divorce.

I wish to show how those accumulating tensions and Kroeber's loss of professional ground to Sapir eventually caused him to drop linguistics until after both Sapir and Boas had died, by which time his ability to contribute to the field had decayed. This sketch of the unequal relationship between Kroeber and Sapir, with Boas as its center of mass, is not intended to suggest that the Boasian Ascendancy was a monolith from which they were shivered by the force of great theoretical collisions – a Superorganic metaphysic in Kroeber's case and an Indo-European linguistic philosophy in

Sapir's. As Opler (1967: 4) pointed out, Boasians never spoke with one voice (though this variety has fostered the false notion that they did not constitute a school). However, it was seldom simply a matter of Boas' students falling out among themselves, either, for he exerted sufficient attractive and repulsive force to keep the orbits of his satellites unstable. Also, much else was at stake in those years, both in the small world of anthropology and in the wider world of politics.

Darnell (1990a: 110-42, 1998: 199-204) suggested that in the course of their correspondence Sapir graduated Kroeber from a descriptive Boasian to a genetic view of languages. Their letters, particularly after 1916, do indeed indicate that Sapir brought Kroeber to a more robust genetic view than he was likely to have attained on his own, though by that time Kroeber was already beginning to pull away from linguistic work. Nevertheless, Kroeber probably had the basic idea first, even though Sapir's linking of languages and language families was far more skillful, widely flung and exuberant. Their correspondence throughout the first half of that decade had orthography as its primary topic, with language consanguinity as a sub-text, as both of them warily circled a priority neither could claim unreservedly. [37]

For his part, and although he did not say so openly at first, well before 1910 Sapir probably believed that languages were genetically related, and for about as long may have intended to elucidate those relationships, even if we may suppose that it was Dixon and Kroeber's work on Hokan and Penutian as collective groupings of California languages, as well as Sapir's own growing conviction regarding the reality of the Na-Dene super-stock and the possibility of relationships between Yurok, Wiyot and the Algonquian languages in eastern North America that galvanized him to begin work on genetic relations in earnest (Eggan, 1986: 3-4). But priority is all-important to scholars, so despite their common cause Sapir would have been ambivalent about Kroeber's progress and reluctant to aid him unnecessarily. This is not the usual image of their collaboration, but it comports with the tenor of their correspondence and with the timing of Kroeber's professional decision-making. It was therefore an important concession when Kroeber acknowledged that Sapir's work on Wiyot and Yurok (Sapir, 1913) "entirely superseded" that which he and Dixon had done (ALKP: ALK-Sapir, 12/30/13). Kroeber knew Sapir had done a far better and more complete job, but wanted at least partial credit for finding the family relations among many stocks.

All this entailed friction with Boas. Sapir deferred to him at first, and as an ethnologist he was cast in the Boasian mold, but his deference did not long pertain in language work. [38] Voegelin (1952: 442-43) suggested that Sapir, "was the incomparably brilliant exemplar of the Boas Plan – when he followed the plan", but as Stocking (1968b) later pointed out, the "Boas Plan" was more a set of guidelines than map or blueprint. Sapir more than anyone else devised its orthography, but he would not always follow the strictures he had suggested for others. Boas had recognized Sapir's brilliance from the start, and this high professional regard did not evaporate after Sapir began linking languages. Lowie (1965/84) claimed that, "Intellectually Boas did for Sapir what Hume did for Kant: he roused him from dogmatic slumbers", and that Sapir long kept his affection for the older man, implying that the more angry their quarrel was the greater was their mutual regret. Although Lowie only maintained that Sapir's regard lasted until about 1923, that much at least seems right, for even much later (in 1930-31) Boas was still trying to get both Kroeber and Sapir to Columbia before he retired so that they could work on American linguistics together.

A Cooperative Phase:

The linguistic opportunities in California and Kroeber's proprietary attitude toward them continued to be a sore though muted issue. If territoriality was among Kroeber's motives in shifting Sapir out of California in 1908, he had a change of heart as the mass of the work to be done weighed down upon him. But his ambivalence deepened as Sapir repeatedly upstaged him during the following decade, all the while remaining his most frequent correspondent, and for a time his closest confidant. Given their somewhat fractious start, their physical distance (they did not meet between early 1908 and late 1915), and perhaps also due to their (actually rather different) Germanic heritages, Kroeber and Sapir were slow to drop formal salutations and mannerisms in letters. Nonetheless, in several exchanges during 1909-10 they were clearly searching for common ground. During 1910 they corresponded about Sapir's job prospects (a touchy subject), the overdue Yana vocabulary and grammar, which Sapir never produced (another touchy subject), recommendations for younger colleagues, and Sapir's work on Takelma and Paiute, which was producing friction with Boas because Sapir was no longer adhering to his program (Darnell, 1990a: 21). By 1911 Sapir had dropped most formalities and wrote expansively on the general progress of linguistics, and 1913 saw their most sustained collaboration; though it was as much a race as a cooperative enterprise.

Their closer, more frequent and most collaborative correspondence began after Sapir made his superior talent for linguistics clear in his reply to Kroeber's paper, "*Noun Incorporation in American Languages*", written for the 16th International Congress of Americanists and published in 1910. Kroeber had called skeptically for proof of the existence of "objective" noun incorporation into verbs – something he believed had often been asserted on insufficient evidence. Sapir, who later made much of this "polysynthesis", showed the phenomenon to be real, even widespread, drawing his examples from many, mostly unrelated languages (Sapir, 1911). Kroeber quickly and graciously acknowledged the superiority of Sapir's reasoning, both in print (Kroeber, 1911d) and in a letter:

> "I am very much interested in your article in the <u>Anthropologist</u>, and delighted with it. If only one or two of the authors who have touched on the problem in regard to a single language had shown as much insight as you did with half-a-dozen, the matter would have been clear long ago, and my paper [Kroeber, 1910b] would never have had to be printed. As it is, I am glad that my challenge was productive to your essay" (ALKP: ALK-Sapir, 11/18/11).

Sapir replied effusively, offering his analysis of some notes on Yana which Kroeber had earlier forwarded to him for comment. His tone already suggested a realistic sense of his superiority as a linguist – a sense that only grew thereafter. After announcing his belief in Uto-Aztecan as a set of related languages in a family grouping Sapir closed with the boast that he believed himself to be "on the trail of several important phonetic laws", a rather non-Boasian goal that bespoke his adherence to the Indo-European paradigm (ALKP: Sapir-ALK, 11/27/11). Just before the yearly AAA meeting, Sapir wrote again to inform Kroeber that he intended to read a paper entitled "Southern Paiute and Nahuatl", which would "establish the soundness of your claims beyond cavil" (ALKP: Sapir-ALK, 12/23/12), by which he meant Kroeber's suggestion that these were parts of a language family and that the Powell classification of North American Indian languages had wrongly kept apart several languages that comprised the Uto-Aztecan stock (particularly Shoshonean, Nahuatl, and Piman; see Golla, 1984: 68). This vindication and acknowledgement of his lumping work was surely gratifying to Kroeber, but it was Sapir and not he who had accomplished it.

The hinges upon which Kroeber and Sapir again turned toward collaboration were the appearance of Ishi toward the end of 1911 (T. Kroeber, 1970), and in 1912-13, Boas' Orthography Committee. Sapir was gratified by Kroeber's offer to let him debrief a "totally wild Yana Indian", and there can be little doubt that for his part Kroeber believed he had found the hook to draw the overdue Yana work out of Sapir. [39] By March 1913 though, Sapir was taking exception to Kroeber's comments on his orthographic proposals (Golla, 1984: Appendix I, "Reply to Kroeber's comments", 3/27/13). Despite Sapir's early and possibly disingenuous suggestion that he was less than fully convinced of the worth of the genetic approach, by that time it was already clear that he was taking the wheel in American linguistics, particularly in linking related languages groups across the continent (Sapir, 1913), and Kroeber began to fear that he might be driving too fast (Darnell, 1990a: 110-21). Sapir was appropriately reluctant to appear less than wholly empirical, or to undermine their common platform. He was therefore slow to put out a general statement of the question, preferring to approach it with concrete arguments for one pair or group of languages after another (e.g., Sapir, 1911, 1913, 1915b, 1916, 1917b and c, 1920). This forbearance eventually resulted in a serious clash with Kroeber over a publication by Paul Radin (below).

The Orthography Committee:

In the opening days of 1912, after discussions at the 1911 annual AAA meeting, a Committee for Phonetic Transcription of Indian Languages was formed at Sapir's urging and under Boas' chairmanship (Darnell, 1990a: 89-91). This body, which nearly all who had to do with it at first believed would answer a crying need, initially consisted of Boas, Goddard and Sapir, but soon included Kroeber and J.P. Harrington of the BAE. Ishi's arrival had already triggered Kroeber and Sapir's most collaborative phase, but working together on orthography offered a parallel field for collaboration. A maximally objective and uniform orthography was desirable for both methodological and theoretical reasons: to promote peer critique and collaboration, and to avoid undue imposition of ethnographic categories upon the subject language – not quite a formally epistemological matter, but a difficult task. These were sound Boasian goals, but this unique instance in which Boas and his most prominent linguistics students launched a project together showed how quickly underlying tensions, some of them connected to the question of genetic relationships among languages, could surface. Work began within the month, like so much Columbia anthropology at Boas' dining table (Golla, 1984: Appendix I). Sapir was enthusiastic, and in announcing to Kroeber in uncharacteristically clipped and businesslike prose that he (Kroeber) was to be on the committee, he also asserted emphatically and a bit grandly that the Powell orthography would be scrapped:

> "I have been instrumental in having a committee appointed at the Cleveland meeting of the AAA …intended to propose a new practical system for phonetic rendering of Indian languages. Chairman: Boas; other members: you, J.P. Harrington, Goddard, and myself. …Our system will, if accepted, become official, i.e. recommended, for AAA and will doubtless be presented at Washington in 1914 [International Congress of Americanists]. This system, which should be adequate, yet not cumbrous, would naturally try, where possible, to adhere to what may be general consistent usage in America, and should also aim

> ...to approximate current European usage. Aim: to further uniformity in American [linguistics] and to bridge over gulf separating American and European usages to some extent. Powell's system to be definitely abandoned. Please write Boas or myself what suggestions you have to offer." (ALKP: Sapir-ALK, 1/1/13, misdated 1912)

Kroeber was slow to agree to sit on the committee (ALKP: ALK-Sapir, 6/20/13; Darnell, 1990a: 88-90), but once on it he was enthusiastic, at least at first, declaring his intention to "serve as a brake on any extremists that may develop" (ALKP: ALK-Sapir, 1/16/13).[40] He also seemed, at least momentarily, to discount the complexity of languages in favor of emphasis upon a greater underlying uniformity. This was in keeping with the kinds of assumptions that any orthography required, but diluted the focus on limitless diversity that Boas usually favored. He continued: "...I'll see trouble from Harrington, probably. He's keen and well informed, but perhaps because of his youth... [has a] ...riotous inclination to indulge in the expression of fine shades of sounds in the symbols used for them."

In addition to the inherent complexity of their task, in effect to parse and standardize the recording and transcription of what Boas' philosophy held to be a sound continuum, the committee worked with tactical disadvantages. First, they set a time limit for themselves, aiming to agree on a system of transcription within a year, before the AAA meeting in December 1913. The follow-on goal was to present it as a unified American position on linguistic recording procedures at the International Congress of Americanists in Washington the following year. European-born or Europe-oriented scholars still considered the ICOA a most prestigious forum for theoretical and methodological validation. In the event, the ICOA meeting was cancelled due to the outbreak of war in Europe, but the deadline could not have been met anyway – indeed, the matter was still not settled in 1935, when Swadesh published a call for uniformity and precision. Secondly, apparently at Harrington's suggestion and with Kroeber's initial support, the committee was committed to unanimity, which made resolution of any serious issue among strong personalities unlikely. Kroeber eventually saw this as a serious handicap (ALKP: ALK-Sapir, 4/22/13, 5/8/13).

In private Sapir was not always sanguine about the prospects for uniform orthography, and believed that Boas was much too strict in his interpretation of how uniform a system ought to be. Sapir wanted every nuance captured, but also believed that many orthographic decisions were best left to the discretion of competent researchers in the field. His own approach was frequently rather intuitive, and his confidence in his abilities and reluctance to accept someone else's system were far greater than those of the average field linguist, who might have been glad of a blueprint. Nor, with a world to win in American historical linguistics, was he inclined to commit himself to any procedure that might inhibit his investigative liberty or means of expression. Therefore he did not engage with the committee in a whole-hearted manner for very long. For his part, Boas needed the most uniform possible set of procedures to impose maximum comparability on the data sets. Given his views on the vagaries of hearing and recording, and dependant as he was upon the work of people who were not always fully trained linguists (a contingency of the rescue ethnography ethic), this was understandable. As Sapir's views gradually prevailed, Boas too temporarily lost interest in the committee, his opportunity for European validation of any new system having literally gone up in smoke anyway.

As the Committee's project dragged on, Kroeber's enthusiasm also gradually waned, though he wanted to finish the job (ALK-Sapir, 3/18/13). In addition to the frustrations of committee work, he was increasingly concerned that a system complex enough to reflect external linguistic reality might be too cumbersome to learn and use, and that the committee was heading in that counter-productive direction. The work went forward in desultory fashion until Kroeber fell out with Harrington in 1916 when, on behalf of E.L. Hewett, he tried to muscle his way back into California linguistics while Kroeber was on sabbatical. [41] During that year the Smithsonian Institution published an interim report on the committee's work, but instead of a single unified system it offered several balanced alternative recommendations on the best available orthographic practices – a sure sign of divided counsel. Sapir was tasked with re-writing this report, but disliked having Boas peering over his shoulder. In March 1915 he wrote to Kroeber that he had put a "third, and I hope final, draft with Boas and Goddard quite a long time ago… [it] has been definitely approved… without reservations of any kind." He indicated that they intended to publish it in the AA, or in "the new linguistic journal (*Language*) that they are talking of inaugurating" (ALKP: Sapir-ALK, 3/15/15). His earnest hope for a final draft probably belied his assertion about no reservations on Boas' part. Either he was being optimistic about Boas' opinion, or he was trying to obtain Kroeber's approval quickly to sway the others.

Kroeber's Genetic Epiphany and the Unspoken Question of Priority:

In the first flurry of language-linking publishing Kroeber won the plume for quantity, Sapir for quality. [42] Ten years after their initial, timid reconnaissance in 1903, Dixon and Kroeber produced *Relationship of the Indian Languages of California* in the February 1913 number of *Science*, along with a more comprehensive article in *AA* that same year. On his own Kroeber also published *The Determination of Linguistic Relationship* (Kroeber, 1913). Between times he had produced substantial sketches of eleven languages and notes on some seventy more, along with five studies of compound nouns and noun incorporation, new linguistic families, and phonetics. However, even well after his first open advocacy of a genetic approach (Dixon and Kroeber, 1913a: 225), he still occasionally professed to be unconvinced of its value, at least in the strong version that Sapir came to propound. This waffling annoyed Sapir, who was coming to doubt Kroeber's abilities (Darnell, 1990a: 111). This pattern repeated itself, turn for turn, over several years, with Kroeber usually erring to the side of caution, trying to brake Sapir's brilliantly intuitive forays into language linkages (ALKP: ALK-Sapir, 1/16/13). [43]

Kroeber made the first overt grab for priority. Crossing in the mails with Sapir's letter about the impending demise of Powell's orthography was Kroeber's account of his sudden conversion event regarding the genetic relations among languages. Kroeber and Dixon had been slowly preparing their 1913 essays on language families in California. While Dixon traveled in India, Kroeber wrote of his renewed interest in Yana and the lexical collecting he and Dixon had done in order to "work out the extent of borrowing" – a phrase too Boasian by half, given what followed:

"I have lately become very much interested in Yana once more. You will remember that for two or three years past Dixon and I have been collecting lexical information on all the California dialects with a view to working out character and extent of borrowing between unrelated languages. We were both convinced that until this information was available it would be impossible to furnish convincing proof of the relationship of Chimariko to Shasta [suggested by Dixon, 1910], and of Costanoan to Miwok [suggested by Kroeber, 1910a], which we both believed in. You will recall being good enough to furnish me with a list of some 250 Yana terms for the purpose, which… proved exceedingly convenient in …our acquaintance with Ishi. Our material and the tabulations …were recently completed and in Dixon's absence in India I have been going over same pretty thoroughly."

By then Kroeber was not much more interested in borrowed vocabulary than Sapir was. Instead, he was tracing both lexical and grammatical commonalties, though he made it sound as though the pre-realization stage grammar had a merely confirming role. He had worked away, making no progress until the scales suddenly fell from his eyes in an (appropriately inductive) epiphany:

"I could, however, get no intelligible result from our data until finally in desperation I dropped the assumption, under which we had been all along been working, that all these resemblances were due to accident or borrowing and assumed genetic relationship between those languages that had the greatest number of similarities. From this time on the skein unwound itself and when I turned to grammatical structure for confirmation it was lying at hand ready made in every instance. My wonder now is that we have overlooked the obvious so long and my only explanation is that we missed the clue and, comparing each language sometimes with the

related and sometimes with unrelated ones until we
were in such a state of demoralization that we gave
up the problem. *I know this is exactly what happened
to me on my first attempt in the same direction ten years
ago* (italics mine). [44]

If Sapir found either the conversion experience, or the claim to
have nearly discovered all this a decade before to be implausible, in
his reply he did not ask whether Kroeber had simply forgotten this
important discovery in the interim. What Kroeber was announcing
amounted to an equal claim to the idea that historical linguistics in
America traced an evolutionary pattern – and he was going public:

> I feel so confident of what we now have in hand that
> I am sending a brief statement to *Science* announcing
> that Wintun, Maidu, Miwok, Costanoan, and Yokuts
> all constitute only one family and that another family
> is made up of Shasta, Chimariko, Pomo, very probably
> Karok and—this will surprise you—possibly Yana.
> In any event, whether they represent relationship
> or borrowing, it is clear that the affinities of Yana
> are all with this last family. On the basis of stems
> alone, I should have no very great hesitation in joining
> Yana with the others, but the structure still seems
> quite different. As we are, however, without available
> information as to Yana grammar beyond what I can
> recall from conversation with you and the list of
> suffixes you were kind enough to send me about a
> year ago, I write to ask you whether you will favor me
> as soon as convenient with answers to the following
> points..." (ALKP: ALK-Sapir, 1/3/13)

In his somewhat delayed reply Sapir's tone was distinctly cool.
He left the meat of the matter until last, and made certain to indicate
the local character of Kroeber's "discovery". As if to emphasize
that he was the acknowledged source of theoretical validation he
answered a question on theoretical soundness which he had not
been asked and sensibly withheld judgment on Dixon and Kroeber's

Penutian-Hokan-Ritwan hypothesis until all the evidence was in. He added a demurrer regarding relations among several of the languages Kroeber had mentioned:

> "Your data in regard to California linguistics are, of course, extremely interesting to me. ...Your new syntheses of linguistic stocks in California are rather exciting, but I see no theoretical reason why they should not be sound. Everything depends, of course, on the matter of your evidence, the presentation of which I am looking forward to with very great interest. As for Yana, I should not have been disposed myself to believe that it is in any way related to Chimariko, Pomo, or Karok, judging from the small amount of material that has been published on these languages. One striking difference between Pomo and Yana is the absolute lack of instrumental prefixes in the latter, Pomo and Chimariko in this respect agreeing with Shoshonean. In fact there is not a single prefix in Yana, a point that will probably have to be considered..." (ALKP: Sapir-ALK: 1/15/13)

There followed a series of additional points on Yana, to which Kroeber replied that the question would be resolved only through more patient fieldwork, along with a measure of intuition about the amount of analytical weight the "spirit" of a language should be given. He seemed happy enough with the implication that they might share priority:

> "...Every point you mention either shows a positive resemblance to the structure of the Shasta group or at least a negative agreement. The lack of prefixes is what all along bothered me most. This seems, however, not to be an insuperable obstacle. Maidu has developed instrumental prefixes which are entirely lacking in the other languages of the group to which it belongs and yet if there is anything at all in our present point of view there can be no question of the connection

of Maidu with the four other stocks. Moreover there are enough striking instances in both Uto-Aztecan and Algonkin of the transfer of certain elements from prefixes to suffixes or vice versa (sic), to make a difference of this sort not insuperable. I have a feeling, however, that the spirit of Yana grammar is quite different from that of the other languages of the northern group and while, in the scarcity of available information, this feeling may be little more than blind intuition which will be dispelled as soon as we know more, it is strong enough to make me go slowly." (ALKP: ALK-Sapir, 1/21/13)

Sapir thereupon threw more cold water on Kroeber's program on grammatical grounds, even briefly alluding to grammar diffusion as an explanation, which at that point they both viewed as an idea generally inimical to the genetic approach:

> "...I do not know if the lack of prefixes in Yana is an insuperable obstacle, but it certainly suggests a fundamental difference of grammatical structure between it and Chimariko, for instance. I do not believe your analogy of Uto-Aztecan and Algonkian is a good one. ...I imagine that ...instrumental prefixes in Maidu might develop as a special form of noun-verb or verb-noun compounds under the influence of Pomo or other non-related language possessing instrumental prefixes..." (ALKP: Sapir-ALK: 1/27/13)

With his grounding in Indo-European linguistics, Sapir must have felt certain that genetic relations would be found to be all but ubiquitous, so either he felt Kroeber was trying to make a good point with bad examples, or he was not keen about Kroeber getting out so far in front. Given some pause by Sapir's evident lack of enthusiasm, Kroeber replied stoutly with some small modifications and a fall-back position. With regard to the evidently unique prefixes in Maidu verbs he was prepared to suggest that a wholly new feature had emerged in a family of languages that sported no such structure elsewhere among its many members. This nodded toward Boas' notion of extreme language plasticity, but also allowed for what nearly amounted to saltation in linguistic evolution.

> "I still agree with you that there seems to be a fundamental structural difference between Yana and the languages of the Shasta group. I believe I attached fully as much weight to the matter of suffixes *versus* prefixes as you do. I am also ready to admit that Algonkian and Uto-Aztekan are only partial parallels. At the same time their analogy is not entirely without point and so far as relationship of Yana to the other languages goes, I am not yet ready to give this up. I unquestionably can not prove it, but so far structural similarities have so regularly followed in the course of lexical resemblances that I will refuse to disbelieve in the connection between Yana and Shasta until it is positively disproved.
>
> I appreciate also the force of your keen remark as to the Maidu prefix. Dixon [ref. to Dixon, 1911] makes it quite clear that at least some of them are merely the first elements of compound verbs. The difficulty that remains therefore is not the prefix, but, as you correctly observe, the existence of the compound. When we know more about the original structure of the group …such compounds may …prove to be a feature retained by the Maidu. If this is not the proper explanation, I can see nothing for it but to take the bull by the horns and admit that Maidu has developed a type of compound entirely new to the family at large. I would rather make this assumption than to throw out of court all the accumulative evidence relating Maidu to the family."

Kroeber ventured a parallel example from Indo-European linguistics, along with an appropriate sop to Sapir's greater expertise in that field:

> "While I see that I must be more careful with you
> than with most people in citing analogies, I will
> take a chance at another in this connection. While
> I know nothing very definite about Indo-European
> philology, am I not correct in believing that Latin,
> for instance, has lost nearly entirely the compounding
> characteristics of Greek and Sanskrit? Is there not
> also a pretty fundamental reversal of method in the
> habit of Romanic languages of putting the qualifying
> element last in noun compounds?" (ALKP: ALK-
> Sapir, 2/4/13)

Once Dixon and Kroeber's note appeared in *Science* the die was cast, and Sapir was keen to be on board. He was even prepared to eat some crow to get there. With defensive phrasing, he retained a few reservations about drawing conclusions from parallel structures rather than painstakingly reconstructing a phylogeny. This may have reflected a difference of opinion between them regarding the nature of acceptable evidence, or perhaps Sapir still maintained that it was such as a delaying tactic. On the whole, Kroeber was more prepared to accept parallel structures as evidence of common descent (a procedure used in both taxonomy and paleontology to distinguish convergence from common descent by discerning analogous and homologous traits). Throughout most of 1913 Sapir insisted that an articulated phylogeny had to be shown to establish the genetic connection. However, his work in the years that followed often took flight well above this fundamentalist empirical approach, becoming at times quite intuitive. This was the last exchange on linguistics between them in which Kroeber kept the upper hand:

> "I have recently read your note in "Science" in regard to
> the linguistic developments in California. I hope you
> do not have the idea that I am personally opposed to
> such syntheses. In fact, I feel strongly that there will be
> more of them as our knowledge progresses. Everything
> naturally depends on the specific evidence. As regards
> parallels, I may say that I am not personally inclined
> to lay much stress on them one way or another, except

as merely suggesting possibilities. The actual historical process must be worked out independently on the evidence supplied by the particular problem. Parallels never constitute evidence. They merely predispose one in favor or prejudice him against accepting specific evidence... Please do not imagine that I think that radical change in grammatical form may not, in the course of time, be brought about within a linguistic stock. ...There are plenty of such developments in Indogermanic that ...seem quite revolutionary. ... [Such developments are] due, at last analysis, to the operation of regular phonetic law... ...if we assume enough time and favoring conditions, almost any change, ...may be ...shown to be possible. All that I personally feel like insisting on is that the evidence itself be such as to force one to adopt such and such conclusions. If you could spare the time, I should be very thankful if you could let me have at least part of the evidence that relates to Yana. Please do not imagine that I have any personal reason for preferring not to have Yana demonstrated as genetically connected with Shasta. In fact, I should be delighted if the total number of linguistic stocks in California should turn out to be very few in number, after all." (ALKP: Sapir-ALK, 2/11/13)

Kroeber briefly pretended to hold back on his evidence regarding Yana, a grammar of which Sapir had owed him for more nearly five years. He was also worried about how little phylogenetic evidence he had presented:

"I agree with you entirely as to parallels. They are nothing but analogies and analogies are never proof. I will be glad to comply with your request to send you the evidence relating to Yana, although in this one case it is almost entirely lexical. It may be some days before I find time to copy it out. ...The resemblances between any two individual languages are never so convincing as those which appear when an entire group is examined. This is in fact the crux of the whole matter. I have been comparing Yokuts and Maidu for a long time, but it was not until I drew in Wintun, Miwok, and Costanoan that the results commenced to be conclusive. I hope you will bear this in mind when examining the rather incomplete material which I shall send you. If you can add any similarities …I shall be very much obliged to you." (ALKP:ALK-Sapir, 2/18/13)

Apparently sensing Kroeber's uncertainty and need for an ally, and unimpressed with the phonetic recording methods he had used in collecting the Yana materials (which Kroeber in fact copied out and sent immediately), Sapir bought more time and gained the high ground once more by seeming to be unconvinced until he could have an opportunity to work with the materials himself. His stated reason was that Kroeber had leaned too much on lexical parallels, whereas real proof required deep grammatical homologies. Sapir also wanted to displace Dixon:

"Thank you for your linguistic material on Yana, which I have looked over with interest… Your material is certainly suggestive, but I cannot feel that I have any right to adopt a definite stand in the matter until I know far more about Sahastan morphology than I do. …It is difficult to know how to weight lexical correspondences without a definite knowledge of grammatical features as well. Some of your examples I should be inclined to erase without much hesitation… Some …seem quite suggestive and … certainly cannot be explained on the basis of mere accident.

I am sorry that the phonetics of the material that you are dealing with leaves so much to be desired. You must realize …that exact phonetic material is indispensable for any solid comparative work. …I rather think that some of your examples would have seemed even stronger had the phonetics of all the languages been as accurate as desirable. …And here let me warn you against Dixon's phonetics. They are indeed deplorable. …In fact, his whole work is amateurish to a degree. When I read his Maidu sketch [Dixon, 1911] I thought it was the last straw. If anything he is supposed to know Maidu, but …his knowledge of that language is quite elementary. He simply cannot hear well, and the more frankly one recognizes the fact the better." (ALKP: Sapir-ALK, 2/27/13)

With Sapir desirous of collaboration, Kroeber was still holding his own. He was not too contrite about the phonetics, for after all they both sat on Boas' committee to fix that problem. He did not miss the hint that Sapir's criticism of Dixon encompassed him, too:

"Thanks for your comments on my Yana list. They will be helpful. I did not expect the list to convince you thoroughly. You will realize as clearly as I that we cannot be finally judged until all our evidence is presented. I am glad that you agree, however, that we already have enough of a showing to make out a case. I am more sorry than you that our phonetics leave so much to be desired, as I realize the handicap under which it placed us. I believe that I am aware of my own deficiencies in this regard, but have hopes that I have heard enough of most of the languages in California to prevent me from falling into very many gross errors. A very cursory examination of the material, even without any knowledge of the language it represents, is enough to reveal the situation. …I am confident that we will come near enough to establishing our points to give work in the California field a new direction, and make it possible for those who are technically better equipped to prove or disprove what we believe." (ALKP: ALK-Sapir, 3/6/13)

Sapir absorbed this, and for two months their correspondence dealt only with the orthography committee and Sapir's long-term efforts to find a position for Paul Radin. In early May, Kroeber reopened their dialogue to offer what he considered to be one of the finds of his career:

> "I have always believed Seri to be Yuman. …I should be surprised if our Hokan group did not prove ultimately to be the nucleus of a very large stock." (ALKP: ALK-Sapir, 5/8/13)

Sapir, too, had been busy. The laconic confidence with which he announced his own candidates for inclusion in a genetic family suggested that he had been working on the idea for some time – certainly well before his earlier exchange with Kroeber about Yana (this became Na Dene, perhaps his greatest contribution to the study of New World languages – see Golla, 1984: 104; Renner, 1995):

> "*A propos* of larger linguistic units, which seem to be somewhat in favor just now, I may say that I have been occupying myself of late with Athabaskan, Tlingit, and Haida, and that I have collected enough evidence to convince myself at least of the genetic relationship of these three." (ALKP: Sapir-ALK:5/30/13)

Kroeber did not reply to this with his usual promptness, and Sapir wrote again, offering some parallels between Yurok and Salish (languages within Kroeber's California fiefdom, but to which Sapir had some claim by virtue of fieldwork years before). He was also beginning to fret about a reaction from Columbia:

> "Do you suppose Yurok might turn out to be related to Salish? Tillamook is not so awfully far away! Don't tell Boas—he'll think I've gone crazy." (ALKP: Sapir-ALK: no date, but dated by Golla to early June 1913 on contextual grounds)

Kroeber offered to help, but also put down a subtly qualified marker that Sapir was not the only person with a claim on those languages:

"The Yurok resemblances look mighty promising. I would be delighted if you were to follow the thing up, and if you run out of Yurok material, let Waterman or me know. ...We seem at last to have got Powell's old fifty-eight families on the run, and the farther we can drive them into a heap, the more fun and profit.

Waterman, the last time he was working on Yurok, told me repeatedly that he was impressed by its fundamental similarity in construction to Tshimshian, on which he had done some work with Boas while in New York. I do not believe he had in mind anything further than similarity of general morphological plan." (ALKP: ALK-Sapir, 6/20/13)

Within twenty-four hours of writing this, Kroeber read a manuscript on Uto-Aztecan vowels which Sapir had sent him on May 30 (mentioned in the letter in which he announced his interest in what later became the Na Dene Superfamily). In the face of this masterly performance Kroeber's tone immediately became more deferential, and his sense of being ahead of his junior colleague in accumulating telling evidence of genetic relations began to deflate. He could not avoid a note of envy as he acknowledged that Sapir was making the case for links between some California languages and a much more widely flung super-taxon of families, and in a way he might have begun but could not have managed. He seemed to be wondering whether he still had time to develop a claim to the general genetic idea, at least as it applied to California languages. He certainly chose an unpropitious time to refer to his failure to offer a position to Sapir five years earlier:

"I have gone through your manuscript with the greatest of interest. I can only congratulate you on your critical ability and capacity for work. Much of what you have accomplished I am scarcely equipped to do, but now that you have covered the ground, I feel that there are some points which I should certainly have worked out some years ago if I had given it my attention instead of having my head full of other and probably less important things. If anyone can still doubt the general proposition of relationship he is obviously prejudiced. I am glad, however, that you have brought the situation to a point where the question is no longer one of fact as to relationship, but one of working out its circumstances and tracking the history of the individual languages.

Do you plan to publish as a unit what you have sent me, or shall you withhold same until the entire monograph is completed?

The feeling …uppermost in my mind is one of regret at our being so small an institution that we could not have provided you with a favorable opening and kept you with us.

With heartiest congratulations…" (ALKP: ALK-Sapir, 6/21/13)

Sapir, who had evidently been preparing this coup for some time, replied to both letters with one. Perhaps put off by Kroeber's implied point about Waterman's work in that area, he damped down Kroeber's enthusiasm for the potential for the Yurok-Salish parallels (which, in fact, Sapir had suggested) on the empirical ground that Salish was so very divergent and so poorly recorded, though he left some room to maneuver on the question. While bemoaning the time it would take to be published he also boasted a bit at his success in placing his Uto-Aztecan materials in a prestigious European journal. In the event, the outbreak of war delayed publication in France, and eventually the material was published both in the French journal and in *American Anthropologist* (ALKP: Sapir-ALK, 11/2/14). It was not just Powell that Sapir wanted on the run. His evolutionary language now suggested greater preparedness to confront Boas on the broader question of genetic relations. Boas had drawn attention to some of those same parallels himself, attributing them to convergence through borrowing:

"I have your letters of June 20 and 21. I wonder if you are not taking my Salish parallels for Yurok somewhat more seriously than facts warrant. While I do not know either Yurok or Salish very thoroughly, it seems fairly obvious that there are tremendous differences between them. Thus, you state [ref. to Kroeber, 1911a] that reduplication is only sparingly used in Yurok, whereas in Salish its use is almost excessive... But perhaps there is something back of my similarities, after all. The trouble with comparing with Salish is itself so terribly split up into divergent dialects that it would require a great deal of specifically Salish work to determine what was really most fundamental in that stock and comparable with other stocks. As Boas has pointed out to me several times, there are remarkable morphological resemblances between Kwakiutl-Nootka and Salish, and ...they may turn out to be genetically related. There are, indeed, quite a few lexical resemblances between Yurok and Tsimshian. Perhaps Waterman did not quite realize that numeral classifiers are not confined to Tsimshian, though they are perhaps more characteristically developed in Tsimshian than in any other West Coast stock.

I am pleased that you thought well of my paper on Uto-Aztecan. I have sent it to Paris to be published in the Journal de la Societe des Americanistes de Paris. I have been informed that its first installment will appear in two successive numbers. This means that the whole paper will be dragged out over a ridiculously long time. If I had known that they were going to split the first installment, I would probably have preferred to have it published elsewhere. As it is, however, I have committed myself. ...Within a couple of weeks or so, I expect to be able to send you for publication in your series, should it prove acceptable, a paper entitled "Notes on Chasta Costa Phonology and Morphology". It is turning out to be a better-rounded paper that I had reason to think it would be, and should prove of at least comparative value for Athabaskan linguistics. ...Perhaps your series could be stretched to include this paper." (ALKP: Sapir-ALK, 6/27/13)

Kroeber defended his Salish–Yurok connection with a deft appeal to the small likelihood that form and meaning could have tracked each other exactly through a multi-stepped diffusion process. He was uncommitted about Sapir's offer of a few notes for UCPAAE:

> "I have never taken ...numeral classifiers, or any similar phenomenon, as indicating anything else other than inter-influence. When, however, you appear to discover resemblances of form corresponding to resemblances of meaning, it is another story...
>
> As regards your paper on Paiute and Aztec, you may be able to make some use of the list of Papago verb stems ...which should appear from our press in a couple of months.
>
> Your Chasta Costa proposition is mighty interesting, and I am keen about getting it for our series, as you suggest. I very much doubt, however, whether this will be possible. The University rule is that University publications shall represent the work of the University. This is interpreted to mean work done by other people on materials acquired or belonging to the University. If your Oregon notes had been acquired as a by-product of your Yana for us, they would, without any question, be available, but as you probably obtained them while on your Takelma expedition, I am afraid they would not be considered eligible. Our rule may be a bit arbitrary, but experience has shown the necessity of drawing a definite line somewhere... I will ...take the matter up with our Editorial Committee..." (ALKP: ALK-Sapir, 7/9/13)

Sapir replied somewhat testily:

> "My Chasta Costa material was obtained in 1906, when I was engaged on Takelma work for the Bureau of American Ethnology. However, this material was obtained at odd moments when I was not on regular

work. It involved no extra expenditure, and I have always considered myself entitled to do what I pleased with it without consulting the Bureau. I thought you might be interested in publishing it in your series, if only for the reason that it is so closely connected with Goddard's Athabaskan work. In fact, I refer constantly to his Hupa, Kato, and Chipewyan material in my paper. I am sending it to you so that you can see and judge for yourself. If, however, the University rules prevent you from publishing it, kindly return it at your earliest convenience, so that I may dispose of it otherwise without too great delay." (ALKP: Sapir-ALK, 7/19/13)

Kroeber put the matter to Berkeley's Editorial Committee, while again trying to get Sapir to produce some components of the long-awaited Yana ethnography and grammar:

"I am submitting [your manuscript] to the Editorial Committee and will advise you promptly. ...I should like nothing better than to publish your paper.

I have rather forgotten the status of your once projected sketch of Yana ethnology. ...You intended ...this for the Putnam volume but ...the material has not yet appeared. Since your Yana grammar does not appear to be making much material progress, would it not be possible for you to whip this smaller contribution into shape...? It would serve to keep your connection with the university fresher... and perhaps ...keep your interest in the institution warmer." (ALKP: ALK-Sapir, 7/26/13)

Sapir's paper was turned down (ALKP: ALK-Sapir, 9/6/13). At about the same time, there was an exchange of letters (some not preserved, see Golla, 1984: 112-13) regarding part of Sapir's main project for 1913, the inclusion of Wiyot and Yurok in the Algonquian Family of languages. This was a coup that Kroeber clearly felt he might have accomplished himself, if he had been more courageous and energetic. At this turning point in their relationship they passed and acknowledged each other in ascent and decline. Out of residual Boasian sentiment or simple envy, Kroeber hesitated regarding Sapir's findings. These were languages to which he had professional claims, and while he had to acquiesce in Sapir publishing the piece, he was clearly chagrined at having missed a highly significant pattern in his own materials. He was coming to regard even marginal evidence as deserving credence and again wished to remind of his long involvement in the issue:

> "Your trump card wins. …I …never dreamed of anything but a coincidence. After this, when I get three aces, I draw to them. No more discards. The whole moral of our California situation is that it doesn't pay to hang back, provided one is reasonably critical to begin with, and I hope you will profit by my many years of sitting on the lid, and cut loose before somebody else does. Our recent comparisons are going to stimulate others.
>
> The pronouns turn the trick, alone, but the rest looks good. My Yurok is in Waterman's hands, my Arapaho locked up in my office, and all the Wiyot I ever had is in my published sketch. …Instead of giving all my Arapaho to Michelson, …I'll hang on to it now until I can follow up this discovery a bit."
> (Golla, 1984, ALK-Sapir, 7/30/13) [45]

This was the starting gun for Kroeber's last sprint in linguistics. He and Dixon were preparing their account of California language families, with enough genetic language philosophy to make it apparent that they had a hand in developing the program. However, it would not top what Sapir was planning to do, as Kroeber knew.

Kroeber and Sapir were not alone in wanting to compress North American languages into fewer families than Powell (1891) had allowed. Among several other interested field workers, Paul Radin had done some work and was in possession of relevant field notes. Sapir had written to Radin earlier in that same month, asking for some of the materials in his keeping, but professing considerable doubt about the whole lumping enterprise. This was a smoke screen, for despite his periodic attempts to help Radin, he did not entirely trust him:

> "The …slaughter of linguistic families, upon which several of us seem to have embarked of late, is going on apace. …I now seriously believe that [Wiyot] and Yurok are related to Algonkin. The consequences of this latest theory are so great that I am hesitating very considerably, even in my own mind, about committing myself, and want to get more and more evidence before I confess to myself that I am convinced." (Sapir-Radin, 7/20/13, in Golla, 1984: 113)

At Sapir's urging, Kroeber went back to his Yurok materials in search of more evidence of Algonkin homologies, and found some. Although he was embarrassed to have Sapir see the primitive character of his early field notes, at Sapir's urging he laboriously copied out and sent the materials to him:

> "My Yurok is in bad shape for comparisons. I never got vocabularies except at the outset, and these are incomplete and horribly written. I have gathered what I can find …for your use. …I find some new and very obvious Wiyot resemblances." (This was followed by several typed pages of vocabulary, ALKP: ALK-Sapir, 8/5/13)

Sapir was working feverishly by this time, so his reply was brief and a little grudging. His use of "phonetic laws" is interesting as an Old World-sounding construction of language as necessarily conforming to some deeper logical imperative:

> "…Several of your resemblances I had already discovered independently. Am trying to work out phonetic laws. …I have accumulated as good evidence as …for genetic unity of Haida, Tlingit, and Athabaskan." (ALKP: Sapir-ALK, 8/5/13)

The following day he wrote at greater length on Kroeber's evidence, skipping among language families, incorporating more grammatical items and putting his mark on the materials Kroeber had provided. He finished gaily, agreeing that Kroeber should publish quickly. Forgotten or dismissed was his insistence seven months earlier that the whole phylogeny must be articulated before descent with modification was to be considered demonstrated:

> "Well, there's something in it all, i' faith! On another sheet I give some extra good ones, tho by no means all I have. There seems to be enough to lift my hypothesis into practical certainty, so why not make people aware? Detailed study can follow."

"His hypothesis" in this instance still referred to sinking Yurok and Wiyot into Algonkin, yet they were both still chary of saying this outright. They traded data freely, but as Sapir worked toward priority he also edged Kroeber away from center stage:

> "…I was thinking of beginning by giving further (chiefly lexical) evidence of genetic relationship of Y. and W. than has been already given [in Kroeber's 1911 sketch, to which he would refer], with due acknowledgment, of course, of your added data. Would this interfere in any way with your own plans? (Sapir-ALK, 8/12/13, in Golla, 1984: 120-21)

As Sapir became more confident and robust Kroeber grew more deferential, especially where the paltry nature of his data was concerned:

> "I enclose a brief list of Arapaho stems which may be of service to you. …However… I imagine that you will be able to make comparatively little use of it. At the time I recorded these words I did not know anything about surd vowels. I imagine that every final vowel in this list is really a surd, and that every final consonant should be followed by a surd vowel. I am

…convinced as ever that you are on the right track. I hope that you can find something in my recent Yurok list." (ALKP: ALK-Sapir, 8/12/13)

The tacit understanding that they were going to present themselves as co-developers of the application of the genetic approach in America was still holding, but the genetic relations of New World languages was an idea "in the air" by 1913, and Kroeber was beginning to fret about their precedence. Sapir had done so much more with his materials that Kroeber was prepared to give up any aspiration to equal him:

> "I hope that …you will be persuaded to publish soon. We are going to have a flood of such cases in the next few years, and the prestige of American Anthropology will be better maintained if at least some of the claims come with the backing of your critical faculty than if they are all made by people in whom the rank and file of us have less confidence. I think this is an important reason, in addition to the purely personal one of securing for yourself what you have found." (ALKP: ALK-Sapir, 9/14/13)

Over several months Kroeber and Sapir trumpeted each new piece of evidence to each other, while Sapir's devotion to Indo-European methods and an evolutionary paradigm became more evident:

> "It is almost humorous to see how stems at first sight very divergent in appearance turn out to be identical when phonetic laws have been worked out. P.S. I finished my paper on "Wiyot and Yurok, Algonkin Languages of California" [Sapir, 1913], and sent it to Hodge (F.W. Hodge, Editor of A.A.). I think my evidence looks convincing enough. Some phonetic laws seem to work out beautifully." (ALKP: Sapir-ALK, 9/12/13)

At year's end Kroeber wrote to Sapir that the article he and Dixon had written on new language families in California (Dixon and Kroeber, 1913b) was in the hands of the Editor of *American Anthropologist*, even though it was, "of course, entirely superseded by your work." (ALKP: ALK-Sapir, 12/30/13). They had modified their piece to take account of Sapir's forthcoming article on Wiyot and Yurok as Algonkin Languages in California (Sapir, 1913), and they wanted to describe Sapir's contribution as "brilliant and startling." Sapir did not reply, and Kroeber wrote to the Editor, F.W. Hodge, that he should go ahead and publish without mentioning Sapir or his "discovery". He added that: "for the first time in my acquaintance with him he is not answering letters." (ALKP: ALK-Hodge, 1/16/14) Hodge did not tell Kroeber that he already had Sapir's paper in hand (Golla, 1984: 133). Sapir later explained that his wife had been ill and there had been a fire in their home, but he probably did not want to reply, either.

The two articles appeared together in the last 1913 issue. In effect, Kroeber had wanted to cite Sapir's "discovery" of the links between Yurok and Wiyot as an example of the general principle he was elucidating, but that was the rub – it was the genetic principle that they both still hoped to elucidate first, both knowing it would only be a real claim if it emerged from much empirical work. Dixon and Kroeber's earlier note in *Science*, while laced with examples, had not been broad enough or sufficiently documented to carry American linguistics into a new paradigm. They had crossed the publication finish line abreast, but Kroeber had to acknowledge that Sapir had established the principle, whereas he had merely illustrated it, and that Sapir had worked on a continental plane, while he had confined himself to California. Thereafter the intensity of their collaboration, measured in the frequency of correspondence and the frequency with which they discussed genetic relations and the shrinking number of language stocks, declined. The tone of Kroeber's letters also became increasingly resigned, while Sapir was no longer so tender of his feelings.

Boas remained at the apex of their triangular relationship. Sapir's "Na-Dene" paper, delivered at the 1914 AAA meeting and subsequently published (Sapir, 1915a), put him somewhat at odds with Boas. Yet Sapir took an opportunity to blacken Kroeber's kettle and to again be counted, however briefly, among the Boasian blessed when Kroeber published his two heretical articles, *Eighteen Professions* (1915a) and *The Superorganic* (1917). Sapir (1917a) derided the latter, especially, as a "metaphysical" exercise – a term of opprobrium among Boasians. In fact, he took more printed notice of Kroeber's Superorganic article than Boas did, and his response to it, along with Robert Lowie's, became the canonical Boasian commentary.

Other challenges brought Kroeber and Sapir together from time to time during the next several years. Sapir was moving fast, perhaps too fast, linking languages across the continent with implications for familial groupings even farther a-field. His lumping of Wiyot and Yurok into Algonkin, which became the template for much of his subsequent work, came under fire. Michelson once again reacted negatively (Michelson, 1914, 1915), this time using Kroeber as his foil. Among his arguments was the devious assertion that someone as intelligent as Kroeber would surely have detected the features of the Yurok Language that Sapir was suddenly claiming as support for his genetic argument. (We are left to wonder what this implied about the degree to which Kroeber's collaboration with Sapir was known at Columbia. The work being done on genetic connections among languages often seems to have been an open secret, but if that was so, surely Michelson would have known more of it.) In need of assurance, in a letter to Kroeber, Sapir betrayed some unease that that he might have gotten out in front of his evidence at times. He also popped a question. Could he defend himself by showing how superficial and inept Kroeber's Wiyot field collecting had been?

> "...I do not think that I shall have any serious trouble in pointing out several weak points in [Michelson's] ... arguments. He may, of course, be right about discarding a few of the particular comparisons of morphologic elements. ...His narrowness of outlook [an excessive use of negative evidence]...is quite apparent. He says himself: 'thus far the phenomena listed have not been reported [i.e., by Kroeber, who did the original fieldwork], ...it is not likely that a skilled investigator like Dr. Kroeber would have overlooked the majority of them." ...Dr. Sapir thinks that as some Yurok adjectives distinguish animate and inanimate, other evidence will show that such a distinction exists elsewhere in the language. If that were the case, Dr. Kroeber probably would have recorded it, as this feature is particularly

easy to determine'. He [i.e. Michelson – who had worked chiefly with written languages] does not realize how long it takes to get wind of even elementary points of structure in a new language [i.e., in the field, by ear]. …I speak of all this to you because I feel that it will be necessary for me to make it clear the Wiyot material published by you [ref. to Dixon and Kroeber, 1903; 1913a and b] is, after all, the result of only a small amount of field work, and it is quite futile to build upon negative evidence under such circumstances. Would you care to give me a statement as to the total length of time spent by you on gathering your Wiyot data, also as to your own feeling in regard to the argumentative value of such negative evidence as Michelson appeals to?" (ALKP: Sapir-ALK, 9/9/14)

This was doubtless a bitter pill, but Kroeber graciously accepted the onus:

"Michelson's review strikes me as puritanical. I have never had any doubt of the validity of your union of Wiyot and Yurok with Algonkin. I'm afraid I cannot give you an estimate of the time I spent in securing the material. …My Wiyot material speaks for itself. The whole sketch is avowedly a slim preliminary treatment.

…I hardly consider it worth while seriously to refute Michelson. …I believe that if you …content yourself with a renewed note on the utter inadequacy of my Wiyot and Yurok materials, which statement I shall be glad to have you make as strong as you like…" (ALKP: ALK-Sapir, 9/15/14)

A month later he gamely wrote to Michelson directly, criticizing his case against Sapir and taking the blame on himself (ALKP: ALK-Michelson, 10/13/14). This was well done, for the historical judgment has been that the linking of Wiyot and Yurok with Algonquian was sound.

The Long Retreat:

For half a decade after 1913-14 Kroeber and Sapir traced out increasingly divergent professional trajectories, but remained linked by their language interests. Indeed, by 1917, only eight years after denying Sapir a position at Berkeley, Kroeber once again wanted him to work in California to help rescue endangered languages (Darnell, 1990a: 110-13). There other factors too, such as the different receptions accorded their respective contributions to lumping linguistics (Penutian and Na Dene), and the fact that it was Sapir who had given the palm of legitimacy to Dixon and Kroeber's long effort.

By 1917 there was also a new personal dimension to their correspondence. Kroeber, who almost never exhibited a need for close confidence, began to display personal and professional angst to Sapir (ALKP: ALK-Sapir, 1/7/16; 9/2/16). This appears to have been concomitant to their mutual interest in psychoanalysis, for it was expressed and examined in those terms, but if it was compassion he wanted Kroeber had mistaken his man. [46] Sapir could be cutting. Even his compliments were often double-edged. For example, when in 1915 he wrote to Kroeber regarding the Orthography Committee, he again panned Dixon's phonetics, knowing that Kroeber had also worked on the system he and Dixon had used (ALKP: Sapir-ALK, 3/15/15). The letter was deviously aggressive in other respects, as well. Sapir was by far the most skillful of the small group of people who were pursuing New World linguistics within an Old World paradigm, and often denigrated language linkages proposed by others. He expressed reservations about the data Kroeber and Dixon had used to link Chontal, Seri and Hokan, and slyly suggested that Chimariko (a language Kroeber failed to study at a time when it was believed that only two speakers remained alive) might have provided the precious link Dixon and Kroeber needed. Sapir called it: [one of the] "greatest misfortunes for American linguistics that Chimariko could not have been studied... No more pressing task for your department than the rescue of what Chimariko material is still available". [47]

What Kroeber may have been saying to his colleagues about Sapir is probably reflected in a letter from T.T. Waterman to Sapir, calling him "an ass" on a point of pedantry. Waterman was mostly in jest, but Sapir, who found such verbal roughhouse repulsive, indignantly forwarded Waterman's letter to Kroeber, hinting that Waterman was mentally unstable (Darnell, 1990a: 143). Kroeber's reply was innocent (ALKP: Sapir-ALK, 9/6/16; ALK-Sapir, 9/12/16), but we may wonder how he was taking Sapir's tendency to occupy the center of substantial linguistic issues, including the theoretical validation of language study as a valuable tool in deep time culture history (Sapir, 1916). This was an area in which Kroeber was deeply interested, and ironically it was he who had urged Sapir to take up the topic. Sapir made of it a triumphant cross-disciplinary foray that captured the enduring favorable attention of archaeologists. [48]

Sapir also played Lowie and Kroeber against each other. After Kroeber published his controversial Superorganic trio of articles he wrote to Lowie (who occupied the very kind of position at Berkeley that Sapir had wanted eight years before), denigrating Kroeber for undervaluing the individual and criticizing his "abstractionist fetishism… and shaky metaphysics" (RLP: Sapir-Lowie, 7/10/17). Given their close working relationship and theoretical differences, it strains credulity to believe that Lowie never mentioned the content of such a letter to Kroeber, and Sapir may have meant for him to do so. Meanwhile, Sapir also wrote to Kroeber about Lowie, softening his own published critique of the Superorganic (Sapir, 1917a) by denigrating Lowie's confounding of culture history with "conceptual science", by which he appears to have meant the history of ideas as opposed to a more distanced behavioral view (ALKP: Sapir-ALK, 10/29/17).

For his part, Kroeber occasionally played Janus between Sapir and Boas, usually seeking common ground and trying to propitiate the old man, something Sapir seldom did. Kroeber had reason to be circumspect, not only because of his recently published heresies in *Eighteen Professions* and *The Superorganic*, but also because he was again having doubts about his professional future in California. He hoped to be considered to head the BAE, an organization he and Boas both had occasionally denigrated, and wanted Boas' backing for the job. [49] This called for propitiation, though there were limits to what he could offer. On the occasion of Boas' review of the problems of American linguistics in the first issue of the *Journal of American Linguistics* Kroeber wrote to him:

"I think you will not find me as far away from your stand on the question of relationship as you may have thought. I should say that relationship was a distinctly extrinsic matter, especially as regards its linguistic considerations, unless its determination proves an instrument for the deeper analysis of individual languages. I consider this to be precisely what Sapir has done with his connection of Paiute and Nahua. It is also what I was planning to do when I reasserted ten years ago the unity of Uto-Aztekan, although I was not equipped to follow up the prospects which I glimpsed and which Sapir has now realized so much better.

In the same way I believe the existence of our Hokan family is justified when Chontal and Seri enable a correction of analyses of Chimariko. I would add that I feel that I have now a much better grounded feeling for the nature of Yokuts and Maidu since I accept them as parts of the Penutian group.

I think you will admit the value of relationship determinations such as these. My position is that the validity and value of unifications are essentially associated.

…On the question of borrowing of form, I was once inclined to take a more positive stand but have become more and more conservative. I am looking forward to the opportunity to discuss this question with you." (FBP: ALK-Boas, 2?/8/17)

This compromise cut it down the middle – indeed, Kroeber almost disappeared into the middle. The nub of the matter, though, was in the last paragraph, where he suggested that he could no longer side with Boas on the question of diffusion of grammar. By that time Sapir would have scoffed at this as faint-hearted ambiguity about their groundbreaking work, but Kroeber preferred to remain on the fence, as he had done for several years. Also, by 1917 he was better attuned to Boas' unsettled state of mind. [50] The phrase, "a distinctly extrinsic matter" seemed to imply an external, etic, perception rather than an intrinsic, emic structure. Sapir would have had none of that, for it would have implied that the structures he found might be his own reified classificatory projections onto languages (reification being the heart of the charge he had laid against Kroeber's Superorganic). Kroeber then qualified even that elliptical statement by alluding to an important exception, while assuming a relationship actually worked analytically "in the deeper analysis of individual languages." He seemed to be casting about for a way to say that the structures of one language sometimes threw light on those of another. If this was true, and those structures had not diffused, as Boas believed they had, their commonalities were probably homologous, having resulted from common origins. He would have done better to come right out with it. However, he had at least served gentle notice of his heresy regarding the diffusion of grammatical structures, and Boas could scarcely have felt that he still had a reliable ally on the matter in Kroeber.

Kroeber had probably begun his withdrawal from linguistics by 1914, but he still had language work to do, some of it potentially controversial. For this he still needed Sapir's help and advice. If any battle appeared to be brewing with Boas over genetic affiliations (happily never joined), then the Penutian Super-family of California languages, proposed by Dixon and Kroeber (1903) and subsequently reinforced (Dixon and Kroeber, 1913a and b), would not have seemed an optimal rallying point. Their claim to have helped to launch a program of language-linking in the manner of Indo-European linguistics rested chiefly upon their work on Penutian. But prior to their joint articles in *Science* and in *Anthropos* in 1913, Kroeber scarcely ever made it explicit that he was seeking to lump as many languages and language families as possible, and merely hinted that his underlying assumptions were evolutionary.

The original Penutian suggestion was for California languages, with Penutian consisting of Utian (Miwok and Costanoan – linked by Kroeber), together with Maiduan, Wintuan, and Yokutsan. But Sapir, whom Kroeber already conceded was the best authority, would not give California Penutian his unqualified *imprimatur* until he had checked their data (see below) and developed a proposal of his own to extend Penutian northward into Oregon, where there was a sibling stock (Takelma, for which he had written a grammar), the

Coosan languages, and Siuslaw. Still later Sapir and Leo Frachtenberg, a student of Boas, included the Kalapuyan and Alsea languages in this northern family. Later Sapir even boldly grouped Boas' beloved Chinook into Penutian. Some linguists still consider Penutian to be undemonstrated, but by the typological evidence Dixon, Kroeber and Sapir were using it seemed sufficiently confirmed. Nonetheless, the way was not straight or easy, and Kroeber seemed to lose heart and back away from the project for a time. Sapir's first positive reaction was to link Hokan with Penutian, but surprisingly Kroeber, who was preparing for a sabbatical at the time, decided to forego an opportunity to comment on this, and also gave up a chance to collaborate on a paper intended to connect Coos and Takelma. Having just finished what he called "one of my scrappy papers" on Arapaho, gleaned from old graduate school field notes (Kroeber, 1916d), he was discouraged and almost ready to give up on linguistics. He had gone beyond praising Sapir's abilities and had begun to denigrate his own. He ended what was in effect a letter of abdication by urging Sapir to do what he believed he could no longer pretend to attempt:

> "I'm quite depressed at not being able to keep up with developments in linguistic relationship. I'm not very fast at work of that kind, my memory being limited, but my real trouble is being loaded up with too many other things. I can do many things in spare moments, but not these comparisons. Well, I'll do the California end of Hokan and Penutian one of these days, and …I'll at least know you'll work it out more thoroughly and more accurately. My only equipment is feeling and perhaps a sense of judgment; the fine analysis fascinates me, but I'm too slow and clumsy to attain it in practice.
>
> I wish you'd line up Beothuk with Algonkin. The case is clear, and with a day's work you'd establish it. It would take me a week or two of mulling around with Algonkin dictionaries." (Golla, 1984: 191-93, ALK-Sapir, 5/29/15)

Kroeber's paper on Arapaho dialects was indeed inconclusive, and when it appeared the following year Sapir quickly appropriated the project, evidently by no authority more explicit than that of his greater expertise:

> "I …read your paper on Arapaho with very real interest. What impressed …me was that once the phonetic laws which differentiate Arapaho are worked out, the divergence of Arapaho from other Algonkin dialects will seem to be very much less than generally believed. I believe there are quite a number of points of comparative interest that have escaped you. As a matter of fact, I have been flirting with the idea of writing a more-or-less formal study of Arapaho comparative morphology. One impression I have gained is that Arapaho and Cheyenne do belong, after all, to a single subdivision of Algonkin. There seem to be some rather important points of resemblance." (ALKP: Sapir-ALK, 8/28/16)

The months between had not served to dispel Kroeber's sense of being outclassed. Recognizing that Sapir was right about Arapaho and Cheyenne, and uncomfortable at having produced an inferior article, he replied dispiritedly, complaining of the difficulty he had in keeping the patterns straight among the many languages they were working with and implying that it had been a mistake to publish:

> "I should have liked to do something real with Arapaho, but in the face of a wide spread group of languages it seemed absurd to try with Michelson and you in the field. I had a sense of duty about bringing out something on the subject after all the time I sunk into it in former years, but my chief sense when the paper was done was one of relief at having extracted myself from a bad and old mess. Apart from such service as the material itself may be, I consider the only point of value in the work to be the definition of the interpretation of the Algonkin verb stem. I am very earnestly convinced that the essential nature of these languages will never be understood until our

understanding of this point is clear. I am also of the opinion that this job will have to be done by you. Michelson has the knowledge, but is either afraid to go to the heart of the issue or incapable of doing so... It is extremely unfortunate that with all our detailed knowledge we should be ...so thoroughly in the dark as to the nature of a group of languages that are (*sic*) perhaps the most characteristic in North America." (ALKP: ALK-Sapir, 9/5/16)

By 1915, particularly in light of his controversial Na-Dene Super-family (Sapir, 1915a and b), Sapir had become the arbiter of matters pertaining to genetic relations among American languages. All this lumping of languages into smaller and smaller numbers of family groups was likely to upset Boas, particularly in that Sapir's Na Dene was composed of Tlingit and Haida (languages in which the older man had considerable professional stake), united with Athabaskan. Kroeber evidently believed that the question had to be confronted, and in New York during November 1915, just after his return from wartime Germany (Boas would have been deeply interested in that trip), he risked a conversation with him on establishing language families with genetic relationships. Evidently he again he portrayed himself as more neutral on this issue than he really was and came off unscathed. He related this little adventure to Sapir:

> "I had a thorough and amiable discussion of relationship with Boas last night. I tried to make him see that no one would quarrel with his stand if he did not feel it necessary to antagonize ours."

This live-and-let-live approach was unlikely to last for long, indeed it had already been overtaken by events, as Sapir was becoming more antagonistic toward Boas. Kroeber again hinted at his own gradual abandonment of linguistics, though he was very interested in Sapir's fast-developing Na Dene hypothesis:

> "I have always thought Zuni was Siouan, but don't think it will hold. I just can't find as much evidence—

> and that mighty little—pointing to Hokan. It is not
> Uto-Aztecan or Athabascan or Algonkin. I have even
> tried Muskogean. I know it is something, but have
> neglected my American linguistics too much of late
> years to be able to trust my instinct very far. I am
> going to go through your Na-Dene carefully." (Golla,
> 1984: 199, ALK-Sapir, 11/28/15)

Kroeber again acquiesced in Sapir's preeminence by waiting for final word from him confirming the validity of the Penutian Super-family in California before publishing. Sapir finally gave his qualified blessing, having found justification in Frachtenberg's work on Siuslaw. Ironically, Kroeber had just denigrated Frachtenberg's linguistic skills in a letter that crossed with Sapir's in the mail (ALKP: ALK-Sapir, 12/8/15). Sapir actually had little faith in Frachtenberg, who was splitting large stocks rather than lumping them. Sapir was even more critical of him than Kroeber was, believing that he had some value as a field collector and recorder, but little as an interpreter of such data and none whatever as a theorist (nonetheless, they later collaborated to develop the Penutian concept by adding the Kalapuyan, Chinookian, and Alsean groups to the original mostly California languages it encompassed):

> "I have been going through Frachtenberg's Lower
> Umpqua (Siuslaw) material and find that Lower
> Umpqua is not only related to Coos but is, …much
> more closely related to it than Takelma is. You may,
> therefore, quote me as maintaining that your Penutian
> stock is continued in Oregon by Takelma, Coos, <u>and</u>
> Lower Umpqua (Siuslaw). Frachtenberg's recently
> announced Siuslaw "stock" is only a joke, even if he
> doesn't know it."

After suggesting further parallels among several other languages, Sapir dropped a bombshell. He was thinking even farther a-field, indeed right up the Pacific Northwest coastal region and into the heart of Boas' ethnographic territory. With the evolutionary character of his project much in evidence, the kind of low-keyed diplomatic smoothing over that Kroeber had engaged in with Boas was unlikely to forefend conflict. There was also a distinct aura of excitement in these exchanges, of the kind that often pertains when a new paradigm shifts the kaleidoscope of data and allows them to tumble into newly coherent configurations.

It is interesting to note how unflinchingly Sapir projected the parts of speech found in European languages onto Native American tongues in this instance, along with his use of the fossil-finding techniques of Indo-European, reminiscent of paleontological totting up vestigial traits in organisms. In addition, Sapir's diagram of language relations as he understood them was configured to denote descent with modification – an unmistakably evolutionary construct. Aware that he was moving fast, Sapir laid down some pre-emptive disclaimers – one of them preparing the ground for assigning blame to Kroeber if the supporting Penutian substructure proved unsound:

> "To you personally (but for Heaven's sake, <u>don't</u> quote me to Boas, Goddard, or anyone else as yet) I don't mind saying that I now believe this enlarged Penutian stock to travel still farther north and to include, though you may blink with incredulity, Chinook! This Chinookan language is greatly specialized, ...but I can explain most of its peculiarities as secondary developments. In its adverbs there are even very clear remnants of old case endings found further south... The verbal prefixes (tense, pronominal, and prepositions) are originally independent particles that have built up a new synthesis.
>
> And now (don't faint!), I think Tsimshian is the most northern outlying member of the stock. Again, greatly specialized, but still exhibiting many startling features in common. ...Of Chinook and Tsimshian I am not as sure as of Lower Umpqua, Coos, and Talekma, but I think my evidence will grow as I work on it. How to group these languages I do not yet know, of course. I would suggest: Mai: to include, Penutian [including Miwok-Costan, Yokuts, Maidu, and Wintun]. Tekelma. W. Oregon [including Coos

and Siuslaw, Alsea]. Chinook. Tsimshian. However, this is premature. We do not even know if Penutian, as first defined, is really a unit. Takelma may turn out to be coordinate with say Yokuts, not Penutian as such. My 'W. Oregon' may eventually have to be grouped with Chinook, though this hardly seems likely.

...Naturally, I am looking forward to Frachtenberg's Alsea and Kalapuya material. If these two fall into line, we have a continuum from Yokuts to Chinook broken only by intrusive Athabaskan between Takelma and Wintun. Only Tsimshian would be really much apart geographically. If its inclusion proves O.K., the Wakashan-Salish-Chemakuan group form an interesting problem from the point of view of movements of population." (ALKP: Sapir-ALK, 12/9/15)

Sapir's preliminary arrangement of these languages turned out to be accurate. A day later he sent another letter, this time endorsing Kroeber's California "Penutian" more enthusiastically, and giving him permission to write a paper on Coos-Penutian, a component of his extension of Penutian northward. By that time Sapir was displaying a quite offhand attitude of authority, tempered only by the realization that by moving so far out ahead of his colleagues he also exposed himself:

"Please go ahead and write your Coos-Penutian paper. In fact I should be glad not to be alone in this new series of developments. My original idea was to write a morphological and phonologic sketch showing that Coos and Takelma are related. Before I got around to [it] ...I discovered ...that both were Penutian. ...Now I feel that we cannot get quite the right perspective until Frachtenberg publishes his Lower Umpqua and Alsea material.

However, it may be well to proceed gradually and to clinch the main point, i.e., show that Penutian has Oregonian cognates, by restricting yourself to Coos and Penutian. In that case would you mind stating that I have independently found that Coos has both morphologic and lexical analogies with Penutian? <u>Or</u> we might collaborate. Write out your Coos-Penutian sketch and I'll add whatever I have that you've missed—morphology and lexical material. I really oughtn't to go on with so much new stuff, as I have a staggering load of descriptive material on my hands." (ALKP: Sapir-ALK, 12/10/15)

On Sabbatical and preoccupied with events in Europe, Kroeber became even more lackadaisical about linguistics, while Sapir, who more and more frequently referred to "working out phonetic laws" for whatever material he was examining (see for example Golla, 1984: 215), grew more assertive. He launched a study of Washo, a seemingly isolated language, and called in data from wherever he could find it. Kroeber, who had once worked on Washo (Kroeber, 1907c), was willing to help, not least because at that point he still intended to discuss at least some linguistic matters in his massive California *Handbook*.

"I shall be very glad if you can settle the status of Washo …My Washo phonetics are particularly rotten… Go ahead on the business as much as you like. You can do it better; and it will relieve me of responsibility that presses. …I'd love to play with the stuff, especially Penutian; but there are many other pleasant things I expect to have to forego; and I'm not as greedy of hopes as I used to be. As to Yuki, I don't know. …I'm open to anything. If you can get the Washo settled soon, I shall be able to get it properly into my California book. By the way, the scope of this [California book] requires the elimination of everything linguistic that has no ethnic or historical bearing, but I am working out some good relations of language to topography on maps." (ALKP: ALK-Sapir, 3/19/16)

The character of Washo was settled the following year. J.P. Harrington had claimed that it was related to Chumash. Linking it to Hokan, Sapir (1917c) called it the penultimate Californian language to be removed from anomalous isolate status. Only Yuki remained to be placed. Sapir had been moving so quickly that Kroeber apparently suspected him of having some surprise in store with regard to Yuki (ALKP: ALK-Sapir, 10/11/17). He repeated his surrender of prior research claim on Washo in favor of Sapir, saying that, "personally, …I am confident that you will make a much better job of it", and obliquely offered to collaborate. More tempting to Sapir than collaboration was Kroeber's offer of materials on the language stored at Berkeley. He wrote back enthusiastically about "pooling resources" and sent his data on Washo to Kroeber and Dixon. He also indulged in a little grandstanding, and since they were using his data, pointedly offered to check their work (we can scarcely imagine Kroeber making such an offer to Sapir):

> "The general morphological resemblances [with Chumash and Hokan], …I have never written down: They are mostly in my head or could easily be verified by a little looking up of source material. There are also a number of phonetic laws that I have worked out that are implicit in the material that I am sending you. …What you might do is let me have a look at the galley of that part of your paper which deals with Washo, so that I might have a final opportunity to correct any misunderstandings on your part in the use of my materials or to suggest further particulars that you might seem to have omitted." (Golla, 1984: Sapir-ALK, 10/17/17)

Kroeber was not enthusiastic about going back to work on a language he scarcely understood (ALKP: ALK-Sapir, 10/23/17), but promised to consider the job in conjunction with Dixon. By return post, after again poking at Kroeber about his recently published "Superorganic", Sapir owned that he had dumped a difficult task on them. He described his own exhaustion after many months of frenetic language work and moaned about the state of the field generally. He could not refrain from again offering to check Kroeber's work for errors:

"What is to become of American linguistic work anyway? Is nobody …interested in the stuff? Please use your own judgment… I leave all matter[s] of policy to you. As I said in my letter, though, I should like to see the galley, …to correct possible misapprehensions, also to have the opportunity of pointing out resemblances of a morphological character that you may inadvertently have overlooked" (ALKP: Sapir-ALK, 10/29/17).

Discouraged, Kroeber wrote back a half-hearted defense of his Superorganic brainchild. But he had at least dared to touch on the theoretical whereas Sapir had not, so he retorted to Sapir's complaint about apathy toward linguistics with a prodding observation that was to have consequences when, somewhat later, Sapir began to write his only big book, *Language*.

"The decadence of linguistics is largely your own fault. You're an individualist and haven't built up a school. Do something general in character and [you] may get opposed. At least I promise you an opponent if you can make me disagree" (ALKP: ALK-Sapir, 11/4/17).

Sapir agreed, and trumped him:

"You have been prodding me so long about linguistic matters that I suppose I shall have to get really mad and sit down and write a book or a series of papers eventually leading up to a book. Years ago…I communicated with Gilbert Murray in regard to writing a more or less popular book on Language. I still have a copy [of the outline] with me, and I am sending it for you to look over and criticize. …Perhaps …I should like to make it rather less popular" (ALKP: Sapir-ALK, 11/28/17).

Thereafter they commiserated on P.E. Goddard's (1915) negative review of Dixon and Kroeber's claims regarding Hokan and Penutian families, and continued a discussion of Paul Radin's worth as an anthropologist (Sapir, as usual, defended him, though this was soon to change). A preview of a new article by Radin (1919a), claiming widespread family connections among New World languages, was making the rounds at this time, for they both seemed cognizant of what he was thinking (he later offered it in the 1919 AAA meeting), but Sapir probably did not dream that it might see the dark of print, or that Kroeber would be the one to print it.

Kroeber Exits:

After a short lapse, during 1920 Sapir launched into a series of fruitful language-lumping efforts, published at 12-month intervals (ALKP: ALK-Sapir, 10/4/20; 10/1/21; 10/1/22). Meanwhile, Boas (1920) assailed the genetic enterprise. Despairing of ever getting a Yana dictionary or grammar out of Sapir, in a letter chiefly concerned with Boas' political travails in the AAA, Kroeber asked him for permission to publish the small collection of Yana vocabulary Sapir had gathered under University of California auspices, by then stored at Berkeley for nearly a decade (ALKP: ALK-Sapir, 1/28/20). Sapir had a measure of proprietary right to the material, and he would be named as the field worker who gathered the data, but Kroeber appears to have expected him to refuse, and was gratified when he agreed. However, there was a condition. Again Sapir wanted to go over Kroeber's work and to correct it before publication (ALKP: Sapir-ALK, 2/4/20). After some maneuvering, Kroeber acquiesced. He had every reason to make amends just then, soon after a confrontational event in which he had seriously angered Sapir and (more hurtful) had earned his scorn.

Kroeber had done this by publishing an article by Paul Radin (1919a) in the University of California's anthropological journal (UCPAAE). Radin, who later called this article "my crime", had put forward a poorly supported assertion that all the native languages of the Americas were genetically related. His evidence was thin and focused mostly on the hypothetical "trunk" from which the language families had evolved, as opposed to describing the branching families themselves. This reflected discredit on the genetic hypothesis by seeming to make a merely speculative endeavor of it, and Boas gleefully referred to Radin's clumsy effort as the best attempt to demonstrate such connections (Boas, 1920; Darnell, 1986: 345; 1990: 118-21; 1998: 241-42). Radin defensively maintained that he was not a linguist and therefore was not accountable for the minute details of his hypothesis. At the same time he tried to upgrade his linguistic credentials by publishing another brief piece in a French journal, linking Huave and Mixe. Whether Radin was qualified or not, Kroeber was meant to be a linguist and was the editor of UCPAAE. It was difficult for him to plead innocence, and equally difficult to know in retrospect what his motivations were.

The idea of genetic relations among American languages had been gaining ground for more than a decade, with several linguists working on it (Hymes, 1961: 9-10). But a comprehensive synthesis – a telltale map of homologies – thus far only partially produced for California by Dixon and Kroeber, was still lacking. Such a thing could only be achieved through painstaking work in many languages, coupled with more than a dash of inspiration, all of which Sapir was providing as quickly as he could. Sapir's pace in this enterprise sometimes gave Kroeber vertigo, but he more than anyone was also privy to the detailed, time-consuming, comparative labor Sapir had expended to prepare his arguments. To be forestalled, his thunder stolen by a lesser light, was quite bad enough (in fact, Radin had given a paper on the genetic approach *in absentia* at the 1919 AAA meeting, so he was not entirely without claim to the topic). But Sapir had been laboriously preparing his own coup, a manifesto on the assumptions and methods of a genetic approach, and was on the verge of delivering it in an address to the anthropological and social science wing (Section H) of the American Association for the Advancement of Science (AAAS), in December 1920. This declaration was to be quickly followed by several concrete studies. Outraged, Sapir put it about that while Radin had suggested a correct conclusion, he had arrived at it through a deeply flawed methodology, and that Kroeber should have known better than to publish it. To Michelson, at the BAE (a sometime colleague but an adversary on the point of the appropriateness of Indo-European methods for unwritten New World languages) he remarked acidly that Kroeber "could easily have thrown out [Radin's article] …on technical grounds, had he known enough" [about linguistics].

Kroeber's motive in publishing Radin's article was never made clear, beyond his half-hearted claim that he wanted to illustrate the logical but too extreme conclusions implicit in Indo-European methods. He certainly was not acting out of friendship toward Radin, for whom he whom felt "repugnance" (FBP: ALK-FB, 1/11/17). [51] It may have been a straightforward but ill-advised attempt to promote the genetic view, but as Sapir noted, Kroeber was too well informed about the technical issues involved to have believed the piece was viable. [52] He may have hoped that if Radin went on the record with a flimsy case and drew fire, the resulting exchanges would call attention to the work he and Dixon had done in linking California languages between 1903 and 1913, but if this was so he miscalculated, and was taken aback by the force of Sapir's reaction.

P.E. Goddard was the Editor of *American Anthropologist* when this row broke out. Delighting in faction, and having small love for Kroeber, he wanted the issue fought out in print. He urged Sapir to write a scathing review of Radin's article. This was the last thing Kroeber wanted, and in an effort to have the affair die with as little notice as possible he wrote to Sapir, anxiously conceding almost all and suggesting oddly that he might have been even more brash than Sapir in linking languages, but simply lacked the ability. His espousal of an evolutionary approach was clear. And he threw Radin overboard:

> "You seem to me to be wholly on the right track... I am confident that at least the vast majority of your findings ...are true.
>
> If I had anything of your facility of absorption I should have been your competitor in this field, making up for your finer discrimination by the greater rashness or at least willingness to be content with slenderer evidence.
>
> Paul's [Radin's] method of leveling everything is essentially repugnant to me. I rather favored his paper for the effect it would have in indicating the limits toward which we were tending. The real interest in the matter however obviously lies not in the fact whether we have one or six or 50 families in America, but how these languages grew out of their origins and what the

causes of the changes have been. The real problems Paul ...wished to discard. The way he took... Yuki, and promptly linked it with antithetical types as Hokan and Penutian, and then went on to tie Shoshonean with Siouan, grates on me. Granted that there was a single proto-American language this has unquestionably evolved in branches of quite different direction. But to blot out the history of these branches on account of an interest in the trunk is as fanatic as Boas' and Goddard's refusal to have anything to do with the trunk even if it exists. ...Paul's actuating motive ...[was] a desire to revolt. He was fighting the established system of classification ...because it was established. It was part of an anthropological world that was cruel to him and he was sideswiping in revenge".

Kroeber panned Radin as a Bolshevik, but revolution had not really been his crime. He had been precipitate and sloppy in trying to call attention to the existence of a proto-language from which most the American languages had evolved without going the difficult way back through the many languages themselves. He made a hypothetical argument for such a language as a logically necessary phylogenetic entity – a violation of inductive scientific procedure and the Boasian moratorium on undue speculation and theorizing. Of course, Sapir intended to establish an evolutionary tree too, with many implications inimical to the Boasian program, making it all the more important for the idea of genetic connections among languages to be seen as solidly empirical. Moreover, in 1920, with Boas' political flap just dying down, it was still needful for Boasians to show solidarity. Kroeber counseled mercy toward Radin and weakly offered some final opinions of his own, asserting himself on a few points, but effectively announcing his retirement from the field.

"I am glad you have retained Eskimo and Na-Dene as distinct. I should have had less faith in your findings had you united them with anything American. As to the Asiatic affiliations of Na-Dene, I am too ignorant to have an opinion, although I do feel strongly that the ultimately monosyllabic and essentially isolating character of Athabascan [will tell]. ...Algonkin also impresses me as very distinctive."

This preserved the possibility of recent Eskimo and some Northwest Coastal peoples' recent immigration, and (perhaps as important), helped to keep Sapir's searchlight away from more languages in which Boas had a professional stake. Sapir (1928b) subsequently retained these as separate language families.

"The most radically new group is Hokan-Siouan. It absorbs the largest number of old stocks and seems to have been the group which the older students were unconsciously thinking of when they attempted [general] formulations.

I share your feeling about Uto-Aztecan not possessing the same degree of distinctiveness as most of the others. I cannot quite feel that it is a blend and therefore expect it to link up with one of the others. ...As for the unplaced languages... Zuni goes into Hokan-Siouan. [53]

Beothuk ...was unquestionably Algonkin. I imagine these peoples were an early branch of Algonkins who got isolated on the island and ... diverged considerably. ...As to the Klamath, I should not be surprised to see it [in] the Penutian classification.

Your idea on polysynthesis as a secondary phenomenon of mainly psychological interest appealed to me strongly. There is not a point ...I should dissent from. I think you should put these ideas into print without waiting until you are able to substantiate them... Boas will think you have turned prophet... but a pronouncement would ...emphasize the nature of the problems that lie ahead. Boas' purely analytic and descriptive work has of course been badly needed and is still, but it is also time that we proved we were not evading the historical problems. I do not believe we need fear [accusations of] ...excessive speculation. Boas' influence is [in] the direction of a soundly critical attitude will remain with us permanently."

Kroeber appeared to be suggesting that Sapir to do something speculative (rather like what Radin had done), and he clearly believed that all or nearly all North American languages would eventually be found to have nested, genetic relationships. Polysynthesis was highly useful to Sapir, whose approach was indeed at times intuitive. [54] The passage about Boas' "soundly critical attitude" was an interesting endorsement of Sapir's methodology, which rested upon, but was quite different from Boas' older, non-evolutionary approach.

Sapir also believed that languages could change by "drifting" in one or another direction, including along the spectrum from analytic to polysynthetic, and that "drift", which did not result primarily from diffusion, was a kind of evolution. He elaborated this in *Language* (Sapir, 1921a). Kroeber harbored a few weak reservations about drift at first, which allowed for Chinese, English, French, among many other languages, becoming more analytic through the course of many centuries, while some American Indian languages (Navajo, Chinook) probably became more synthetic in time. In Boas' view his well-worked Chinook was being used as an example of an evolutionary process in which he did not believe, while the different adaptive cultural levels for different languages might give aid and comfort to those who supported the idea that it was more progressive to "drift" from analytic to synthetic than the reverse.

I hope you will really put through a distributional survey of structural features. I am sure this will prove a meeting ground for all of us. Some years ago Boas urged me to undertake such a review. ...However, I shall never more than dabble in linguistics and you are clearly the indicated man for the job. ...Boas' point was that we should probably find many structural features which had been transmitted like culture elements between distinct stocks. I am inclined to think he is probably over-sanguine on this point...

> As to Goddard, I would suggest leaving him alone.
> He is in a difficult position… He is over 50… and not
> essentially nearer a really comparative Athabascan
> grammar than he was 20 years ago. Treat him with as
> much consideration as possible." (ALKP: ALK-Sapir,
> 12/27/20)

The "distributional survey" Kroeber mentioned probably
represented what in his view was the only feasible way to convince
Boas that grammar was linguistic inheritance and not diffused, and
that grammatical similarities indicated common ancestry. The fact
that Boas had once urged the project himself would have made it
the more persuasive if the results told against his own position. The
reference to Goddard (then working with Boas) concerned Sapir's
trespass into Athabascan, to which Goddard objected by right of
prior fieldwork.

Almost immediately thereafter (the above letter may still have
been in the mail), and despite Radin's scoop, Sapir presented his bold
hypothesis on the genetic relations among languages at the December
1920 Chicago meeting of Section H of the American Association for
the Advancement of Science, highlighting the importance of "drift"
in language change, and advancing his general model for North
American linguistics (Sapir, 1921b). Analogous to the relationship
between genetic isolation, drift, and speciation, this was the tendency
for more-or-less isolated dialects of a language to accumulate differences
over time. Kroeber claimed that they were in basic agreement, but still
balked at an open endorsement, confessing:

> "I gasped a bit when I realized that you had really
> presented this outline at Chicago. …I had always been
> strongly impressed by your caution. …You must have
> a lot of ammunition salted away." (ALKP, ALK-Sapir,
> 1/20/21)

Golla (1986) discussed Sapir's motives in this meeting, suggesting
that he intended to sum the analytical work he and others had done
on the genetic relations of American languages, and to preamble a
wider and deeper effort which, in the event, he never completed.

Whatever his reasons for preparing his presentation, suppressing Radin's premature claim must have been foremost in his mind when he gave it. From a standpoint of personal and professional loyalties it was still difficult to come out against the Boas on a key point of methodology, especially before the prestigious AAAS. For his part, Sapir (selectively oblivious to wider political considerations, while Kroeber was hypersensitive to them), seems to have been ready to assume the mantle of leadership in American linguistics. He continued to write to Kroeber on linguistic topics after Kroeber had ceased to be very responsive on them. In one of the longest letters in their correspondence he outlined his reasons for believing that his Nadene (no longer hyphenated) was connected to "Indo-Chinese" – geographically his greatest linking leap yet:

> "I have long wanted to write you about Nadene and Indo-Chinese, but my evidence accumulates so fast that it is hard to sit down and give an idea. …If the morphological and lexical accord which I find on every hand between Nadene and Indo-Chinese is "accidental," then every analogy on God's earth is an accident. It is all so powerfully cumulative and integrated that when you tumble to one point a lot of others fall into line. I am now so thoroughly accustomed to the idea that it no longer startles me. For a while I resisted the notion. Now I can no longer do so.
>
> …I shall not broach the Indo-Chinese part of the problem until I have moored myself more completely in Nadene. (…Don't blab too much about my Indo-Chinese just yet. It's not wise. *Einem Narren zeigt man nicht die halbe Arbeit*, and 99% of one's fellowmen are damned fools.) (ALKP: Sapir-ALK, 10/1/21)

Whether Kroeber believed Sapir to be approaching apotheosis or nemesis, he was no longer prepared to simply follow in his wake. The flow of his language work, already waning during World War One, stopped during 1920-1921. By exploiting his privileged access to the Uhle Peruvian collections at Berkeley, materials of enormous value, both aesthetically and for sorting out the artistic traditions of the Andes, he eventually found a new line of work in archaeology, in which he had successfully dabbled in 1916. He wrote nothing more of substance in linguistics until he reviewed Sapir's *Language* the following year, and after that little more before the last decade of his life. That masterful book, written at his urging, established Sapir as the preeminent linguist in the United States. When *The Dial* asked Kroeber to review the book he hesitated, writing to Sapir that it was not a question of money, "but of finding something to say" (ALKP: ALK-Sapir, 1/11/22). Once persuaded, he wrote a graceful swan song, by that time having shed his residual reservations about Sapir's "drift" concept, which played a large part in the book. The divergence of dialects into languages was like divergence in biological species, and left a like pattern. [55] The review said as much about Kroeber as it did about Sapir, but Kroeber was entitled to mixed feelings. Having yielded the field he had less to lose, but he must have still been worried about such an explicit re-introduction of evolutionary thought into cultural anthropology. He acknowledged the clarity and elegance of *Language*, suggesting that it was the quest for just these qualities in language patterns that had first drawn him to linguistics:

> "The technique of modern philology has something superb about it. It is as austere as anything in the world. The work of an accepted leader like Brugmann …unsurpassed in any branch of learning, …cannot be popularized…" (Kroeber, 1922)

Karl Brugmann was an Indo-Europeanist "neogrammarian" whose comparative methods for reconstruction of prehistoric languages both Sapir and Kroeber had believed would profit New World research. "Popularized" was the single sour note in the review. Sapir had written for the intelligent layman, eschewing footnotes, a comprehensive bibliography and other trappings of scholarship. Yet he had produced a milestone in American linguistics that gave it scientific standing independent of anthropology.

Kroeber's linguistic swoon cannot be put solely to Sapir's account. Undoubtedly other things contributed to it. The press of academic business kept him chronically short of time (one of the excuses he offered to beg off contributing to Boas' *Handbook of American Indian Languages* was that he had no time to gather fresh material – something Boas might have marked down against the wisdom of his continued control of California anthropology). However, his discouragement was surely a large factor in the ensuing topical sea change in his extraordinary annual publication output. His second wife and biographer described the late teens and early twenties of the century as a period of personal conflict and depression for him. Several years widowed, he was also exhibiting symptoms of a frightening undiagnosed illness that robbed him of his sense of balance and eventually of his hearing in one ear (it was Meunier's Disease, but he feared a brain tumor or madness). Along with this went much professional self-questioning. As Theodora Kroeber did not know him then, he was her chief source for that time and her account of his mental state was in effect his own (T. Kroeber, 1970: 87-119).

If Kroeber was in bad psychological repair during those years, he was far from immobilized. Indeed, he made a project of his depression, continuing to undergo and to practice psychoanalysis, a field in which he had been interested for nearly a decade (ALKP: ALK-Wheeler, 3/2/09). He even briefly (and uncharacteristically) hoped that psychology might elucidate the mental connections between individuals and their cultures. He was seldom inclined to consider culture in relation to individuals, and believed that psychoanalysis in ethnography was mostly a wash, perhaps because he read it in German but practiced it in English and was sensible of its cultural specificity. As one who had once denied the objective existence of individual minds (Kroeber, 1915a), he had to reach far to connect individual minds (except geniuses) with whole cultures.

Depression did not paralyze him in other areas of anthropological work, either. His output in ethnology, sustained throughout most of his long career, was quite heavy between 1918 and 1923, totaling thirty-one articles and twenty reviews. This was the more impressive in view of a heavy writing commitment during that period (his 1923 textbook *Anthropology*). However, his bibliography reveals his unsettled state of mind, for his attention skipped from linguistics through psychology to ethnography and then to archaeology. This was almost giddy flight for a person ordinarily so focused, and bespoke his search for a more secure berth, within or without anthropology.

An Aborted Return:

In 1927, a year during which Kroeber exhausted himself in archaeological fieldwork and writing (ALKP: ALK-Davies, 10/10/27), an attractive opportunity to return to linguistic work briefly presented itself. In the intervening years the relationship between Boas and Sapir had continued to deteriorate. That between Kroeber and Sapir stagnated professionally, but became warmer again after Kroeber turned to archaeology (by the late 1920s their exchanges were mostly about poetry and psychoanalysis). The occasion for Kroeber's bid to return was the announcement of $100,000 in grant money for the study of American Indian Languages, given through the American Council of Learned Societies (ACLS) to its Committee on Research in Native American Languages, chaired by Boas. By virtue of that chairmanship, as well as that of the Committee on American Indian Linguistics, Boas exerted considerable control over the ACLS funds. Ultimately, control of the money and the committee seats determined who was running the field. The ACLS windfall, nearly the only funding support available for language work other than occasional grants from the Rockefeller Foundation, was disbursed over ten years between 1927 and 1937 and did much to keep American field linguistics alive through the Great Depression (Stocking, 1976: 27). Even in those latter days of heady economic optimism it was evident that the ACLS grant represented an opportunity that was not likely to recur, and it ignited a scramble for the money that both uncovered and created fault lines within the Boasian group.

Kroeber, Sapir, and Boas all had their own agendas with regard to this funding event, and with the field in such a fiscally excited state, alliances were ephemeral and partly determined by who crowded whom. Characteristically, Boas crowded first and hardest, pressing Kroeber to sit on the Board of Advisors to the Committee on Indian Linguistic Research, the vehicle in which he intended to play keep-away with the money (FBP: Boas-ALK, 4/18/27). Boas and Sapir quickly produced preliminary sketches of comprehensive proposals, but their comparative worth as linguistic science was not the primary issue early in 1927, when the grant was announced.

Rather it would be whether the money would be best used to finance work focused on a unified goal like Boas' *Handbook*, or spread over a wider range of linguistic research activities, as Sapir wished. Boas not only wanted to bankroll more projects that would build upon the model of his (just being completed) *Handbook*, he also wanted to galvanize research in California, America's linguistic mother lode, where the field had lain almost fallow since Kroeber stopped working nearly a decade before. He therefore indicated openly (and perhaps almost innocently at that point) that much of the work he wanted done was to be done there. For Kroeber this presented turf problems.

Sapir's proposal glossed his underlying agenda, which was to weaken Boas' grip on the Committee. He clearly viewed the ACLS funding as an opportunity to capture leadership of American linguistics, which Boas still occupied by patriarchal right and through the advantages of his several national-level chairmanships. Sapir, who had begun his field career obediently using Boas' methods, believed that the "Boas Plan" had exhausted its potential, and that the publication of the third and final volume of the *Handbook* was a logical cut-off point. Both Kroeber and Sapir wanted more diversity than the *Handbook* project offered, and neither of them wanted Boas to simply dictate how the ACLS money would be spent. Because they did not want it to be simply scattered to the winds either, they aimed for a middle path, agreeing that the Committee should control allocations rather than farming portions out to many institutions for diffused decision-making. Seats on the committee therefore quickly became tactical goals, and its chair a strategic one (ALKP: ALK-Sapir, 2/21/27).

If the time for changing the guard had arrived, Boas was viscerally unwilling to cede anything while there was breath in him, least of all to Sapir, who in turn had his own reasons to refuse to compromise, some of them quite sound, if vengeance is a worthy motivation. Boas had recently recommended first another student, A.A. Goldenweisser, and thereafter the BAE's Indo-European linguist, T. Michelson, rather than Sapir for a University of Chicago position, although Sapir had solicited his recommendation (Darnell, 1990a: 195-236). Boas' dislike for genetic assumptions in linguistic work may have had something to do with this, but in fact he had very high regard for Sapir's abilities (after this small flap died down and before the larger blow-up of the mid-1930s Boas worked to get both Kroeber and Sapir to Columbia to do Native American linguistics). It seems likely that there was another explanation, and a growing awareness that Sapir meant to displace him would have served. Conveniently enough, Boas could also claim that by recommending Michelson he was showing that he did not oppose the whole framework of historical linguistics in an Indo-European mode. (Despite being an Indo-Europeanist, Michelson opposed Sapir's genetic scheme because almost all American languages were unwritten, and therefore did not present the necessary concrete "fossil forms" for analysis.)

Kroeber's goals were more modest and defensive. As the situation was shaping up to be a re-apportionment of linguistic field research responsibilities, any seat on the board promised to be hot-spot, and he paused before agreeing to occupy it. Even though he was not yet ready to propose any viable plan of action for new fieldwork, he wanted a share of the ACLS money at work in California, though not at the expense of his leadership there. This was unrealistic, for the field had grown considerably, with more students in play. He was still territorial about anthropology in a state in which he had failed to exert leadership in linguistics for nearly a decade, but unless he could quickly do something to make Berkeley look more active linguistically, he had little claim to the new money. If it was not entirely too late to re-hydrate the California language program in response to the new funding opportunity, it certainly would not be an easy matter to do so. [56]

Because Boas feared that the ACLS money might prove soft or ephemeral he wanted it obligated in a timely manner, and proposals were wanted quickly. Kroeber scratched one out but held it close (he sent a *précis* to Sapir, but did not immediately give it to Boas or anyone else). He had good reason to be circumspect, for he had no students to carry out the work he proposed and accepting other people's students was simply a less direct way of surrendering control. In February 1927 there was still uncertainty regarding how and by whom allotments would be made. When drafts of the plans being drawn up were made available to him Kroeber quickly saw that Sapir's proposal was far better than his, and indicated to Sapir that he would withhold his in its favor. Recognition that his plan did not measure up to Sapir's was not his only motive. Kroeber believed the money should be disbursed in such a way that would encourage further donations. He would throw in his hand with Sapir, but he advocated a compromise that he believed Boas might accept. He was also after a better deal than Boas was offering on a personal matter:

> "I [have] been thinking about this matter... and settling in the conviction that Boas' proposition is inherently the less desirable approach. I am not now referring to the little angle of it that touches me personally. I believe I have got reasonably objective about that. In fact I am ready to accept any arrangement that lets me go without flagrant humiliation.
>
> I do think, however, that the principle is undesirable of asking for money for projects ... built essentially around the particular needs and opportunities of individuals. ...I believe that the chances for systematic continuance of funds will be better if your plan is adopted, even if the specific allotments are much as proposed by Boas." (ALKP: ALK-Sapir, 2/21/27)

But it was the blocking of one particular allotment that formed Kroeber's primary motive in siding with Sapir, though in the end he could not get his way. Among the proposed grants was one to Jaime de Angulo, and Kroeber was determined that it should not go through. De Angulo's wife was also to be funded to complete some earlier work, and Kroeber was even highly ambivalent about this. De Angelo was a Franco-Hispanic ethnographer and ethnomusicologist of independent means and eccentric mind; a sometime marginal associate of the Berkeley Department (de Angulo, 1995).[57] As late as the end of 1921 Kroeber had still been able to write to Sapir about de Angulo in measured terms, claiming to know him mostly on a personal plane, and praising his intellect while decrying his "infantile emotional vehemence", which Kroeber kept at arm's length as a "defense mechanism" (ALKP: ALK-Sapir, 11/20/21). But during the time between a more serious clash, tinged with sexual jealousy, developed between them. In 1923 De Angulo, who occasioned more poisonous remarks than any other person mentioned in Kroeber's correspondence, "stole" Nancy Freeland, the Department's star graduate student, married her, and in Kroeber's view, expropriated her Berkeley-funded work while reducing her to support work for his projects. There were also some old disagreements about recording projects on Mexican and Californian languages in which de Angulo was remiss, but the worst thing he had done was to attract Freeland, who married him (Kroeber's antithesis), instead of responding to Kroeber.

Recognizing de Angulo's worth as a field linguist, Boas ignored this matter, which must have seemed minor to him (he did not meet de Angulo until he traveled to California in August of 1927, so perhaps Lowie recommended him). As his immediate goal at that point was to get Kroeber to cooperate with his committee, Boas said nothing of this to him at first, so Kroeber was taken aback when it emerged that de Angelo would have funding for an independent project. He complained to Sapir that Boas was high-handedly granting funds without adequate consultation with the rest of the senior anthropological community (Sapir's own initial complaint, and a strong motive for siding with him), but Kroeber fell between the stools. He continued to drag his feet about sitting on the committee, and despite his assurance to Sapir that he would withhold his proposal, he continued to discuss it with Boas. Meanwhile, he also tried to propitiate Boas with an offer of his old Yurok Language field notes for a Columbia student to work up, without apparent effect.

Before any concrete assignments could be given, a stock-taking of the state of linguistic research in California was needed, and on this Kroeber was prepared to work hard, even though it would inevitably turn out to be a roster of his uncompleted projects. Before he could produce this survey, he wrote back to Boas, reluctantly and provisionally agreeing to most of the funding decisions. His displeasure was plainer than his acquiescence, and his decade-old abandonment of linguistics was painfully on display:

> "For twenty-five years responsibility for the study of California Indian languages has, practically by common consent, been left to us. The resources available have sufficed to carry out only part of our

program and we shall be glad to turn over to your committee such parts of this project as it can better provide for." (FBP: ALK-Boas, 4/25/27)

Dissatisfied with this vacuous reply and anxious to move the money before opposition could further solidify, Boas sent back a stiff and preemptory letter, outlining his own plan and requiring Kroeber's (FBP: FB-ALK, 4/30/27). Boas proposed that a student of Sapir's should work on Athapascan, Jaime de Angulo on Karo or Tonkawag (in Southeast Texas), Melville Jacobs on Sahaptin (in Oregon), Frans Olbrechts on Cherokee or Osage, and Gladys Reichard on any available language. Boas' proposal showed that matters were already well-advanced. If Kroeber wanted to retain any prominent role in California linguistics he would do well to produce his plan and take a place on the Board.

After posting this brusque letter Boas evidently thought better of its tone, and on the same day wrote another, softer one. He wanted to explain matters in the Committee on Indian Linguistic Research "personally". He complained that at the 1925 meeting of the Linguistic Society, Sapir and Bloomfield had "...balled up the affairs of the Linguistics Committee", meaning they had advocated expanding that body by adding Sapir or someone of his choosing. Only Boas' "personal intervention" had saved the day (in fact, Bloomfield had supported Boas in that gathering, and may even have acted on his behalf). Kroeber's presence was needed to prevent a repetition of that untoward event in the new committee. Boas indicated that he did not envision interfering in Kroeber's plans for California linguistics (assuming he had any). Instead, he promised soothingly that, "...we shall be guided entirely by your wishes". Apparently he believed Kroeber could still influence Sapir, though in fact they had not had much professional contact for several years. At some point during this exchange Boas realized that Sapir himself, and not one of his students, would be going to California that summer. This may have prompted him to accept the invitation of the California State Board of Education to give a series of talks in August. A gathering of all three of them in San Francisco might have been an opportunity to patch matters up, but it did not work out that way.

Although he could scarcely deny that he no longer occupied the driver's seat in California linguistics, Kroeber remained determined to prevent de Angulo from having any part in it, though with a juggernaut advancing from Columbia he also saw the need for some kind of compromise. He wrote accepting a position on the Board, sending with this letter his summary of linguistic work in California accomplished or in progress to that date – apparently an expanded version of the plan of work he had withdrawn in favor of Sapir's several months earlier. It was a fine summary (some details are below), but it highlighted the embarrassing fact that almost no linguistic work had been done at Berkeley for seven years, which did not recommend him as either a linguist or a manager of linguistic field programs. It must also have reduced Boas' sense of obligation to be guided by Kroeber's wishes, but there was still some common ground. Kroeber favored publication of existing bodies of data over new collection work, something Boas likewise advocated; certainly in the difficult case of the wayward J.P. Harrington, who was hard to keep pinned to a job. Such an arrangement would have left Kroeber in nominal control.

> "I am wholly in sympathy with your attitude that grants should involve not only field research but the working out of manuscripts; also that disposal of manuscripts as regards publication should be within the committee's power.
>
> In cases of chronic delay of working up materials… I hope you will be rigorous in your stand that the Committee will encourage preparation of arrears before new collecting."

There followed what Boas must have read as excuse-making:

> …The situation in California is… we have always had some funds for linguistic fieldwork; and the university has …been… willing to publish… The supply of people capable of doing satisfactory work has however been somewhat fluctuating. Further, as we have often been unable to provide compensation or assistance, the working up of data has been regrettably delayed in a

number of cases. For instance, Drs. Goddard, Sapir, Mason, Radin, myself, and others are all from five to fifteen years in arrears in certain linguistic researches…
…your committee could ultimately aid our endeavors most if such help is in accord with its policies.

I enclose a statement of work done, or undone… …
We have work in progress, though not always actively, in Yurok, Yuki, Wappo, Washo, Miwok, Yokuts, Luiseno, Papago; that there is need of new work to be undertaken, which we are not in a position to perform, in Karok, Pomo, Wintun, Lutuami, and several Shosonean groups. …As regards Shasta and Achowami we have left the field to Dr. Dixon, and Chumash and Yuman to J.P. Harrington." (ALKP: ALK-Boas, 5/4/27)

Kroeber also recommended that J. Alden Mason continue his work on Papago, that Grace Dangberg revise and extend her grammar of Washo, that a small grant be given to edit Paul Radin's nearly complete Wappo grammar, and that he (Kroeber) should resume work on Yurok and Luiseno. He also urged Boas' committee to communicate with the University of Pennsylvania to negotiate publishing Sapir's delayed monograph on Southern Paiute. This set of suggestions may have seemed too self-serving, or too vague, or just insufficiently ambitious for Boas. He shot back a reply, again asking for more specifics about to whom money ought to be given (ALKP: Boas-ALK, 5/13/27). Kroeber, who had had already provided all the specifics he had, conceded:

"My detailed statement was for the orientation of yourself and your committee… I have at the present time no requests or recommendations to make… on behalf of anyone here… I have not offered for several years the language course which I used to give, and none of our present students or assistants are trained to do independent work in language."

This abdication effectively gave *carte blanche* to Boas' committee to install whom they wished in California linguistic fieldwork, and effectively dispensed with Boas' promise to be guided by Kroeber's wishes. Kroeber still hoped to prevent one thing:

> "As regards Mrs. De Angulo, the situation is so complicated that I recommend letting matters lie for the present. Inasmuch as her work on Miwok, in distinction to her husband's various undertakings in the linguistic field, was done... while she held a university position, I would appreciate it if your committee would leave to me ...steps directed toward resumption of [her] work... From what I have written to you, you will realize that the situation is somewhat difficult." (FBP: ALK-Boas, 5/16?/27)

Not even this was granted. Kroeber was blocking Freeland's participation unless he received redress for a past wrong that was of little interest to Boas, who would not put obstacles in the paths of competent field workers when every hand was needed. She and her husband were to be enlisted. When Kroeber at last forlornly suggested that he hoped to train some graduate students beginning in the fall, Boas must have seen it as much too little, much too late. On the same busy day on which he sent off his summary, Kroeber wrote yet another letter to Boas on the matter that seemed to worry him as much as the question of who was going to be running anthropology in California. Boas still intended to fund de Angelo, and Kroeber again insisted futilely that he must not work through Berkeley.

Kroeber's summary of progress in the study of California languages was a valuable snapshot of California linguistics in the nineteen-twenties. In his view, *Wiyot* was adequately covered by a monograph by R. Gladys. *Yuki,* which both he and Sapir had classified in the Hokan-Siouan super-family, Kroeber claimed to be actively preparing (in roughly concurrent letters to Sapir he also claimed to be back at work on Yurok – so his efforts must have been scattered). [58] He also maintained a claim to *Yokuts*, a language already partly covered by his early monograph (Kroeber, 1907a). [59] Paul Radin's work on *Wappo* (a *Yuki* language) needed only some editing and copy work before going to press. *Lutuami* (*Klamath-Modoc*) had not been studied, except for a sketch by de Angulo. Kroeber suggested that it might be related to languages farther north. *Shasta* and *Achowami* had scarcely been touched since Dixon had worked on them some twenty years before (though Kroeber later grudgingly admitted that de Angulo had "worked considerably in *Achowami*"). [60] *Shasta* was almost extinct and had to be studied soon.

Kroeber was apologetic for not having worked up his data on *Karok*, and indicated that he was ready to turn his notes over to some competent student. [61] Some dialects of *Pomo* (probably a misnomer, as it was the name of a village, classified by Kroeber and Dixon as a Hokan language, and later by Sapir as Hokan-Siouan) were rapidly disappearing, represented only by Kroeber's early sketch of the Eastern dialect and some notes by Paul Radin on the Southwestern. *Washo* had seen a good beginning by Grace Dangberg and needed only funding and some prompting to have her complete it. [62] *Yuman*, which J. P. Harrington had undertaken to study, was a whole language family, but one with many surviving speakers, so there was little urgency for rescue recording work. *Wintun*, particularly its *Patwin* dialect, was heading for extinction, with only some preliminary sketches by Dixon and Radin extant. [63] Although *Maidu* had been studied and published by Dixon (1911), he had neglected the Southern dialects, which represented more than half the stock. *Miwok*, on which Nancy Freeland had made a good beginning, needed further work. She was the best qualified person, if she would do it. [64]

Kroeber had done some work on *Luiseno*, a Shoshonean language spoken in the area of California just east of San Diego, in order to elucidate the earlier manuscript materials of Philip S. Sparkman (1908). [65] He had brought new information provided by a native informant to bear, and he believed it wanted only the services of a competent student to bring a good study to publication. [66] *Serrano* was still unrecorded and in danger of extinction. [67] *Cahuilla* (in the Mohave and Sonora Deserts), on which Harrington had gathered some notes, seemed close to *Luiseno* but was probably extinct. The unique *Tubatalabal* dialect in the Kem River valley of central California was still "intact" (more than 100 speakers survived), but in need of study. Northern *Paiute* was represented by the texts of K.

Marsden, for which the phonetics needed revision but which were otherwise "excellent".[68] *Papago* (Sonora and Arizona), studied by J.A. Mason and Juan Dolores, was past the fieldwork stage and into the work-up process. *Chimariko*, *Esselen*, and *Chumash* were all extinct by 1927, *Coatanoan* and *Salinan* nearly so. Linguistic extinction without record was the Boasian nightmare.[69]

Flush with his share of funds from the ACLS pot, Sapir (by then at the University of Chicago) planned a trip to California during the summer of 1927 to investigate details of the Hupa language in the Hoopa Valley and adjacent areas. Despite his dissatisfaction with the funding process, Kroeber was galvanized by the prospect of fieldwork with Sapir, and wrote to him, welcoming the opportunity to, "do a little Yurok with you" (ALKP: ALK-Sapir, 6/2/27). In a subsequent letter he declared himself once again, after so long a hiatus, enthusiastic about linguistics (ALKP: ALK-Sapir, 6/9/27). He proposed working on tones in Yuki using a "kymograph", an early voice recording device he had tried out earlier in San Francisco, where Chinese were asked to listen to recorded Mandarin and report on tones. The planning for this hybrid field project ended a hiatus in their correspondence, with a clear difference in tone from the early years. Kroeber now needed Sapir's advice, and also to show him how far he had gone in his Yuki work.

Sapir did well (Sapir, 1928a) but the summer did not turn out at all as Kroeber wished. The initial plan was to have several Yurok and Yuki informants travel to Berkeley, though there were also hints of Kroeber and Sapir traveling together up to Hoopa. In the event Sapir went to Hoopa alone and remained there until the beginning of September, Kroeber's project having become troublesome, taking up so much time that he could not join him. By July he was writing to Sapir about the alarming possibility that Yuki contained tones and glottal stops, which would invalidate most of the records he had made and necessitate doing much of the work on the language over again. The Kymograph was not very useful and Kroeber again sheepishly admitted the inadequacy of his early recording methods (ALKP: ALK-Sapir, 7/19/27). Thereafter he escaped to the East for a meeting, just after Boas arrived in California to give his Board of Education talks and see how the ACLS money for the season's work was being spent. Their schedules overlapped by less than a week, so

Kroeber saw very little of him on this rare visitation (FBP: ALK-FB, 5/16/27). To his dismay however, de Angulo, funding in hand, swooped in by pre-arrangement with Boas to manage the old man's stay. Boas seemed happy enough to be chauffeured about and waited on, and Kroeber wrote bitterly of how, with astonishing *chutzpah*, de Angulo:

> "DASHED from the far north to squat for the next to the last two hours before him [Boas] on the terrace in front of our dining room. Sapir used the last two [*illeg.* days?] to formulate his impressions. Boas was in Berkeley for a week to lecture at Mills, so Familie de Angulo drove him down and back every morning. Otherwise I hear little of them."

He was later further dismayed to learn that in his absence Lowie had allowed de Angelo to monitor a seminar to sharpen his fieldwork skills – something he would never have permitted. Apparently this matter, of such emotional importance to him, was a source of mirth to some of his colleagues. Lowie may have done it to tweak him, or perhaps because Boas urged him to do the most expeditious thing (de Angulo also threw good parties – ever Lowie's weakness). By then there was also a serious glitch in Kroeber's project. As he had feared, Yuk was a tonal language:

> "I did Yuki in early summer with fat little Ralph, wound it up, and found it had tones, so must do it all over again. Sapir, who went to Hoopa for tones, found it had none, curse his luck." (ALKP: ALK-Pinner, 8/21/27)

A month later, commiserating with Sapir over alleged plagiarism of his notes on glottal stops by Harrington, Kroeber still would not admit failure. Instead, he pleaded a lack of time due to the unexpected complexity of Yuki tones (ALK-Sapir, 9/26/27). In fact, his linguistic comeback had failed, and it must have seemed terribly unfair that Sapir should have had such an easy time of it while he fumbled about with his recording machine, made mistakes, and ultimately found himself without publishable results. Furthermore, Boas' committee was positioned to do California linguistics energetically on a broad front. Thus dethroned, Kroeber wrote no article about his work with "fat little Ralph" until 1959, the year before he died. Uncertain of his memory by then, he framed it as some possible Athabascan influences on Yuki and published it as a one-page note in a journal to which he had seldom contributed. [70] The rest of 1927 saw his archaeological reputation much enhanced as he published his Peruvian fieldwork, and A.V. Kidder invited him to take pride of place in his famous first Pecos Conference (he and Sapir both attended in 1929). As matters turned out he had already done his last archaeological fieldwork, but stung by his treatment by Boas, and by the way his attempt to return to linguistics had turned out, he gave every indication of turning to archeology for good.

The 1934 Linguistic Train Wreck:

Another crisis in linguistics, seven years after Kroeber's fieldwork failure of 1927, involved him once again in the oedipal clash between Sapir and Boas and ensured that he would stay away from language work all but permanently. Sapir had taken the chair of the Division of Anthropology and Psychology of the National Research Council, and tried to enact some changes in the way funding decisions were taken. This was a stronger power base than any he had inhabited previously and it put him in contact with philanthropic foundations, such as the Rockefeller Foundation, on regular basis. At the 1934 AAA meeting Sapir, again trying to grab the helm in American linguistics, brashly proposed to alter the size and character of the Association's Committee on American Indian Linguistics. Among the things he suggested was that Kroeber might take the chair. This was an attempt to both stack the committee and to gain control of funding. In addition, the Smithsonian Institution and the BAE, never benign venues for Boas, were reacting favorably to Sapir's suggestions that a new Handbook of American Indians should be written along more "scientific" lines (ALKP: Sapir-ALK, 9/25/34, 10/18/34).

This was an assault on Boas' leadership position. Originally formed at Boas' behest, the AAA linguistics committee was his creature and the primary venue for the Boas Plan for recording American Indian languages. The quorum core of the Committee usually consisted of Boas, Bloomfield (whom Sapir considered to be under Boas' thumb), and Sapir himself. Several other linguists and anthropologists occasionally sat on it as well. Sapir wanted a permanently expanded committee, chaired by A.V. Kidder (an archaeologist) or some other "neutral" person. Among those he put forward was his own student, Morris Swadesh, whose work in glottochronology Kroeber was to greatly admire later, but who could scarcely have been called impartial in that venue. Kidder's suggested titular presence was a red herring, for Sapir really wanted to eject anyone who was not a linguist first and foremost, and one man (Bloomfield), who was. As Kroeber feared, Sapir's gambit, aimed at stacking the Committee and gaining more control of resources, immediately ignited a crisis as old resentments re-boiled. Already indignant at this power-grab, Boas was outraged when Sapir put it about at the meeting that he was as critical of Boas' business acumen as he was of his linguistic methods. In those bleak depression years it may have rung oddly to have the aesthetic and fiscally inexperienced Sapir talking about sound business methods, but few would have taken that part of his argument seriously. What Sapir most disliked was that Boas continued to use his heft in committee to push through funding for projects that suited his plan of research, but of which he (Sapir) did not approve. Boas was also pushing for the AAA's linguistic efforts to be extended into Latin America, with the same old program for fieldwork. [71]

Either W.G. Leland (then the Permanent Secretary of ACLS) or Sapir quickly approached Kidder, who appears to have given some initial offhand assent to chair an expanded committee. Perhaps he was unaware of how vitriolic the atmosphere had become, but he was famously in favor of interdisciplinary cooperation and this probably looked like more of it to him. He should have been more wary, for he had stood against Boas in the censure vote in the AAA Council in 1919, an affront Boas was unlikely to have forgotten. [72] Hard words were spoken and the meeting broke up in disarray, with nothing voted. After a brief visit with Sapir in New Haven, Kroeber wired Kidder, counseling him to decline the chair as Sapir's roster of proposed members would leave him "open to misconstruction", "griefs" (*sic*), and conflict "not now on surface" (ALKP: ALK-A.V. Kidder telegram, 12/16/34). They met soon thereafter, at Kroeber's invitation, in New York. His views carried weight with Kidder, with whom (before the Depression set in) he had planned an ethnographic and archaeological project to link the culture histories of California, the Southwest, and Mesoamerica. Boas, too, made his views plain to Kidder, who backed away hastily. This did not dissuade Sapir, who continued to press his points, while Kroeber, happy in the momentary and mistaken belief that he had forestalled a crisis, returned to California.

A week later, as the situation worsened and schism loomed, Kroeber thought better of having Kidder out of it so completely, and wrote a long letter, asking him to weigh in on the side of reason with Boas. A little implausibly (after all, he'd only just returned to Berkeley), he pleaded ignorance of the situation due to distance and suggested trying for some compromise. He saw two propositions that Boas would have great difficulty swallowing, but which were necessary for reconciliation. The first was that the value of the new linguistic program Sapir had championed forward be recognized. The second was that Boas had should accept that the time had arrived to pass the torch, and to someone he had come to view as an enemy. [73] His configuration of Boas' approach as "the work of the past" was an interesting acknowledgement of his belief in the need for a new paradigm; presumably something he would not have said to Boas. Apparently forgetting the wording of his earlier telegram to Kidder, he also affected to have just heard from Boas about the details of Sapir's proposal:

> "All the way across the continent I've been thinking about the linguistic mess (*scratched*: "muddle"). My first reaction was mostly about what it means in the way of tragedy for the two principals. But each day I sense more fully what it will do in setting back the work, and damaging anthropology, and I've been trying to find a way to prevent a complete smash.
>
> Unfortunately I know almost nothing of the history of the case. I hadn't even known that for the last two years the old committee had received funds for publication. Now Sapir has told me at length what is wrong with Boas' aims, standards, business methods, and personality; and Boas the same about Sapir. The one fact I learned from Boas was that there was to be

a new committee to replace the old one of three: you chairman; Boas, Sapir, Swadesh, Newman, Hoyer, Edgerton, perhaps one or two others: Bloomfield left off and Androde not on. Whatever this selection was meant to accomplish, it certainly looks loaded and would be so construed. ...Wissler told me that you had refused to serve; which I think Boas did not know, at any rate did not mention. Anyhow, you're well out of it.

That's the extent of my knowledge of events; and it's not much to build on. I <u>am</u> sure that the split between Boas and Sapir is personally irreparable. ... But the two between them represent the undoubted primacy of American Linguistics. Will they succeed in pulling the whole edifice down with their (*scratched*: "personality") clash, or is there still a chance to effect a solution which will let them disrupt and hate each other (*scratched*: "to the full") and yet force them to work together with a larger group which is uninvolved in the personal difference?

Both men are first of all anthropologists; and the threat is not to general but to Native American Linguistics. ...Here is a plan:

1. You ask Leland to hold all horses a couple of months while we see what can be straightened out.

2. Ask Cole to appoint (and his successor to confirm) an AAA committee on linguistics of four. This to consist of you; ...Tozzer; Cole, and myself. I am regretfully not suggesting Wissler because this ... would put an unbearably heavy strain on the unbiassedness (*sic*) which... he is held in high repute for. ...I'll ...do what I can by letter, and ...[will] consider coming east, even if I have to dig into my own pocket.

3. This AAA committee not to go into old grievances... but to club Boas and Sapir into

agreeing to... start fresh. This fresh start to consist of the old Boas-Sapir-Bloomfield committee voting to enlarge itself... by adding us four... Also some non-American... to balance Bloomfield, whom Sapir considers to be under Boas' influence.

4. This ...committee to work out a program on the following four bases:

   A. The work of the past (Boas dominated) is agreed to have been sound, valuable, productive, and in the main wise in its limitations, for the initial period, and work along these lines should be continued....

   B. Extension of the method, in part perhaps semi-experimental (Sapir – stimulated), as now warranted, as an addition.

   C. Agree extension to Latin America, [this] is urgently import.

   D. ...The committee to continue in charge of policies and appropriations, a few of the ablest younger linguists to be added gradually...

What do you think? Has this any chance? Tozzer and I can handle Boas, I think. He will put himself in the hands of those he considers to be his friends, even when under fire. The Cambridge meeting in 1919 showed that. Otherwise he fights to the limit, regardless of consequences. Sapir is no stand-up fighter, and will fall into line when faced with a solid front; but he doesn't know what he has started with Boas. He has evidently picked and picked (no doubt with good reason) until B[oas] declared war, and now S[apir] wails that it isn't he but Leland who has the grievance. He should have stood up to the domineering old man instead of running to Leland... and now sheltering behind him.

Ted, there's one ridiculous – sad angle to it. At bottom the row is this: Without his knowing it, Boas has for years owned and run American linguistics, and, also without knowing it, now S[apir] wants to take it away from him and own it. They are... the two great stars in the field... I have intense affection ... admiration for both of them.... The only difference now is that S[apir] blinds himself to the ruin ahead, B[oas] sees it but doesn't lay off. ...Us dumber but less emotional people [must] jump in and sit on both of them to keep them from not only wrecking themselves but the house and all its fixtures. Will you join in...?

Well, this is a mean one, but here's hoping you'll take hold once more." (ALKP: ALK-AV Kidder, 12/23/34)

Still eager to help, Kidder did indeed take hold (ALKP: Kidder-ALK, 12/26/34, 1/2/35; Kidder-Leland, 12/25/34). With everyone's holiday season spoiled, and himself down with the flu (Boas, too, caught the flu at the AAA meeting, so it must have struck down many others), he gamely spent Christmas orchestrating action along the lines Kroeber had suggested. Copies of the armistice proposal were sent to F.C. Cole at the University of Chicago, A.M. Tozzer, the Harvard Mayanist, and C. Wissler at the American Museum of Natural History. Kidder fretted briefly about Tozzer's dislike for Sapir, but believed that he would act in an even-handed manner. Kroeber also wrote directly to Tozzer, whom he correctly believed could influence Boas. Fortunately the letter he sent was toned down considerably from the one he first composed, for unbeknownst to Kroeber, Tozzer had for many years reported everything he knew, and much that he only thought he knew, to Boas. An anachronistic reading yields imagery worse than anything Kroeber intended to conjure, but given the year and Boas' frame of mind about events in Germany, a glimpse of Kroeber's first, frustrated draft would have estranged them completely:

"Has Kidder talked to you about the Linguistics smash? It's up to a few of us Gentiles to …keep the Jewish engineers from wrecking the train…

With Boas I recommend a frankly personal attitude. We, his friends, are in the matter to see he gets justice, but in return he must trust us and put himself in our hands. He will consent ungraciously, but he will consent, if you hold him to it flatly. Sapir has no fight in him and will line up as soon as he sees there is a real clash impending. A suggestion of that, and a chance for him to feel that the offered solution is more or less of his own making, will probably bring him around…

Don't rate me an anti-Semite yet, but Sapir's way of killing off the goose… is really too crude. Think of it: Boas, (*scratched* Jew), Sapir (*scratched* Jew), Bloomfield (*scratched* Jew), Swadesh (*scratched* Jew), Newman (*scratched* Jew), Michelson (*scratched* Jew), Edgerton (*scratched* Aryan) Sanskritist, Kidder (Aryan) an archaeologist. When there are first magnitude Jewish stars, we have all wanted them to shine. But after all, this is a Gentile Cosmos, and when anthropology becomes a Jewish battlefield, I join those who walk out of it. I believe that our first principle should be that a majority of this committee should remain Gentile controlled for some years, if only to protect the Jews against themselves, and Leland should be so informed.

Anything I write to you goes for Ted [Kidder], without saying, so, again, a good 1935." ALKP: ALK-Tozzer, 1/2/35)

Along with this letter to Tozzer, Kroeber enclosed one to Boas (ALKP: ALK-Tozzer, 1/2/35; 1/24/35; ALK-Boas, 1/3/35; see also FBP, Tozzer-Boas, 1/15/35). He had previously hinted to Boas that he felt that Sapir was going too far, and maintained that linguistics in America was properly part of anthropology and should remain so. On this occasion he remained on the fence:

"I am asking Tozzer to give you this letter when he sees or writes to you. A number of us who are genuinely neutral are likely to be injected into the linguistic problem in the hope of avoiding a general smash which would kill off all prospects for support. I think you can rest assured that whoever is brought into the matter will be detached and fair, and that you can count on Tozzer and me as representatives of your own point of view. In return, we would ask you to for the present, to ignore all criticisms, and to make no moves of any sort, until we feel that the difficult and delicate situation is on the way toward a constructive solution. We think such a one can be found, and when it is, not only will the work of the Committee under your chairmanship during the past eight years be automatically vindicated, but a foundation be laid for continuance along the right lines.

Tozzer will lay the plans before you as soon as he is authorized to. Meanwhile I would only ask of you as a personal favor, to do nothing whatever in the premises without his previous approval, so as not to embarrass those of us who are working for a prosperous resumption instead of the threatened termination of the work." (FBP: ALK- FB, 1/3/35)

Then to Tozzer he wrote: "You're in charge of the rescue party now, and good luck to you," which would have seemed ironic to Tozzer, who had often complained to Boas of Kroeber's excuses for not getting involved in East Coast AAA affairs.

In the event Tozzer did an outstanding job. He counseled Boas that caution was in order, and in a strong letter to Sapir called upon him, as the junior man, to make the first gesture by offering compromise proposals regarding the composition of the committee. He courageously undertook to see to it that Boas would in some sense "give in" once this gesture was made by hinting to the old man that this was what the his supporters wanted (ALKP: Tozzer-ALK, 2/6/35, preserved with a copy of Tozzer-Sapir, 1/15/35). He also arranged a meeting between Boas and Sapir. This was perilous, but his luck held. The antagonists talked throughout an afternoon and shelved their quarrel. However, Sapir's most important aim, an expanded committee, was thwarted for the time being.

> "Boas and Sapir met in New York and ironed out, so far as I can ascertain, their difficulties. I have heard nothing from Sapir since… but Boas was here for… the ACLS. I told Leland that… the Linguistic Committee would cooperate and work together effectively toward a common end.
>
> In order to accomplish this meeting I had to write Sapir a second letter even stronger than the one, a copy of which I sent you. I think he approached this meeting reluctantly but they had a five-hours' talk together. …I see no reason for changing the original committee of Bloomfield, Boas, and Sapir.
>
> In the budget …Boas wangled another $1000… in spite of the fact that several other items… were decreased. Boas did this, the only increase in the whole list… Leland approved the increase before Boas proposed it.
>
> I am very thankful that …peace has been established." (ALKP: Tozzer-ALK, 2/6/35)

Tozzer misread the degree to which real peace had been established, but he had brokered an impressive truce. Of course, Boas certainly would have angrily denied Tozzer's implication that he had somehow been bought off to simmer down, had such a thing ever been said to him. In the meantime, Kroeber found himself caught out when Tozzer, for reasons that can only be speculated about, forwarded to Sapir a copy of his January 3 letter to Boas. Although Kroeber's wording had been diplomatic, Sapir was indignant. He wrote to Kroeber to deny any culpability, while remaining unrepentant with regard to his desire to have funding allocated by almost anyone other than Boas. He took a very dim view of Kroeber's version of the suggestion for an American Anthropological Association committee to take hold of the situation, which would have militated against the linguistic secession he sought to achieve. In fact, he denied just about everything:

"Your letter of January 3 (*sic*), forwarded to Tozzer, was relayed to me by him. I regret that you did not send your letter directly to me.

I believe I can be trusted to be reasonable about the linguistic situation, so far as my part in the argument is concerned. …Any ideas that may be afloat as to my desire to wrest power from Boas are utterly unfounded. I did not take the initiative in the proposed reorganization of the Committee and I have tried to keep my personal grievances against Boas, which are very real and very profound, to myself.

I do not agree with you that there is anything in particular at stake for either anthropology or linguistics in the present excitement, which seems to me to be largely the product of Boas' imagination. My feeling is …that there is every intention to continue with American Indian linguistic work, and …it can be done either through some form of committee management or through local university allocation of funds.

I think your suggestion for a Committee of the American Anthropological Association to look into the matter or advise the ACLS or Rockefeller Foundation …is extremely unfortunate. I am inclined to believe that the mess that will then result will be far in excess of the present one, which can, by silence, charity, and good will, be allowed to work itself out to a perfectly pacific conclusion." (ALKP: Sapir-ALK, 1/19/35)

Kroeber responded to this on January 28 (the letter is not preserved), and succeeded in eliciting a softer reply from Sapir, who was still not inclined to recognize that the situation was real or, if it was, that he had any hand in starting it. Instead he implausibly used the breathing space afforded by his meeting with Boas to once again appear to line up with the patriarch, as though defense of Boas' sensibilities had been one of his concerns right along. He also appeared to be less than fully informed about Kroeber's role in deciding the composition of the AAA committee, and perhaps less than frank about his own (it may have been Sapir who first suggested Kidder for this role):

"...What I protested against was the idea of a strictly non-linguistic committee, taking action on problems that have recently come up in the ACLS.

With regard to the new committee, there are several misunderstandings, for which I am in no way responsible. The idea of the new committee was suggested by Leland and came to me as something of a shock. That Kidder be the chairman of this committee was his idea and not mine. Personally, I think it was a wrong idea, and I believe that it was this particular element in the situation that Boas resented more than any other. Boas should have been asked to serve as chairman.

...I had a conference recently with Boas in New York and it was perfectly evident to me that he is prepared, as am I to go ahead amicably and without interruption of previous work. I found no 'situation' to worry about, in spite of the fact that I spent the greater part of the day with him." (ALKP: Sapir-ALK, 2/4/35)

In later years Kroeber remembered himself as the central mediator in this affair. In fact, with Tozzer's considerable help, the principals had cooled down of their own accord, though the grudge continued until Sapir's death in 1939 (flaring again briefly over committee work in 1938). In any event, the linguistic field could have seemed no more hospitable to Kroeber in the nineteen-thirties than it had in the nineteen-teens and twenties, and he did not return to it even superficially until the other two men were dead. When asked to contribute something to Kroeber's *festschrift* two years later, Sapir handed in a brief piece on Hupa tattoos. Perhaps he did not want even a brief linguistic note to be buried in an obscure publication, but the result was that there was no linguistic article among thirty-seven items in the Table of Contents, except maybe that little piece on Papago nicknames.

Kroeber, White, and Bidney: Triangulating the Superorganic

What follows is discussion of a triangular correspondence among A.L. Kroeber, Leslie White, and David Bidney during the decade following World War Two. The first two men need no introduction, but the third may. Bidney first essayed to be American Anthropology's philosopher by summing and synthesizing its several theoreticians, Kroeber among them. He published articles in the early post-World War II years and throughout the nineteen-fifties, and wrote an ambitious book, *Theoretical Anthropology* (1953/1967).

Alfred Louis Kroeber is regarded as a ranking if occasionally heretical Boasian whose credentials lay chiefly in devotion to empirical research and defense of Franz Boas in several professional crises. However, his philosophy of work was largely at odds with the Boasian program, a tension most apparent in his linguistic efforts prior to 1920 (in cooperative competition with Edward Sapir), as well as in his latter-life enterprise, which can be summed as the natural-cultural history of whole civilizations. Kroeber believed in cultures, but his devotion was to Culture. Of all his theoretical writings, the *Superorganic* (Kroeber 1917), his persistent notion of Culture, drew the most fire over decades. He never really fought shy of this partly Spencerian, partly Durkheimian, and partly Teutonic-Romantic emergent evolutionary concept. He had to qualify it often, and disavowed it at least once (Kroeber, 1952: 23), but it re-emerged in different forms in his work. The 1917 article annunciating his world-view contained the seeds of several ideas he put forward over the course of his career: the spatial-temporal grouping of geniuses, the utility of statistics in telling culture traits, and cultural evolution. The Superorganic encompassed his greatest difference from the Boasian Ascendancy during the early stages of his career. In his last years, when he had unaccountably come to be held as authoritative on evolutionary topics (Kroeber, 1960b), it constituted his strongest claim to have thought deeply about general cultural evolution.

The Superorganic was not popular among ethnologists. Sapir and Clyde Kluckhohn both strongly criticized it, and Kluckhohn, together with David Bidney, nudged Kroeber away from it temporarily during the early nineteen-fifties. Leslie White pulled him back. White did not accept Kroeber's version of the Superorganic unreservedly, but was possessed of a similar conceptual framework in his "Culturology" and in his model of cultural evolution. On this score Kroeber's Boasian *persona* did him a disservice, for he was so wary of the term "evolution" that, like Holmes' celebrated dog that failed to bark in the night, for almost all of his professional life its lack left lacunae in his work. This may have been his greatest missed opportunity, for it is reasonably clear that he entertained a notion of cultural evolution that was actually quite close to White's. He maintained several times in correspondence that their views were similar, but due to polity or discretion he declined to say this in print. By the nineteen-fifties White had the lead and was well past having to defer to him as an intellectual progenitor, or call upon him as a patron, and would have objected to claim-jumping or unseemly intellectual piggybacking by such a senior scholar. Harris (1968: 332), concerned to minimize Kroeber's influence, fixed upon the latter's untoward reluctance to credit the evolutionary ideas of his most accomplished student, Julian Steward. Harris was therefore puzzled by White's approval of *Configurations of Culture Growth* (Kroeber, 1944). He did not see what White saw clearly: that much of what Kroeber wrote suggested cultural evolution, even necessitated it, without invoking it. Furthermore, Kroeber's notion of cultural evolution was that of the nineteenth century variety. Others saw this. For example, Wolf (1964: 57-59) put his pen squarely on Kroeber, writing that Kroeber and White had broken with relativism and "… returned American anthropology to an ancestral problem… [to] … the central concern of Lewis Henry Morgan and the evolutionists, to a view of the cultural process as universal, moving along a continuum from… primitive to civil society."

David Bidney, American anthropology's first avowed philosopher, acknowledged Kroeber as his antecedent. Bidney was part of a primary theoretical thrust of post-war anthropology – the problem of the nature of culture. Kroeber's *Configurations of culture growth* attracted his attention, but it was his critique of the Superorganic that first put them together (Bidney, 1944). Bidney, gradually wooed from an initial interest in Edward Sapir, was co-opted by generous attention even as he showed himself rather too well versed in Kroeber's work for Kroeber's own comfort. Seizing his opportunity to get to the heart of American anthropology and conduct interviews there he quickly spun up a searching correspondence. Kroeber, apparently sensing that Bidney could do him either good or harm, gradually allowed himself to be drawn out on theoretical and philosophical topics that he usually avoided. Meanwhile, he used Bidney as a foil in his half-friendly duel with White, in a triangular circuit of which Bidney may not have been aware.

Bidney began aggressively, calling Kroeber's Superorganic an idealist "culturalistic fallacy" (Bidney, 1944: 42). Idealism" here meant that Kroeber believed in the existence, even the mass of non-material things, but the thrust of the whole phrase was to invoke the opposite of the reductionist "naturalistic fallacy" committed by those who saw environmental determinism as the paramount force in culture history, or explained culture with reference to the biological levels below. In Bidney's view White had committed both errors at once. For Kroeber, Culture was *sui generis* and autonomous, while Boas, Dixon, and Sapir were "realists", who held culture to have no objective existence of its own, but rather to "exist" only in the minds of practitioners and in its semiotic transmission. Bidney therefore saw the Superorganic as a reification that took the Boasian notion of culture to a dizzy height, sacrificing the uniqueness of cultures to the autonomy of Culture. By not ruling out the possibility of degrees of Culture, it also undermined cultural relativism. He closed with a pious and somewhat pompous assertion:

> "Culture, we maintain, is a historical creation of Man and depends for its continuity upon free, conscious transmission and invention. ...[and] neither natural forces nor cultural achievements taken separately or by themselves can serve to explain the emergence and evolution of cultural life."

This opening salvo might have developed into the sort of grand theorizing Kroeber sometimes enjoyed, but his advanced age, ill health, and generally negative experiences with controversies must have made it seem like a lot of trouble for little gain. He had claimed privately to be heartily sick of talking about the Superorganic, and wished aloud on at least one occasion that he had never written about it (T. Kroeber, 1970: 223-30). Drawing Bidney close through letters, a tactic he preferred with formidable critics, was the easier and safer course. For his part, Bidney came to admire Kroeber almost unreservedly, eventually saying that he "rivaled Boas" (Bidney 1967: 467), and praising his ethnographic efforts in California as the perfect grounding for many theoretical contributions. Because Bidney's view of Kroeber was in good part dictated by Kroeber, we may take it as nearly a case of Kroeber discussing himself.

The "Dean of American Anthropology" wrote with surprising diffidence to Bidney (ALKP: ALK-Bidney, 3/26/45 – this earliest preserved correspondence between them mentioned an earlier letter that did not survive), disavowing theoretical aspirations while drawing the younger man out on his brash use of ancient philosophy to attack a problem in modern social science. Bidney was flattered by mail from Olympus, and happily expanded upon these themes. Kroeber responded carefully but fully, claiming (implausibly) to be unread in philosophy and unfamiliar with the Aristotelian definitions of causation, which Bidney believed key to an optimal explanation of culture. He also claimed (quite incredibly) not to know what Bidney meant by the term "emergent evolution":

> "I am not used to being read with such care… I am really unread in formal philosophy: I had to look up Aristotle's four kinds of causes and what Emergent Evolution meant. I wish I did know more. I certainly want to be rigorously logical, even if anything methodological or philosophical I do has been essentially a by-product of concrete work. …any slurs… were directed at social science activities like economic theory, or material-content philosophies like Spencer's and Compte's. If not, point out the passages and make me retract….
>
> As I think I said in my last, I have no doubt overstated my case [i.e., regarding the Superorganic]. I grant that *persona* are invariably the efficient causes of cultural phenomena.
>
> …In your terms, I would say that formal (and perhaps material) causes are more significant for

understanding culture (<u>not</u> man) than the efficient causes. Is this an extreme position or an absurd one?"

As to Emergent Evolution, thanks for the enlightenment. I'm without prejudice as to the label. As for idealism, I can see why you class my point of view with Marx's or Spengler's, but not with Hegel (whom I could never understand) nor with Plato (if I at all understand his doctrine of ideas). Not that I mind that name either."

Kroeber touted the empirical approach as the royal road to understanding, a customary piety undercut by the whole thrust of the Superorganic. Technology got its due as part of culture, and he offered a sense of what kinds of technology impressed him. He cleverly linked the first and last elements in the chain of "culture over minds over material substrate" to show culture ruling both minds (which were merely parts of societies), and matter. He wavered on the Superorganic, but was not yet talked out of it:

"…A curious thing about levels is that culture at the top – being most epiphenomenological – affects not only minds but organisms and inorganic nature. Without culture, would human minds and bodies dam the Colorado and the Boulder? I can't quite figure out what kind of causation that is; but it seems that the specific precipitating factor must be TNT and steam-shovels – artifacts, and therefore part of a cultural system."

The way to understand a superorganic entity was the (quite Boasian) empirical study of its manifestations:

"I grant of course that "psychobiological references (or implications) are indispensable" — both to the immediately efficient media (persons) and to the psychosomatic organisms as a limiting framework or condition. (Incidentally, this was held by Terde,

Wundt, Tyler, and Boas before Sapir and Malinowski.)
What I maintain boils down to this: to understand
culture one has to understand the variety of its
individuations, and for this, knowledge of related
culture manifestations – related in time, space, origin,
and type – is the first prerequisite. Undoubtedly this
alone will not yield exhaustive final understanding;
but without it, we shan't even begin to grapple with
it. At least, such is the precipitate of my trying to
grapple with it for 47 years." (ALKP: ALK-David
Bidney, 3/26/45) [74]

Bidney was careful of Kroeber's good name even when
criticizing him, so with growing trust their correspondence continued
throughout the decade between 1944 and 1954. Because Kroeber
wanted an alliance, he touted Bidney's worth at every opportunity,
sometimes chafing at the younger man's slow work habits and fear
of publishing (ALKP: ALK-Guggenheim Foundation, 3/9/51). For
his debut, Bidney Bidney joined forces with Kroeber to rebut Leslie
White's *An Anti-Evolutionist Fallacy*, (Bidney, 1946). Those who
hoped that Kroeber might lend his magisterial hand to bat away this
annoying gad-fly were disappointed. He produced a cautious, polite
piece (Kroeber, 1946b), in which he chided White for draining the
content from history to feed evolutionism, but delivered no heavy
strokes and left White plenty of room to maneuver. These were the
early stages of the re-introduction of evolutionism into American
Anthropology, and evidently people were feeling their way.

Eighteen months later Bidney had become rather dependent upon
Kroeber's feedback, while Kroeber, still somewhat wary, was more
in charge. In the wake of White's review of Kroeber's *Configurations
of Culture Growth*, a huge catalogue of culture-producing geniuses
plotted in time and space, Bidney's interest was shifting to a fuller
consideration of that massive work. At first he found *Configurations*
flawed (like White he focused first on Kroeber's too-expansive use
of the term "history" and his essentially bio-geographic approach
to ordering culture history). Bidney was a nitpicker, and Kroeber,
disappointed with the public response to *Configurations,* and with
his hands full with White, was losing patience with philosophical
vocabulary and discourse:

"Your searching comment is good for the soul, but trying to one's complacency. Of course you are right that time and space are both essential for history. As usual, I overstated my case in trying to be emphatic, when I spoke of "timeless history". It really is history with the time element held constant to a moment – highly "limited" as you say. I agree that the significance of such a moment is in its context of temporal continuity…"

This was, of course, a method of natural history, applied to culture. If he could get Bidney to stop philosophizing and get down to evaluating fieldwork, they would be in the natural history of cultures business, with an emphasis on history, and away from mentalist blind alleys:

"I understand that a cultural configuration *per se* (not in space-time) may be the object of an aesthetic analysis. But what do you mean by a "phenomenological analysis" which is non-historical but also alternative to "aesthetic"? Is it "science", or what? What is its purpose…? I am …much interested, because I suspect a lot of ethnological work may be just that. To me, personally, it becomes history, because as I read it or hear it I weave it into a space-time context, and therewith it acquires relational meaning also… I've often wondered what Lowie gets out of reading ethnology: his historic sense is good, but his historic interest seems rather mild, compared with mine. Perhaps what he does with the material is just your "phenomenological analysis". But what end does that serve?

…Of course there is a psychological process or activity (and physiological, too) in every cultural one. And I have always been interested in it. Much so, geographical environment cannot be left out. I wrote a volume on it – *Cultural and Natural Areas*.

But only a Huntington thinks he can <u>derive</u> cultural
qualities and events out of land and climate. So rebus
symbolism has its psychological bases, syllabification
as part of the resistance to abstracting phonemes ditto,
acrophony ditto. But no psychology, of course, will
explain how a symbol of an ox head came to stand for
A and not B, or how the language happened to have
an Aleph."

To shift Bidney's attention away from the Superorganic Kroeber
gave him credit for convincing him of some of the weaknesses of that
concept, while acknowledging, perhaps enviously, that regarding
meta-structures in history White had walked in where he (Kroeber)
had feared to tread. Ever a professor, he gave a little preemptive
homework – to list the points in his writings that Bidney thought
weak (and might criticize later):

"...As to psychologizing – aren't you aware that
you have caused me to modify my intransigeant
(*sic*) position of reification of culture? There again,
my old stand was an overstatement. The specificities
(*sic*) of culture will never be usefully, or specifically
explained by psychology alone; nor from purely social
phenomena; they must first of all be related to other
cultural phenomena. That much I saw, and still hold
to. Where I went too far was in stretching culture from
a system of viewing... phenomena into a closed system
of reality of its own. This I mean to take back publicly
as soon as I get around to it.

...I grant that reification of the Superorganic
involves immanent determinism. I think I've had
inclinations that way, but also hesitations. I dipped
my foot in, but kept pulling it out; White plunged
in. I mean to keep my foot dry from now on, thanks
to you.

...Now do something for me. As a philosopher,
I'm an amateur and though rash am not wholly lacking
in humility. As an anthropologist, I have professional

self-respect. Has the tendency to reification invaded
my construal of specific cultural situations to the point
of vitiating them, so far as you know? If so, will you
cite chapter and verse?"

There was another half-concession, though one putting behavior
in its place with all the data of sociology *underneath* and *underlying*
culture, the emergent phenomenon:

"I'm ready to accept culture as an attribute of human
behavior. Are you ready to concede that cultural
phenomena have to be operated with on the cultural
level before being resolved into psychology?" (ALKP:
ALK-Bidney, 8/1/46)

"Attribute" may have implied epiphenomenal status, but
Kroeber lost little in conceding this, for he had always thought that
Culture had evolved. However, it had also leaped a Rubicon. If not
exactly shifting his position, Kroeber was responding to Bidney's
(and Kluckhohn's) nudges, but White's pull was also in evidence. He
didn't "get around" to renouncing the Superorganic until 1952, and
when he did, he retained culture as a realm of its own, though with
more roots in the levels below. He may already have been leaning
toward White, and back toward the Superorganic, and wanted
Bidney to show his hand. He conceded the obvious, but demurred
on its implication: culture ultimately came from people's heads, but
just as phenotypes ultimately came from genes, the relation did not
relegate genes to a lesser order of reality.

Bidney, uncharacteristically neglecting to read the fine print,
was delighted with Kroeber's renunciation of the Superorganic as
a separate "level of cultural reality" (Kroeber, 1952: 23). With that
letter as evidence, he thereafter credited himself with having brought
that renunciation about (Bidney, 1953/1967, especially pp. 467-81).
He tested Kroeber once more on it, from a more philosophical
direction, and elicited another, even stronger renunciation of the
Superorganic as a real thing in the world, though with the caveat
that the corresponding sciences that addressed the many emergent
levels of organization were, after all, studying *something*. On the

crucial matter of culture as the highest of the emergent levels in the natural world, Kroeber fired back with a Kantian juxtaposition of the phenomenal *versus* reality:

> "As to levels. These seem to be generally accepted – but as to what? Granted they are not levels of reality, what are they levels of? Phenomena, perhaps. ...Or conceptual structures? Or perhaps another word is more fitting than "level". In short, is your description directed at levels as such, or at levels being construed as realities? If the latter, you needn't enlarge; I admit the point that culture is no more a thing than mind or life is. [At this point Kroeber crossed out an entire page and began again, only to write the same thing, *verbatim*.] ...But if the former, I am thoroughly at sea. The hierarchy of sciences is a commonplace; and to each group of sciences there corresponds a fairly definable class of phenomena."

Bidney was not finished with the question of "timeless" history, which was the standard gambit for anyone who wanted to take issue with Kroeber's badly explained bio-geographical approach to culture history - a product of his early years, when the archaeological record was largely a blank and the comparison of the distribution of traits in present-day cultures promised to be a more reliable guide to the past. In linguistics as well as ethnology, the framework of interpretation was much the same as in bio-geographic triangulation on past states, whether one was discussing the possibility of Ural-Altaic dialects scattered in Iberian mountains, the distribution of pottery styles, or the variety of beak forms among Galapagos finches. Bidney did not get along with White, but used White's arguments to prod Kroeber. This time he prodded him far from the Boasian approach and the path got crooked. Kroeber wrote:

> "...As to timeless history, ...I believe what I said in the White article about historic significances (*sic*) being dependent upon breadth (ultimately totality) of context, is evidence that timelessness is a

special phase, or limit, of historical approach, not a categorically distinct species. When dating fails one, or there never was any, so that a stretch of events has to be handled as a block, we don't therefore throw that material away. We extrapolate, with a degree of speculation; or infer (also somewhat speculative) time events from space distributions. One always aims as well as space and event... [Words missing from draft] ...definition of history. Holding either time or space fixed in a given piece of work doesn't make it unhistorical, I would say, as long as it relates to a larger context which includes time and space. Perhaps ..."timeless" is what you stick at. Would synchronic be more acceptable?

...In short, I do not define history non-temporally. It consists of characterizations of phenomena ("events") in space and in time setting. The characterization (narration, description, physiognomy) is primary, because without it the space and time frames obviously are empty; whereas if either of them is lacking, there is always the chance of the deficiency being supplied later."

That much was unambiguous, but then he became unclear:

"...Either the time or space element can be temporarily held fixed (synchronous instead of diachronic presentation), i.e. may be apparently suppressed, for special purposes, or for lack of data; though any such presentation resumes its full significance only on re-incorporation into the total time-space frame. This re-incorporation may be implicit while the work is being done; or subsequent, or ultimately potential."

The bio-geographical approach was born of necessity – a lack of data in time depth. Kroeber's pronouncements on it had been taken out of context. However, his attempt to affix blame for aspects of an approach that had characterized his work for decades on the need to answer Radcliffe-Brown and Leslie White was not convincing. His admiration for White remained grudging and clandestine:

> "The whole time-suppression business is an incident, a minor angle. It is a protest against White, Radcliffe-Brown and Co. trying to define the historical approach over-variously, ...as something of which time is the only essential or distinguishing factor – As if you could leave significance out of history! Read again how White imagines a history of the alphabet: a meaningless meandering of an atomic phenomenon through time and space... and this after I had written a story full of change and process and significance! And R[adcliffe-[B]rown's dictum that history is good when it operates with dated documents – unsound otherwise!
>
> I evidently expressed myself unfortunately somewhere; and if you misunderstood, others may, and I'll take occasion to refine or correct my expression, if I can. But if you think that I consider history basically timeless, you're barking up the wrong tree. I agree with you, on all but the extreme farther edge. Tell me what you see "evolution" as being over and above the obviously historical part; or more about levels; or about P[henomenological] A[pproach] – in all of which I do not see as far as I'd like to – and I'll be grateful. But in this timelessness business you're tilting at some venial excess, or slip, or inaccuracy of mine, which is of no real importance. When you say that I'm also infected with Whititis only I cover it up more, I haven't denied it: I've listened for more. But you've got to put it on different grounds than a marginal indiscretion."(ALKP: ALK-Bidney, 9/17/46)

Kroeber was straining at the Boasian leash on evolution, but not in Darwin's direction. A little over a decade later he was to preside, somewhat incongruously, over a Darwinian Centennial Symposium on evolution, but in the late nineteen-forties he had little to recommend him as a Darwinian, for he still mistook evolutionary patterns for evolutionary process:

> "As to 'evolution': I have always been pretty guarded as to accepting or defining it. So far as it is not history, or is more than history, I don't know what it is; and I said so in the paper on [Leslie] White."

Bidney's *Theoretical anthropology* was shot through with Kroeber's influence and references to his work (Kroeber was the most cited author other than Bidney himself – White was third). The second edition (Bidney, 1967: 467-81) was dedicated to Kroeber, and contained an extensive appendix on his contribution to contemporary anthropology. Bidney owed him that tribute, for Kroeber had buffed and polished him for his debut and supported him thereafter. Even the Superorganic, which Bidney had assailed vigorously a decade before, was treated with restraint and given its due. In Bidney's mature view, however wrong-headed, the Superorganic was Kroeber's most fertile idea:

> "Kroeber is perhaps best known for his paper on "The "Superorganic" ...first introduced by Herbert Spencer, he reinterpreted and adapted it to the uses of ethnology... a superpsychic, autonomous level of phenomenal reality independent of the processes of biology and psychology. Later, he differentiated the cultural Superorganic from the level of society as well. His objective was to establish cultural anthropology as an autonomous science, and to preclude the reduction of cultural phenomena to those of a lower level of reality, such as psychology and biology. Individuals were regarded as the passive carriers of culture, and all cultural phenomena were to be explained historically and causally in terms of other cultural phenomena. Culture as a whole was viewed as a historical and evolutionary level of reality subject to its own laws. ... The majority of the anthropological profession ...in America at least, tended to accept [the Superorganic] and incorporate it in their textbooks."

We are entitled to question whether Kroeber's notion of the Superorganic was ever as popular as that with ethnologists, for almost all of them had reacted badly to it, as had Bidney, who could not resist a little third person lime-lighting:

> "As a matter of record, it was not till Kroeber's view was challenged by David Bidney in his article on *The concept of culture and some cultural fallacies…* that the former began to re-consider and modify his views in a series of papers. The revised edition of Kroeber's *Anthropology* (1946 *sic*) testifies to this fundamental change, and the preface to the reprinted of the original version on *The Superorganic* in *The nature of culture…* frankly acknowledges the limitation of his paper."

Bidney, aware of Kroeber's ability to evade easy categorization, wanted to transfix him before helping him on toward apotheosis, but this still said much about the flexibility of a man many characterized as never having changed his mind about much of anything. As if to compensate for the flexibility he had just implied, Bidney – who was still probably unaware of White's gravitational pull on Kroeber, grumbled about how difficult it had been to move him even a short distance:

> "In revising his views, Kroeber still adhered to the thesis that culture should be regarded for purely methodological or heuristic purposes 'as if' it were independent of individuals and minds, even though it is not actually so. Cultural achievements and products were to be studied impersonally, 'as if' they were independent of individuals and societies, in order to establish useful correlations, patterns, and configurations, but this did not mean, he insisted, that culture was an autonomous process, *sui generis*. This purely methodological reinterpretation of cultural phenomena enabled Kroeber to retain and validate his program of research of the culture element distribution in North America as well as his method of surveying the configurations of classical civilizations."

That rings true, and it is interesting that Bidney believed that such data-bound studies as Kroeber's on culture element distributions were grounded in the Superorganic. The idea has merit, for the "styles" Kroeber invoked and expounded throughout his later life were planks in a platform that supported the Superorganic.

Leslie White became anthropology's *enfant terrible* during the early post-war years, but laid his groundwork well before. In *Science is Sciencing* (1938), he established that culture was as open to scientific investigation as other natural phenomena. This he had from Kroeber, for the Superorganic pre-supposed it, as Kroeber and Kluckhohn (1952) were still pointing out nearly fifteen years later. White had other debts to Kroeber (1915, 1917, 1918, 1936), particularly in arranging natural phenomena alongside the sciences that explained them on emergent levels. In *Mind is Minding* (1939), he dispensed with the need for human minds as objects of scientific interest, identifying them as merely the activity of brains - a commonplace among clinical psychologists that had not yet percolated through disciplinary firewalls into anthropology. He put cultural evolution back on the theoretical agenda while suggesting that if it could be studied scientifically as well as historically, then its general processes (if not its specific events) might be predicted as well as reconstructed.

The greatest impediment to collaboration between Kroeber and White was White's crusade against the heritage of Franz Boas and the surviving incumbents of the latter-day Boasian Ascendancy. With Boas only a few years dead, White was accusing him of suppressing the scientific development of American anthropology with a dictatorial, wrong-headed attitude toward both evolution and the scientific method. In White's view, this was all simply a means of sweeping evolution under the rug and forcing a generation of American anthropologists into a fruitless and apparently endless quest for mere facts. White began to be obstreperous about this in print during 1945, with *History, Evolutionism, and Functionalism: Three Types of Interpretation of Culture* (his contribution to the first number of SWJA), and *Diffusion versus Evolution: An Anti-evolutionist Fallacy*. In the former he added "Evolutionism" to "history" and "science" as modes of study of the human career, claiming that temporal aspects of the record yielded to history, its formal aspects yielded to science, and that the temporal–formal together were the proper subject matter of evolutionism.

As chief among those White considered to have confounded history and evolution, Kroeber was a target of this exercise. In *An Anti-Evolutionist Fallacy* White discounted diffusion, a mechanism for culture change that the Boasian program had long favored, and that Kroeber had elaborated five years earlier (Kroeber, 1940). The diffusion model explained little, in White's view, but covered for an overriding and unjustified Boasian assumption that everything was always in an ineffable process of change, and that the meaning of cultural phenomena could not be traced from one culture to another. Like Harris (1968: 275-77) after him, White assailed as a non-issue the dichotomy between history and science over which Kroeber had Boas had quarreled during the nineteen-thirties (Kroeber, 1935), claiming that they had befuddled themselves by mistakenly subsuming the evolutionary in the historical. Kroeber (1946, 1948d) could only reply that White had subsumed the historical into the evolutionary.

White could be embarrassing as well as annoying. In the late 1940s he was only slowly shedding his (by then perilous) pre-war pro-Soviet political convictions. Morganian stages of historical development were a necessary Marxian component of his thought, and he never disguised allegiances or shrank from confrontation. A letter Ralph Linton wrote to W.D Strong contained a glimpse of White as his pre-war contemporaries knew him. With the capitalist world collapsing and the Soviet model seemingly ascendant, like many another Western intellectual White visited the Soviet Union in 1930 to find a hero in Stalin. Linton, a veteran of the Great War, was not sympathetic: "It will be amusing to see [White] among the conservatives [at the University of Michigan], for he is an out-and-out Bolshi since his Russian experience" (WDSP: R. Linton-W.D. Strong, 11/29/30).

White could not be to Kroeber's taste as a public fellow traveler, but he had dared where Kroeber had not, and had produced what Kroeber, in a career of gingerly poking at the question of culture change, had not - a mechanism. In *Energy and the Evolution of Culture* (White, 1943/1949), bolstered by the influential writings of the archaeologist V.G. Childe (whom Kroeber too greatly admired), he put forward the concept of energy capture and use as both mechanism and potential measure of technological progress. White explicitly denied that any but "culturological" (mostly technical-economic) factors were in play, dismissing out of hand race, instinct, intelligence, consciousness, the moral sense, personality, and individual minds (including geniuses), as unscientific. He thus offered a motive force for the Superorganic that operated right in front of anthropologist's eyes, if means could be found to measure it.

White (1946) reviewed Kroeber's *Configurations of Culture Growth* positively. He sent a preview draft of what was more a feature-length article than a book review to Kroeber, along with a letter explaining that such a lengthy book required lengthy treatment. He carefully distinguished himself from Kroeber (who might have had some prior intellectual claim in "culturology"), but largely approved of a book many considered Kroeber's weakest. White felt that since Kroeber was propping up a Superorganic view of Culture he would have done better to treat it as a whole rather than teasing it into more Boasian parts. In short, Kroeber had failed grandly. Nonetheless, White admired his ability to think outside the Boasian box. The review was: "...Not calculated to enhance my popularity in the AAA. But it is honest and sincere as it is plain spoken. I feel that anything else would be unworthy of both of us" (ALKP: White-ALK, 1/10/49).

White also noted the work of Wihelm Ostwald, whom some believed deserved credit for the science and the term "culturology", about which White was quite proprietary. The point here, of course, was not so much to dismiss Ostwald's claim as to forestall Kroeber's, which we cannot imagine he ever intended to press. Kroeber responded with a very long letter, acknowledging for the only time I am aware of his compulsive trait counting. He seemed circumspect, even fearful of this newly powerful junior colleague who was so forward with ideas he (Kroeber) had kept under wraps. As with Bidney, he wanted to establish a dialogue to pull White close rather than thrust him away. The overall flavor was chatty, almost gaseous with the forced charm of one who must whistle his way past the graveyard, and with hollow-sounding claims to have largely accomplished what he had intended in his big book. He was able to claim, therefore, that he was not (much) disappointed, though in letters to others he gave clear indications of how much he had taken the book's failure to heart. He deployed his concurrent correspondence with Bidney about Aristotelian causation, wrapped in compromise language that intoned, "we don't really disagree much, we are all in this together, and have a long way to go". On the prevailing mode of research into culture and personality, then in vogue, they found common ground:

> "I liked your review article. You've treated me in a most friendly spirit. …I don't feel in the least I failed (pp. 7. 12). First of all, I had a fine time satisfying an inner need. And then I think I sharpened or corrected a good many particular interpretations of fair breadth, and adumbrated some new ones, besides emphasizing an attitude. To have emerged with something bigger would have been grand, but there was no real disappointment."

> "…Entire agreement with your point that if we abandon culture for ink-blots etc., who will deal with it (pp.15, 16)?
>
> P. 17, etc. On force and cause. I think here is where we all bog down by using words in different senses. I have used them differently at different times. Bidney's recent *American Anthropologist* article, though too technically logical, has value in making clear some of our implications. I think it must be admitted with him, and Boas, that the <u>efficient</u> causes of culture are men; but its <u>formal</u> causes are cultural; and that of the two, the efficient causes have little relevance or significance as against the formal ones – provided one is interested in culture. Of course, if interest is rather in men and how culture affects them, or they it, the formal causes matter less than the efficient; they can then be treated or assumed as if constant while men and their interactions vary – as in *Configurations* I have virtually held men constant while I watched how cultural forms changed."

There followed a sentence of cosmic reach, with vaporous theological imagery intended to convince that the search for ultimate origins and causes was pointless. He gestured toward his concurrent dialogue with Bidney over the meaning of "timelessness":

> "What you cite from me on p. 19, paragraph three as to our not understanding very much is probably connected with the ambiguity as to causality. Given certain cultures or cult[ural] forms to start with, I feel we can go quite a long way (in time or timelessly) in understanding a good deal about them by analyzing out their interrelations or "formal causes". But sooner or later, as we go backward (or forward), we reach a point where this universe ends... where the formal-cause thought-process is no longer operative, and where we ultimately have to bring in the "first or productive causes of cult[ture] which we still see so dimly. ...I think we know a lot about the nature of culture, but we do not really understand either its origin or its fundamental nature."

White still believed that Kroeber had confounded history and evolution, and Kroeber's response prefigured his rejoinder in SWJA several months later, except that, as with Bidney, he assigned some homework. Also, it didn't hurt to pull rank where languages were concerned:

> "The matter of history and evolution, (History *versus* Evolution, you say) I'd like awfully to talk over with you some time. I see only a difference of degree or emphasis, not of kind. Have you read Hugh Miller's *History and Science* of a few years ago? —He is a philosopher at UCLA. Try it, and give me a reaction. He accepts history outright as evolution in the broad sense. The limitation of Rickert is in being under the ban of the German *Geisteswissenschaft* concept, which he partly freed himself of by converting *Geist* into *Kultur*, but then didn't know what to do with

> evolutionary biology and geology, and wavered
> between ignoring them and assigning them outright
> to [be] science! There's a lot of basic methodology still
> to be clarified in this area."

White, whose use of energy was entirely materialistic, had called Kroeber on his almost vitalistic uses of "force" and "energy" in cultures and civilizations. Kroeber ducked this and glanced safely off the question of environmental determinism. Here he could not suppress a note of disappointment about the reception *Configurations* had received:

> "As to technology and energy, pp. 20-21, this too
> is something I would like to talk out with you.
> Subsistence and technology are primary, of course
> – as antecedents – but I'm not so sure they are as
> causes. As to energy, while I talk metaphorically of
> "cultural energy", aren't you talking of physical energy
> controlled by cultures?
>
> p.23: Culture whole: I'd rather have tackled it,
> but the pieces were good sized hunks to chew. In the
> next-to-last chapter on "Nations" I did try to deal with
> whole cultures, one after the other; and that chapter
> probably satisfied me the best in the book. But as yet
> no one else has paid any attention to it.
>
> Your article has given me a lot of stimulation, as
> you see. I'd like to keep the copy, if you don't need
> it, and do some further thinking about the problems
> it raises, while it's in the press."(ALKP: ALK-White,
> 9/11/45)

These theoretical points regarding evolution and cultural wholes moved between them easily because they shared the concept of the Superorganic. But they were dealing with more than theory. They were also adjusting their positions with regard to the man who was White's primary target, and who had loomed behind Kroeber since before the century dawned. But Kroeber's defense of Boas as a dutiful empiricist in fieldwork was half-hearted. He noted his old teacher's preference for removing interpretations rather than adding them on:

> "I agree that there is no substitute for creative imagination (p.14). The difference presumably is that the inductionist keeps coming back to his data, the deductionist leaves them as soon as possible. I would credit Boas with plenty of power of imagination, but also the obsession of only using it critically, that is negatively."

It is instructive to have White's later remarks about Boas as he configured them for Kroeber, who had written to him to take exception to White's *History, Evolutionism, and Functionalism: Three Types of Interpretation of Culture* and *Diffusion versus Evolution; an Anti-Evolutionist Fallacy* (1945b). White criticized Boas in ways that Kroeber may have wished to, and touched on Kroeber's ambivalence on evolution:

> "I was very much interested in what you had to say about Boas and about such matters as greatness, achievement, and recognition in general.
>
> With regard to my 'feelings about Boas'; I do not believe that my feeling about him is any stronger than the feeling of dozens of his admirers – or, as you once said, of his disciples who 'literally worshipped him'. The only exceptional thing about my feeling is that it is negative rather than positive. Intense loyalty and admiration or even worship of Boas seems to be taken for granted but a severely critical attitude …seems to require some explanation. …He has been regarded as perhaps the greatest anthropologist of all time and has been held up before the world as the very essence of the scientific spirit, …whereas I am convinced … that he was quite muddle-headed, incapable of creative imagination, and philosophic synthesis, and at … directly opposed to the spirit and procedure of science. …He has done American anthropology a great injury

and …it will take a long time [for it] to recover…I would agree …that my opposition to Boas does not rest upon evolutionism alone… Boas and I are at opposite poles on almost all subjects. But I would not agree with you … that I have been tolerant in 'letting you off' on this score. It is true that you have paid lip service to the anti-evolutionist point of view, as for example in the early pages of your *Anthropology*. But I cannot see that you have carried your anti-evolutionism beyond lip service. On the other hand, I believe that there is abundant evidence in many of your writings which indicate that you have thought and worked in the spirit of evolutionism…

…About our exchange …[on 'History and evolution'], …two separate and distinct kinds of processes in culture can and should be distinguished. Whether we designate these …'history' and 'evolution' …or some other terms, does not matter…" (ALKP: White-ALK, 2/27/47).

So White too wanted a truce, if not an alliance, while Kroeber was ready to concede that the Boasian Ascendancy had stifled some crucial kinds of research, particularly where evolutionary thought was concerned. Apparently not much came of this near miss of minds, for their correspondence thereafter was infrequent and unexceptional. Certainly Bidney (1967: 71-72, 329-30) later believed that Kroeber had dropped the whole notion of general evolution of a Superorganic (at his prodding), and that White had picked it up. What seems clear is that White's remarks about Kroeber's ambivalence were on the money.

List of Abbreviations

AA: *American Anthropologist*
AAA: American Anthropological Association
AAAS: American Association for the Advancement of Science
ACLS: American Council of Learned Societies
AHP: Ales Hrdlicka Papers
ALKP: Alfred Louis Kroeber Papers
APS: American Philosophical Society
Amer. Antiq.: *American Antiquity*
BAE: Bureau of American Ethnology
BAMNH: *Bulletin of the American Museum of Natural History*
CA: *Current Anthropology*
FBP: Franz Boas Papers
HAN: *History of Anthropology Newsletter*
HOA: *History of Anthropology*
JAFL: *Journal of American Folklore*
RLP: Robert Lowie Papers
SWJA: *Southwest Journal of Anthropology*
UCPAAE: *University of California Papers in Archeology, Anthropology and Ethnology*
WDSP: William Duncan Strong Papers

References Cited

Alsberg, C. L.

1936   (With R. Lowie). Alfred Kroeber, Personal Reminiscences and Professional Appreciation. In, *Essays in Anthropology Presented to A.L. Kroeber in Celebration of his Sixtieth Birthday, June 11, 1936.* Freeport. Books for Libraries Press.

Anderson, S.

1990   Sapir's Approach to Typology and Current Issues in Morphology. In, D. Dresler *et al, Contemporary Morphology* (pp. 277-95). Mouton. De Gruyter.

Beals, R.

1968   Kroeber, A.L. In, *International Encyclopedia of the Social Sciences,* New York. Macmillan.

Benedict, R.

1939   Edward Sapir. *AA,* 41: 465-68. Reprinted in Koerner, 1984.

Bidney, D.

1944   On the Concept of Culture and Some Cultural Fallacies. *AA,* 66: 293-97.

1946   On the So-Called Anti-Evolutionist Fallacy: A reply to Leslie White. *AA,* 48: 293-97.

1953/67 *Theoretical Anthropology.* New York. Schocken.

1965   The Contribution of A. L. Kroeber to Contemporary Anthropology. *Intl. Jour. Compar. Sociol.* 7: 266-77.

Bloomfield, L.

1926   A Set of Postulates for the Study of Language. *Language*, 2: 153-64.

1933   *Language*. New York. Holt.

Boas, F.

1889   On Alternating Sounds. *AA* (Old Series), 2: 47-53.

1893/94 Classification of the Languages of the North Pacific Coast. Paper read at the International Congress of Anthropology, Chicago (1893) and published in *Mem. of the Intl. Cong. of Anth.* (1894). Reprinted in Stocking, 1974b.

1894a   The Anthropometry of the Northwest Coast Indians. In, C.S. Wake, *Memoirs of the International Congress of Anthropology.* Chicago. Schulte.

1894b   Chinook Texts. *BAE Bulletin No.* 20. GPO. Wash. DC.

1897   Decorative Art of the Indians of the North pacific Coast. *AMNH Bulletin*, 9: 123-76.

1911   Handbook of American Indian Languages, Part 1. *Bulletin No. 40 of the BAE*. GPO, Wash. DC.

1920   The Classification of American Languages. *AA*, 22: 367-76.

1922   Handbook of American Indian Languages, Part 2. *Bulletin No. 40b of the BAE*. GPO. Wash. DC.

1924   Evolution or Diffusion. *AA* (New Series), 26: 340-344.

1938   *General Anthropology.* New York. D.C. Heath and Co.

Brightman, R.

2004   Jaime de Angulo and Alfred Kroeber: Bohemians and Bourgeois in Berkeley Anthropology. In, R. Handler (ed.), *Significant Others. Interpersonal and Professional Commitments in Anthropology*. History of Anthropology, vol. 10: pp. 158-195.

Buckley, T.

1996   The Little History of Pitiful Events: The Epistemological and Moral Contexts of Kroeber's California Ethnology.

In, G. Stocking (ed.) *Volksgeist as Method and Ethic. Essays on Boasian Ethnography and the German Anthropological Tradition.* History of Anthropology, Vol. 8. Univ. of Wisconsin Press.

Campbell, L.

1998   *Historical Linguistics.* Cambridge. MIT Press.

Carmichael, P.H.

1998   (ed.) *The Archaeology and Pottery of Nazca, Peru.* Alfred Kroeber's 1926 Expedition. Walnut Creek and London. Alta Mira.

W. Cowan, M.K. Foster, and K. Koerner

1986   (eds.) New Perspectives in Language, Culture, and Personality. *Proceedings of the Edward Sapir Centenary Conference.* John Benjamins. Amsterdam and Philadelphia.

Darnell, R.

1971   The Revision of the Powell Classification. *Papers in Linguistics,* 4: 70- 110.

1976   The Sapir Years at the National Museum, Ottawa. In: J. Freedman (ed.) *The History of Canadian Anthropology.* Hamilton. Canadian Ethnological Society (also reprinted in Koerner, 1984).

1986   The Emergence of Sapir's Mature Thought. In: *New Perspectives in Language, Culture, and Personality.* Proceedings of the Edward Sapir Centenary Conference. W. Cowan, M.K. Foster, and K. Koerner (eds.). John Benjamins. Amsterdam and Philadelphia.

1990a   *Edward Sapir: Linguist, Anthropologist, Humanist.* Berkeley. Univ. of California Press.

1990b   Franz Boas, Edward Sapir, and the Americanist Tradition. *Historiographia Linguistica* XVII: 129-144.

1998   *And Along Came Boas. Continuity and Revolution in Americanist Anthropology.* Amsterdam. John Benjamins.

2001   *Invisible Genealogies: A History of Americanist Anthropology.* Lincoln. Univ. of Nebraska Press.

J.T Irvine, and R. Handler
1999   *The Collected Works of Edward Sapir*. New York. Walter de Gruyter.

De Angulo, G.
1995   *The Old Coyote of Big Sur: The Life of Jaime de Angulo*. Berkeley. Stonegarden Press.

Dixon, R.B.
1910   The Chimariko Indians and Language. *UCPAAE*, 5: 293-380.
1911   Maidu. In, F. Boas (ed.), *Handbook of American Indian Languages*, Part 1, BAE Bull. 40, Washington D.C.

Dixon, R.B., and A.L. Kroeber
1903   The Native Languages of California. *AA*, 5: 1-26.
1907   Numeral Systems of the Languages of California. *AA*, 9: 4: 319-56.
1913a   Relationship of the Indian Languages of California. *Science*. 37: 225.
1913b   New Linguistic Families in California. *AA*, 15: 647-55.
1919   Linguistic Families of California. *UCPAAE*, 16, 3: 47-118.

Driver, H.E.
1962   The Contribution of A. L. Kroeber to Culture Area Theory and Practice. *Indiana University Publications In Anthropology and Linguistics*, #18. Durr, M. and E. Renner.
1995   The History of the Na-Dene Controversy: A sketch. In, M. Durr, M. E. Renner, and W. Oleschinski (eds.), *Language and Culture in Native North America. Studies in Honor of Heinz-Jurgen Pinnow*: pp. 3-18. Newcastle. Lincom.

Eggan, F.
1986   An Overview of Edward Sapir's Career. In: *New Perspectives in Language, Culture, and Personality. Proceedings of the Edward Sapir Centenary Conference*. W. Cowan, M.K. Foster, and K. Koerner (eds.). John Benjamins. Amsterdam and Philadelphia.

Eldredge, N.
1999   *The Pattern of Evolution*. New York. Phoenix.

Gibbs, G.
1863   Instructions for Research Relative to the Ethnology and Philology of America. *Smithsonian Misc. Coll.*, 160: 13-17. Washington. Smithsonian.

Gifford, E.W.
1916   Composition of California Shell Mounds. *UCPAAE*, 12 (1):1-29.

Goddard, P.E.
1915   The New Stock Names Announced for California. *AA*, 17: 413.
1920   Has Tlingit a Genetic Relation to Athabascan? *IJAL*, 1: 266-79.

Goldschmidt, W.
1959   (ed.) The Anthropology of Franz Boas. *American Anthropological Association Memoir* No. 89.

Golla, V.
1984   *The Sapir-Kroeber Correspondence*. Rep.#6, Survey of California and Other Indian Languages. Berkeley. University of California.
1986   Sapir, Kroeber, and North American linguistic Classification. *Studies in the History of the Language Sciences*, 41 (New Perspectives in Language, Culture, and Personality): 17-39. Philadelphia and Amsterdam. John Benjamins.
2005   *The Attractions of American Indian languages*. Paper presented at the 79th Annual Meeting of the Linguistic Society of America. Oakland, CA. Jan. 7, 2005.

Gould, S.J.
1989   *Wonderful life*. London. Hutchinson Radius.

Greenberg, J. H.
1950   Review of David. G. Mandelbaum's Selected Writings of

Edward Sapir in Language, Culture, and Society. *A.A.*, 52: 516-18.

Handler, R.
1986   Vigorous Male and Aspiring Female: Poetry, Personality, and Culture in Edward Sapir and Ruth Benedict. In, G. Stocking (ed.) *Malinowski, Rivers, Benedict, and others.* University of Wisconsin Press.

Harris, M.
1968   *The Rise of Anthropological Theory.* New York. Crowell.

Harris, Z.
1951   Review of D.G. Mandelbaum's Selected Writings of Edward Sapir. *Language*, 27: 288-333 (Reprinted in Koerner, 1984).

Hatch, E.
1973   *Theories of Man and culture.* New York. Columbia.

Hobsbawm, E.
1964   *The Age of Revolution*, 1789 – 1848. New York. Mentor.

Hoijer, H.
1951   Review of D.G. Mandelbaum's Selected Writings of Edward Sapir in Language, Culture, and Society. *Romance Philology*, 4: 4, 311-15 (Reprinted in Koerner, 1984).
1954a   (ed.) Language in culture. *Proceedings of a Conference on the Interrelations of Language and other Aspects of Culture.* AAA Memoir no. 79.
1954b   Comments on American Indian Linguistics in the Southwest. *AA,* 56: 637-39.

Hymes, D.
1961   Alfred Louis Kroeber. *Language*, 37, 1: 1-28.
1964   (ed.). *Language in Culture and Society.* New York. Harper and Row.

Jacobs, M
1959   Folklore. In: W. Goldschmidt (ed.) *The Anthropology*

of *Franz Boas*. American Anthropological Association Memoir No. 89.

Koerner, K.

1984   (ed.) *Edward Sapir: Appraisals of his Life and Work.* Amsterdam Studies in the Theory and History of Linguistic Science, Series III, Studies in the History of the Language Sciences, Vol. 36. Amsterdam and Philadelphia. John Benjamins.

Kraus, M.

1984   Edward Sapir and Athabaskan Linguistics. In: *New Perspectives in Language, Culture, and Personality.* Proceedings of the Edward Sapir Centenary Conference. W. Cowan, M.K. Foster, and K. Koerner (eds.). John Benjamins. Amsterdam and Philadelphia.

Kroeber, A.L.

1899a   Animal Tales of the Eskimo. *JAFL*, 12, XLV: 17-23.

1899b   Tales of the Smith Sound Eskimo. *JAFL*, 12, XLVI: 166-82.

1900   The Eskimo of Smith Sound. Bull. of the *AMNH*, 12: 265-327.

1902   A Preliminary Sketch of the Mohave Indians. *AA*, 4, 2: 276-85.

1903   The Coast Yuki of California, *AA* n.s. 5: 729-30.

1904a   The Languages of the Coast of California South of San Francisco. *UCPAAE*, 2, 2: 29-80.

1904b   Types of Indian Culture in California. *UCPAAE*, 2, 3: 91-103.

1906a   The Yokuts and Yuki Languages. *Boas Anniversary Volume. Anthropological Papers Written in Honor of Franz Boas*, 64-79. New York. Stechert.

1907a   The Yokuts Language of South Central California. *UCPAAE*, 2, 5: 165-377.

1906b   The Dialectic Divisions of the Moquelumnan Family in Relation to the Internal Differentiation of the Other Linguistic Families in California. *AA*, 8, 4: 653-63.

1907b   Shoshonean Dialects of California. *UCPAAE*, 4, 3: 65-165.

1907c   The Washo Language of East Central California and Nevada. *UCPAAE*, 4, 5: 251-317.

1908   Anthropology of California. *UCPAAE*, 4, 3: 65-165.

1909   Classificatory Systems of Relationship. *Jour. Royal Anthropological Society*, (also published in Kroeber, 1952).

1910a   The Chumash and Costanoan Languages. *UCPAAE*, 9: 259-63.

1910b   Noun Composition in American Languages. *Anthropos*, Band 5: 204-218.

1910c   Noun Incorporation in American languages. *Verhandlungen des XVI. Internationalen Amerikanistan-Kongresses*, Wien 9. Bis 14.

1911a   The languages of the Coast of California North of San Francisco. *UCPAAE*, 9: 273-435.

1911b   Phonetic Constituents of the Native Languages of California. *UCPAAE*, 10: 1-12.

1911c   Phonetics of the Micronesian Language of the Marshall Islands. *AA*, 13, 3: 380-93.

1911d   Incorporation as a Linguistic Process. *AA*, 13, 4: 577-84.

1911e   The Languages of the American Indians. *Popular Science Monthly*, 78, 5: 500-15.

1913   The Determination of Linguistic Relationship. *Anthropos*. Band 8: 389-401.

1914   Chontal, Seri and Yuman. *Science*, n.s., 40, #1030: 448.

1915a   Eighteen Professions. *AA*, 17,#2: 283-288.

1915b   Serian, Tequistlatecan, and Hokan. *UCPAAE*, 11: 279-90.

1916a   Floral Relations among the Galapagos Islands. *University of California Publications in Botany*. 6, 9: 199-220.

1916b   Zuni Culture Sequences. *Proc. Nat. Acad. Sci.*, 2, 1: 42-45.

1916c   Zuni Potsherds. *AMNH Anthro.* Papers, #vol. 18, part 1. New York. AMNH.

1916d   Arapaho Dialects. *UCPAAE*, 12, 3: 71-138.

1916e   Speech of a Zuni Child. *AA*, n.s., 18, 4: 529-36.

1917   The Superorganic. *AA*, 19: 163-213.

1919a   On the Principle of Order in Civilization as Exemplified by Changes of Fashion. *AA*, 21, 3: 235-63.

1919b   Peoples of the Philippines. *AMNH Handbook Series*, #8. New York. AMNH.

1919c   Review of E. Sapir (1916) Time Perspective in Aboriginal American Culture, a study in method. *AA*, n.s., 21: 75-77.

1922   Review of E. Sapir's "A Study of Language". *The Dial*, 72: 3: 314-17.

1923a   *Anthropology*. New York. Harcourt, Brace, and Co.

1923b   Relationship of the Australian Languages. *Journal and Proceedings of the Royal Society of New South Wales for 1923*, vol. 57 (Oct. 16): 101-17.

1925   Handbook of the Indians of California. Wash. D.C., *BAE Bull*. 78.

1935   History and Science in Anthropology. *AA*, n.s, 37: 539-69.

1936   So-called Social Science. *Jour. of Social Philosophy*, 1, 4: 317-40.

1937a   Quantitative Classification of Indo-European Languages (with D. Chretian). *Language*, 13, 2: 83-103.

1937b   Athabaskan Kin Term systems. *AA*, n.s. 39: 602-08.

1939   Cultural Intensity and Climax. In, Kroeber, 1952.

1940a   (with J. Richardson). Three Centuries of Women's Dress Fashions; A Quantitative Analysis. *Anthropological Records*, 5, 2: 111-53.

1940b   Stimulus Diffusion. *AA*, 42: 1-20.

1940c   Statistical Classification. *Amer. Antiq.* 6, 1: 29-44.

1941   Some Relations of Linguistics and Ethnology. *Language*, 17: 287-91.

1943   Structure, Function, and Pattern in Biology and Anthropology. *The Scientific Monthly*, 16, 2: 105-13.

1944   *Configurations of Culture Growth*. Berkeley. Univ. of California Press.

1946a   The Ancient *Oikoumene* as an Historic Culture Aggregate. *Huxley Memorial lecture for 1945*. Roy. Anth. Inst. of Gr. Brit.

1946b   History and Evolution. *SWJA*, 2: 1-15.

1948a   *Anthropology* (2nd ed.). New York. Harcourt Brace.

1948b   Have Civilizations a Life History? Centennial, *AAAS*. Wash., D.C.

1948c   Seven Mohave Myths. *UCPAR*, 11, 1: 1-70.

1948d   White's View of Culture. *AA*, 50, 3: 405-15.

1952   *The Nature of Culture*. Chicago. Univ. of Chicago Press.

1953   The Delimitation of Civilizations. *Jour. Hist. Ideas*, XIV, 2: 264-75.

1955   On Human Nature. *SWJA*, 2, #3:195-204.

1958   *Flow and Reconstitution in Civilizations*. Paper given at the Wenner Gren Foundation, New York. Reprinted in Kroeber, 1963.

1959   Possible Athabascan Influence on Yuki. *Intl. Jour. of Amer. Ling.*, 25, 1: 59.

1960a   Preface: *Yana Dictionary* (M.R. Haas, ed.), UCPL, vol. 22.

1960b   Evolution, History, and Culture. In: S. Tax (ed.) *Evolution after Darwin*. Chicago. Univ. of Chicago Press.

1963   (*op. post.*) *An Anthropologist Looks at History*. Berkeley and Los Angeles. Univ. of California Press.

1964   (*op. post.*) On taxonomy of Languages and Cultures. Forward to D. Hymes Language and culture in Society.

Kroeber, T.

1970   *Alfred Kroeber, A Personal Configuration*. Berkeley. Univ. of Calif. Press.

Lewis, H.S.

2001   Boas, Darwin, Science, and Anthropology. *CA*, 42, 3: 381 – 406.

Lowie, R.H.

1923   Review of Language. *AA* 25: 90-93.

1948   Some Facts about Boas. *SWJA*, 4: 69-70.

1965/84 Comments on Edward Sapir, His Personality and Scholarship. Privately printed in 1965 and reprinted in Koerner, 1984.

Lowie, R. H and C. L. Alsberg.

1936   Alfred L. Kroeber: Personal Reminiscences and Professional Appreciation. In, *Essays in Anthropology Presented to A.L.*

Kroeber in Celebration of His Sixtieth Birthday. New York. Books for Libraries Press.

Mackert, M.

1993   The Roots of Franz Boas' View of Linguistic Categories as a Window to the Human Mind. *Historiographia Linguistica* XX:2/3: 331-51.

Mandelbaum, D.G.

1949   *Selected Writings of Edward Sapir in Language, Culture, and Personality*. Berkeley. Univ. of Calif. Press.

Michelson, T.

1914   Two Alleged Algonquian Languages of California. *AA*, 16: 361-67.

1915   Rejoinder. *AA*, 17: 194-98.

Murray, S. O.

1983   The Creation of Linguistic Structure. *AA*, 85: 356-61.

1984   Notes on the History of Linguistic Anthropology. *Historiographia Linguistica*, XI: 3, 449-60.

Nelson, N.C.

1909   Shell Mounds of the San Francisco Bay Region. Berkeley. *UCPAAE*, 7, 4: 319-48.

1910   The Ellis Landing Shell mound. *Ibid*, 7 (5): 357-426.

Opler, M.

1967   Franz Boas: Religion and Theory. *AA*, 69: 741-44.

Powell, J.W.

1891   Indian Linguistic Families in America, North of Mexico. *BAE-AR 7* (1885-86): 1-142.

Radin, P.

1919a   The Genetic Relationship of the North American Indian Languages. *UCPAAE*, 14: 489-502.

1919b   The Genetic Relationship of Huave and Mixe. *Journal de la Societe des Americainistes de Paris*, 11: 489-99.

Renner, E.

1995   The History of the Na Dene Controversy: A sketch. In, *Language and culture in Native North America – Studies in Honor of Hans Jurgen Pinnow.* M. Durr, E. Renner, and W. Oleschinski, Eds. Munchen and Newcastle. Lincom

Rensch, B.

1947/60 *Evolution above the Species Level.* New York. Columbia University Press.

Rivers, W.H.R.

1907   On the Origin of the Classificatory System of Relationships. In Rivers, 1924, *Social organization.*

Rowe, J.H.

1962   Alfred Louis Kroeber, 1876-1960. *Amer. Antiq.*, 27, 3: 395-415.

Sapir, E.

1910   Some Fundamental Characteristics of the Ute Language. *Science*, 31: 350-52.

1911   The Problem of Noun Incorporation in American Languages. *AA*, 13: 240-82, and in Societe des Americanistes de Paris, 10: 379-425.

1913   Wiyot and Yurok, Algonkin Languages of California. *AA*, 15: 617-46.

1914   Southern Paiute and Nahuatl, a Study in Uto-Aztecan. Part 2. *AA*, 17: 98-120, 306-28.

1915a   Algonkin Languages of California. A Reply. *AA*, 17: 188-94.

1915b   The Na-Dene Languages, A Preliminary Report. *AA*, 17: 534-58.

1915c   Epilogue to Michelson's Rejoinder to Sapir (1915a). *AA*, 17: 198.

1916   Time Perspective in Aboriginal American Culture: A Study in Method. Anthropological Series 13. *Memoirs of the Canadian Geological Survey*, 90. Ottawa.

1917a   Do we need a Superorganic? *AA*, 19: 441-47.

1917b   The Position of Yana in the Hokan Stock. *UCPAAE*, 13: 1-34.

1917c   The Status of Washo. *AA*, 18: 449-50.

1918   Yana Terms of Relationship. *UCPAAE*, 13, 4: 153-73.

1920   The Hokan and Coahuiltecan Languages. *IJAL*, 1: 280-90.

1921a   *Language: An Introduction to the Study of Speech*. New York. Harcourt, Brace and Company.

1921b   A Bird's Eye View of American Languages North of Mexico. *Science*, 54: 408.

1921c   A Characteristic Penutian Form of Stem. *IJAL*, 2:68-72.

1922a   The Takelma Language of Southwestern Oregon. Reprinted in: The Handbook of American Indian Languages. *BAE Bull*. 40, 2: 1-296.

1922b   The fundamental Elements of Northern Yana. *UCPAAE*, 13, 6: 215-34.

1922c   Athabaskan Tone. *AA*, 24: 390-91.

1923   Text Analyses of Three Yana Dialects. *UCPAAE*, 20: 263-94.

1925   Sound Patterns in Language. *Language*, 1: 37-51.

1928a   A Summary Report of Field Work among the Hupa, Summer of 1927. *AA*, 30: 359-61.

1928b   Central and North American Languages. *Encyclopedia Britannica* (14th Ed.), 5: 138-41.

1929   The Status of Linguistics as a Science. *Language*, 5: 207-14.

1933a   The Psychological Reality of Phonemes (in French). *Journal de Psychologie Normale et Pathologique*. 30: 247-265.

1933b   Language. *Encyclopedia of the Social Sciences*.

Silverstein, M.

1986   The Diachrony of Sapir's Synchronic Linguistic Description; Or, Sapir's "Cosmographical" Linguistics. In: *New Perspectives in Language, Culture, and Personality. Proceedings of the Edward Sapir Centenary Conference.* W. Cowan, M.K. Foster, and K. Koerner (eds.). John Benjamins. Amsterdam and Philadelphia.

Sparkman, P. S.

1908   The Culture of the Luiseno Indians. *UCPAAE*, 8 (4): 187-234.

Steward, J.

1961   Alfred Louis Kroeber; Obituary. *AA*, 63: 1038-87.

1973   *Alfred Louis Kroeber*. New York. Columbia University Press.

Stocking, G. W.

1960   Franz Boas and the Founding of the American Anthropological Association. *AA*, 62: 1-17.

1966   Franz Boas and the Culture Concept in Historical Perspective. *AA*, 68: 867-84.

1968a   *Race, Culture, and Evolution*. New York. The Free Press.

1968b/74 The Boas Plan for the Study of American Indian languages. In, D. Hymes (ed.), *Traditions and Paradigms in the History of Linguistics*. Bloomington. Indiana University Press.

1974b   *A Franz Boas reader: The Shaping of American Anthropology*. Chicago. Univ. of Chicago Press.

1974c   Some Problems in the Understanding of Nineteenth Century Evolutionism. In, R. Darnell (ed.), *Readings in the History of Anthropology*. New York. Harper. pp. 407-25.

1976   (ed.) *Selected Papers from the American Anthropologist*, 1921-1945. Washington. The American Anthropological Association.

1977   The aims of Boasian Ethnography: Creating the Materials for Traditional Humanistic Scholarship. *HAN*, 4 (2): 9-12.

1979   Anthropology as *Kulturkampf*: Science and Politics in the Career of Franz Boas. In, W. Goldschmidt (ed.) *The Uses of Anthropology*. AAA, Special Publication 11.

1987   *Victorian Anthropology*. New York. The Free Press.

1992   The Ethnographer's Magic and Other Essays in the History of Anthropology. Madison. Univ. of Wisconsin Press.

1996   (ed.) *Volksgeist* as Method and Ethic. Essays on Boasian Ethnography and the German Anthropological Tradition. *HOA*, Vol. 8. Madison. Univ. of Wisconsin Press.

Swadesh, M.

1935   A Method toward Correctness and Accuracy in Phonetic Transcription. *AA*, 39.

1939   Edward Sapir. *Language*, 15: 132-35 (Reprinted in Koerner, 1984).

1951   Diffusional Cumulation and Archaic Residue. *SWJA*, 7: 1-21.

1959   Linguistics as an Instrument of Prehistory. *SWJA*, 15: 20-35.

Voegelin, C.F.

1952   The Boas Plan for the Presentation of American Indian Languages. *Proc. Am. Phil. Soc.* 96, 4: 439-51.

White, L.

1938   Science is Sciencing. *Philosophy of Science*, 5: 369-89.

1939   Mind is Minding. *Scientific Monthly*, 48: 169.

1943/49 Energy and the Evolution of Culture. *AA*, 45: 335-56.

1945a   History, Evolutionism, and Functionalism: Three Types of Interpretation of Culture. *SWJA*, 1: 221-48.

1945b   Diffusion vs. Evolution; an Anti-Evolutionist Fallacy. *AA*, 47: 339-56

1946   Kroeber's "Configurations of Culture Growth". *AA*, 48: 78-93.

1947   Evolutionary Stages, Progress, and the Evolution of Cultures. *Ibid*, 3: 165-92.

1963   The ethnography and ethnology of Franz Boas. *Bulletin 6, Texas Memorial Museum*. Austin. University of Texas.

Whorf, B.

1939/56 The Relationship of Habitual Thought and Behavior to Language. In, J.B. Carroll (ed.) *Selected Writings of Benjamin Lee Whorf*. Cambridge. MIT Press.

Willey, G.R.

1988   *Portraits in American Archaeology*. Albuquerque. University of New Mexico.

Notes

1. George Stocking's *Victorian Anthropology* (1987) and *After Tylor* (1995), contain full accounts of the wide range of ideas that came to be lumped under the general term "evolutionary" during the latter nineteenth century. An earlier essay by Stocking on the character of nineteenth century evolutionism is reprinted in Darnell, 1974.

2. It is interesting to read the obituaries and eulogies accorded Sapir just after his death and to compare them with more mature reassessments of his work in later years (many such pieces are gathered in Koerner, 1984). Among other things, some varied interpretations of what Sapir meant by "drift" in languages are in evidence. Only a few years past their most serious clash, in his eulogy for Sapir, Franz Boas (1939) offered only a bare-bones roster of his work along with a seemingly grudging acknowledgment of his genius. Ruth Benedict (1939) was more generous, describing Sapir as benefiting from his training in Indo-German philology, and also calling attention to his poetic side. A youthful Morris Swadesh (1939) likewise noted his grounding in Old World languages and linguistics. Two years later, writing for a Jewish journal in a time of slaughter, David Mandelbaum gave a more nuanced account of some of the range

of issues Sapir addressed, but couched his vision of Sapir's significance in terms of a Jewish activism which Sapir himself did not publically emphasize.

Reviews of *Language: An Introduction to the Study of Speech*, Sapir's *magnum opus,* and later reviews of collections of his articles are also interesting. Reference, direct and indirect, to the matter of language evolution can be distilled from contemporary discussions of Sapir's work. Reactions varied, but the quality of his thought seems to have been seldom in question; just his conclusions and the manner of his presentation. In his (1922) review of *Language* Kroeber noted that the book lacked the attributes (or the impediments) of scholarly publication, but made a virtue of that. Bloomfield's (1922) review was more backhanded, recommending the book to "the general reader". Lowie (1923), ever the Boas loyalist, enthused about *Language*, but also made substantial mention of Sapir's "somewhat heretical position" with regard to the historical relationships among languages (an evolutionary question on which Sapir's views had become clearer over the previous half decade and which forms part of the story I wish to relate). He also dwelt on an issue that troubled those who wished to support the more evolutionary view, *viz.* that independent evolution of similar grammatical structures seemed a less elegant and less powerful explanation of parallel structures than to simply admit that large and complex grammatical structures could diffuse, a proposition which, once accepted, made a hash of any historical reconstruction that purported to reflect genealogy or degrees of relatedness.

After Sapir's death in 1939, reappraisals of his work were somewhat slow in coming, in part because of the war, and in part because his writings were so scattered and diverse. In 1949 D.G. Mandelbaum published *Selected Writings of Edward Sapir in Language, Culture, and Personality*, which appears to have rekindled student interest in his work, overshadowed for two decades by Bloomfield's unified and less wide-ranging paradigmatic approach. Cultural evolution had not quite yet been entirely rehabilitated as a respectable question in American anthropology, but it was visible below the surface of discussions of Sapir. In reviewing Mandelbaum's edited collection J. Greenberg (1950) noted that "Sapir's achievements in historic linguistics rest largely on the application of the well-tested methods of Indo-Europeanist linguistics to the field of American Indian languages, but much also derives from Sapir's feeling for linguistic structure on the historical level. ...Thus an exceptional form, descriptively of little moment in the present stage of a language, may... provide the clue to a distant and unsuspected relationship." H. Hoijer's (1951) review of *Selected Writings* likewise referred to Sapir's Indo-European training and offered a brief quoted account of linguistic "drift" that emphasized its evolutionary content. A more extensive review by Z.S. Harris (1951), without referring to evolutionary thought or assumptions, called into doubt whether Sapir's approach had ever been "genetic" in any real sense, because he had used structural evidence right along and his observations had therefore been taxonomic; a difference in data and methodology similar to that pertaining between the use of biological (chiefly reproductive) *versus* morphological criteria for defining species.

3. Stocking 1960, 1968a and b, 1974a, 1977, 1979, and Darnell 1998, are two among recent Boas champions, and their bibliographies contain the gamut of writings about him. Robert Lowie's paean (Lowie, 1937: 128- 155) and an ill-tempered pamphlet by Leslie White (1963) typify the extreme range of opinions about him. The AAA *Memoire* edited by Walter Goldschmidt (1959) contained more varied and less extreme opinions. As Jacobs (1959) noted with regard to Boas' folklore studies, his personal influence on specific anthropological issues waned as he aged and the field became larger and more diverse. However, I

agree with Stocking and Darnell, whom I paraphrase to say that there was a moral quality to the culturally relativistic aspects Boas' program for ethnology, which found its time. However much those relativistic aspects were later overblown, they were focused on a target that called for moral imperative, and they could only have gained further momentum in the traumatic years after his death.

4. Koerner (1984) gathered many appraisals of Edward Sapir's work, including those by Kroeber. Sapir differed from Kroeber on some technically important matters, such as the role of cultural or linguistic areas in language evolution, with which I do not deal here. See Anderson (1990) on Sapir's language typology.

5. Sapir's career will take another generation to elucidate comprehensively. Mandelbaum (1949) edited the initial collection of Sapir's writings a decade after his death. The real work was begun by Darnell (1971, 1976), Golla (1984), Koerner (1984), and the other participants in the Edward Sapir Centenary Conference (Cowen *et al*, 1986). Darnell's sketch of Sapir in that volume has been augmented by her biography of him (1990a), and he also figures large in her study of Boas (1998). Silverstein (also in Cowen, *et al*) emphasized Sapir's essentially Boasian view of language on both emotional and philosophical planes. Goddard (*ibid*) showed the roots of Sapir's comparative method in Indo-European linguistics and Kraus (*ibid*) treated his work on Athabaskan. There has since been collaboration in the massive job of publishing Sapir's unpublished writings and re-publishing some of what he put into print (Darnell, Irvine, and Handler, 1999).

6. Anderson (1990) was the most recent of several writers to notice that. Harris (1951) and Hoijer (1954b) both saw the parallel, as Silverstein (1986: 80-81*cf*) noted.

7. Sapir was justifiably proud of his prose (see Darnell, 1986: 576-77).

8. Murray, 1983: 357; 1984: 452-53 alluded to this.

9. Roland B. Dixon was Kroeber's collaborator for many years. For a good sense of his work see Dixon 1910, 1911; Kroeber, 1907b, 1910a, 1913, 1964 (*op. Post.*). See also Darnell, 1998: 199-241. Dixon studied Achowami, Maidu, Wintu, Chimariko, and Shasta on his own. In 1910 he described the last two of these as genetically related. He and Kroeber collaborated on *The Native Languages of California* (1903), *Relationship of the Indian Languages of California* (1912, re-published with revisions in the Journal *Science* in 1913), *New linguistic Families in California* (1913b), *Relationship of the Indian Languages of California* (1913a), and *Linguistic Families in California* (1919).

10. See especially Kroeber, 1955 and 1963. Chary of recanting a recantation, he dealt with these questions more in correspondence than in print. See: ALKP: ALK-Bidney: 3/26/45, 8/1/46/, 9/17/46, 12/18/46, 1/24/47, 6/3/54; ALK-Beardsley, 4/27/48; ALK-Gray, 9/17/56, 12/4/58, ALK-Kerr, 5/20/53, ALK-Mason, 11/21/52; ALK-Morgenbesser, 2/22/60; ALK-L. White, 9/11/45.

11. Soon after Sapir's death and shortly before Boas', Kroeber (1941) published a short article entitled *Some Relations of Linguistics and Ethnology*, returning to the question of whether grammar diffused among languages – something that Boas maintained happened regularly and Sapir believed happened seldom, if ever. Kroeber framed the question but did not answer it, though he seemed to suggest that Sapir's focus upon Indo-European languages may have blinded him to the phenomenon in other linguistic families. Kroeber never felt sure about this matter, having sided with Boas on it as late as 1913 in his *The Determination of Linguistic Relationship*. Boas was more right than Sapir.

12. This and seriation were almost the only methods Kroeber used in archaeology (he was not a skilled

stratigrapher), where he sought patterns and traceable bits of meaning, especially in decorative motives, and treated them like so many morphemes and roots. He was always more prepared to discern and classify units of meaning than he was to explain them. This, together with his customary aversion to enthusiastic, controversial ideas helps to explain why, much later, he was not more receptive to the "language is culture" hypothesis of Benjamin Whorf (1939/1956), of which he said it was hypothetical only to the extent that it was testable, something he believed would be very difficult (Kroeber, in Tax, *et al*, 1953). He offered the penetrating observation that Whorf's idea would "prove both true and false at different levels" (not damning in discussing emergent evolution, surely) and that "new methods" and "a new approach" would be needed to make it testable. He repeated these remarks in Hoijer's *Language in Culture* (1954a: 231-32).

13. As Kroeber's stature as the leading New World anthropologist grew so did the number of inquiries about such matters. Late in life, in a letter to David Bidney, he was still being cagey on evolution (ALKP: ALK-Bidney, 3/26/45). Bidney suggested that his philosophy of culture history was a close parallel to the doctrine of emergent evolution. Kroeber feigned philosophical innocence at first but eventually accepted the interpretation.

14. Kroeber meant *Configurations* to be his masterpiece, his defining book. It could not be the former, but certainly was the latter. In some ways the work was perfect as an illustration of the breadth of his interests and intellectuality, as well as the limitations of his methods. It was characteristic of him to take a phenomenon (genius) that was identifiable but indefinable, and then to simply count instances of it in time and space. If nothing else, genius is a quality of mind so exquisite (though also often affective and effective in the outside world) as to count as the very pinnacle of Civilization

– the great cultural phenomenon he most wanted to elucidate. At the same time genius (and indeed mind) is composed of *qualia,* and is ultimately unverifiable by anyone other than its possessor, who has privileged, exclusive access to it. Kroeber tried to count his way to the top of Civilization by counting instances of its most rarified furnishing, and one which by definition could not be made more concrete or accessible.

15. There are interesting parallels, as well as distinctions between Boas' program for anthropology and the tenets and goals of Darwinian evolution and population biology, many of them most described by Lewis (2001). Boas wanted to focus on the internal workings of single cultures (read "populations") and to document short-range, short-term changes in the frequencies of traits and structures (as opposed to longer-term evolutionary trends). He emphasized variance over central tendency within units and avoided discussions of comparability with other units. He put no limit to the range of "trait" diffusion, but the overall trajectory of such movement was void of cultural meaning in the terms of any given culture through which the traits passed. That is, Boas believed that the range of meaning diffusion was very limited – meaning being all but culture-specific and being what gave cultures their individual character. This was a parochial and essentialist-sounding position given the catholicity of the rest of the argument, but he needed meaning as a boundary for cultures, lest the dissolving power of the relativistic principle reduce everything cultural to a nominalistic field. Boas didn't want to melt cultures, but to fortify their uniqueness. Of course, this contrasted with Darwin's parallel but opposite strategy regarding species, which he did not wish to fortify, but rather to meld at their temporal-spatial peripheries. Another difference between them: Darwin focused on descent with modification in the diachronic dimension, produced by a largely synchronic selective mechanism, but illustrated by ages of fossil strata and

comparisons of homologous traits in otherwise very different taxa. Boas had small use for diachronic views or long-distance ones, and eschewed comparison (the heart of historical linguistics) most of all.

16. Kroeber was certainly not oblivious to variance in statistics or in cultural entities, but unlike Boas he had an affinity for the centers, the foci, as he called them, as defining the taxon or type. In his study of culture areas (Kroeber, 1939: 5) he observed:

> "The weakest feature of any mapping of culture wholes is …the boundaries. Where the influences of two culture climaxes or foci meet in equal strength is where a line must be drawn, if boundaries are to be indicated at all. Yet it is just there that differences often are slight. …what boundaries really show is not so much clefts occurring in nature, as relative extent and strength of influences emanating from foci."

17. Kroeber (1923b), keen to show language divergence, later rejected this idea in one of his few post-1920 and pre-1950 linguistic publications (a brief piece that chiefly addressed a topic beyond his bailiwick, the relations of Australian languages).

18. Dixon and Kroeber (1907) also published a study of number systems in California that paralleled the language families in their degrees of divergence in "numerical classifiers" (i.e., named groups of numbers), an innovative piece that was not widely appreciated. Sapir appears to have later believed that they had postulated something innately psychological about different human approaches to numbering, an odd thing to propose about counting, which is not, at last, open to a very wide range of interpretation. Kroeber sensibly denied that he had postulated anything but simple diffusion of methods of counting (ALKP: ALK-Sapir, 7/9/13), which can occur in large and complex

components, if our continued use of Babylonian 60-based sky-search methods for observing celestial phenomena is any indication.

19. Kroeber did some anthropometry among the groups he studied during his first years in California, and dabbled in this sideline occasionally for about five years. In 1909 he asked Boas for data he had gathered at Hupa in order to incorporate these into a study (FBP: ALK-Boas, 11/2/03; ALK - Boas, 1/15/09).

20. Even a less than exhaustive list of his early linguistic efforts shows this: Kroeber 1904a and b, 1906a and b, 1907a, b and c, 1909, 1910a, b and c, 1911a, b, d and e, 1913, 1914, 1915b, 1916c and d.

21. Kroeber, 1964 (*op. post.*). See also ALKP: ALK-Sapir, 9/2/16, 9/5/16, wherein linguistic work meshed seamlessly with ethnography. When Sapir wanted to know how much time Kroeber had spent on specific problems in the field he replied that his, "linguistic notes were thoroughly intertwined with ethnological ones." (ALKP: ALK-Sapir, 9/15/14)

22. See Kroeber, 1925, 1-97 and 726-780, for his first full treatment of both tribes. He began publishing on the Mohave quite early (Kroeber, 1902). He reluctantly surrendered some of his "rights" to the Mohave to M. R. Harrington (a protégé of E.L. Hewett) a decade later (ALKP: ALK-T.T. Waterman, 1/20/16).

23. This is to say that Kroeber was not cheated of credit for ideas regarding the applicability of Indo-European linguistics methods in the Americas because he never really claimed even the full measure that was his due, and vacillated about the worth of the genetic approach that had produced them for many years. The closest he came to laying a claim in a public venue was an address he gave at Berkeley on the 20th anniversary of Sapir's death, and only a year before his own. It was recorded, but not transcribed until much later, and published by Koerner (1984). On that occasion Kroeber spoke

the plain truth of the matter as he saw it, saying a bit wistfully that Sapir, "…took the modest beginnings that were made by Dixon and myself and others of about that same period, and carried them infinitely farther." That tracks perfectly with the tenor of their correspondence. In short, he saw and acknowledged that the qualitative difference in their work was what counted most.

24. How Boas came by this conviction before the Sino-Sphere was well known is not clear. It may simply have been a concomitant of Historical Particularism and his convictions regarding diffusion of other aspects of culture. He also may have had it more concretely, from an early exposure to Yiddish, a dialect of German that contains some Slavic grammar. If that was the case, it is difficult to see why Sapir did not have, or resisted, the same insight.

25. See the reminiscence of Sapir by Swadesh in Koerner, 1984. Swadesh was hounded out of American academia for his Communist sympathies. Kroeber, along with several others, courageously tried to support him (ALKP: ALK-Moe, 3/11/47; ALK-Swadesh, 5/26/48; ALK-APS, 4/10/51, ALK-Guggenheim Foundation, 2/3/50), but Swadesh could be his own worst enemy. In 1949, at the height of the red scare, he circulated a mimeographed circular through American Ethnological Society, decrying the firing of Communist faculty members by universities. This was brave, but by itself probably would not have sealed his fate. Unfortunately, he also flaunted reckless admiration for Stalin. He eventually left the United States in search of academic work. He went first to Chile, where the wrath of the State Department followed, revoking his passport. Despite Kroeber's recommendation, the Chileans refused him entry (ALKP: ALK-Hamuy, 3/6/52). Swadesh then went to Mexico, where he was allowed to remain, though under suspicion. His war record with the War Department and the OSS in

Burma did not help him in the domestic political circumstances of the Korean War. Indeed it was the root of his troubles, for much worse than being simply a red academic, he was viewed as a turncoat intelligence operative.

26. Some of the arguments eventually brought to bear against historical linguistics and its glotto-chronological tool had a Boasian ring. For example, it was accused of false analogy with biology and with containing a misleading genealogical metaphor. True believers might reply that it was not a metaphor, but an isomorphism, but they could not well answer the discrepancy between the selective mechanisms and the ultimate patterns (divergent *versus* both divergent and convergent) traced by organic and linguistic phylogenies, respectively.

27. See Steward's 1961 Kroeber bibliography, nos. 501, 520, 531, 532), also see Kroeber, in Hymes, 1964.

28. Voegelin, (1952) described Boas' statistical criterion for deciding sibling status for dialects, based upon a percent of mostly lexical cognates.

29. He eventually asked Boas for this favor (ALKP: ALK-Boas, 5/8/04).

30. Boas' devotion to an empirical and relativistic approach was early and unwavering. In *On Alternating Sounds* (1889) he already displayed characteristically relativistic aspects of his thinking about languages (Stocking, 1992: 74-79), effectively countering the notion that primitive languages were more variable than modern Western ones, and therefore less capable of containing and conveying complex meaning. He found the mote in the ear of the non-native hearer and confronted classifiers of sounds with evidence that a sound unfamiliar to any two of them was likely to be recorded and described in different ways. Viewed as performance, utterances employed segments of a continuum of mouth and throat formations and

resulting sounds. It followed that classification of such segments was bound to be variable and arbitrary, even for a native speaker. From the standpoint of perception, if hearing was arbitrary, any system of classification based upon it was infected with the same, ever widening lack of certitude. This perception of the continuous, non-quantum nature of cultural information was more than a cautionary point on linguistic recording methods – it was a worldview that focused on variance and relations, on the active ionizing edges of the larger, residual, mean-and-mode-defined entities that might otherwise be taken for cultural reality.

This was an approach, a method, more than an assertion of what constituted cultural or linguistic reality. Thus, as Hymes (1961: 23-24) noted, the image of Boas gratuitously resisting Kroeber's and Sapir's innovative suggestions on the genetic affiliations of American languages was too simple. Darnell, (1998: 217) concurred, both of them apparently referring to Swadesh (1951, in Hymes, 1964), who configured the differences between Boas and Sapir as one of "diffusional cumulation versus archaic residue" – in other words exchange within *habitus versus* the homologies of heritage. Structurally their argument paralleled that regarding heritage *versus habitus* in contemporary physical anthropology, except that in linguistics, due perhaps to the political problems of Boasian professional loyalties, the debate was not as an open one. Boas was not blind to the structural similarities among American languages, having once called attention to them (Boas, 1893, 1894b: 342; see also Darnell, 2001: 47). Indeed, Sapir once remarked to Kroeber that Boas had pointed out, "the remarkable morphological resemblances between Kwakiutl-Nootka and Salish", which Sapir was trying to show were "genetically related" (ALKP: Sapir-ALK, 6/27/13). It is quite possible that he was against acting on the idea, but was not altogether against the idea itself.

31. Mackert (1993) suggested an interesting and rather more philosophical reason for Boas' approach to language and hence his aversion to using Indo-European assumptions and methods to study American Languages. It was centered on Boas' philosophical commitment to a "Steinthalian notion of the inner forms of language and linguistic relativism". This is plausible, and Boas certainly "rejected the evaluation and hierarchical arrangement of languages". However, considering the rather kinetic environment in which Boas and his students operated, I believe his immediate motivations to have been concretely methodological and interpersonal.

32. The structure of this argument, which follows from a general reluctance on the part of natural science to grapple with the imponderables of ultimate origins, characterizes a whole moiety of anthropological thinking, and as a philosophy has underlain many arguments in archaeology, anthropology, and paleontology. For example, S.J. Gould (1989), discussing the misinterpretation of the fossil content of the Burgess Shales, was concerned to show that the old evolutionary idea of ever-increasing diversity of forms was both wrong and wrong-headed. Instead, from some unknowable point(s) of origin, a huge array of forms proliferated. In Gould's view, Charles Walcott (incidentally, Boas' nemesis at AMNH), committed multiple taxonomic sins of conservatism by classifying almost every life form represented in the shale in some already established phyletic category. Actually, wholly different (and now extinct) phyla were in evidence. With regard to cultures and languages, the telling point was not only that the search for origins was futile, but that searching out genetic relations (segments of the increasing cone of diversity) was

equally futile. Cultures and languages were to be studied as conceptual and structural wholes.

33. Ironically, Boas' defense of the uniqueness of each culture, and his insistence that similarities among languages did not indicate common descent with modification, left him (on a philosophical view he would have dismissed), defending a position curiously like that of Professor Owen arguing against Darwin half a century before, insisting upon the essential uniqueness of species. The salient difference, of course, was that Boas did not regard cultures as created, eternal, or possessed of essences.

34. Kroeber won his turf fight with Merriam and Goddard by becoming chairman of the Department upon Putnam's retirement, but it cannot be said that he was ever particularly effective as an administrator or as a bureaucratic in-fighter within the university. His department languished in a "temporary" corrugated metal shed throughout his long career and was always starved of university funds (Steward, 1961: 17-21). This contrasts oddly with his considerable skill in getting money from funding organizations for individual researchers and projects. Indeed, toward the end of his life he came to be a dominant voice in funding decisions for anthropology both at Viking (Wenner-Gren) and the Ford Foundation.Kroeber probably believed that he struck the right balance between administration and scholarship, keeping his department alive and fostering moderate growth through difficult economic times. The faculty remained small, but student attendance at undergraduate courses was good. In fact, Kroeber and his colleagues held the common run of students in low regard (ALKP: ALK-A. Fletcher, 6/4/09; ALK-E.C. Moore, 12/26/22, 8/20/28; ALK-Pinner, 11/14?/30). Nonetheless, Berkeley's graduate program produced renowned anthropologists and archaeologists. Kroeber turned out a large and steady stream of scholarly writing, and the University of *California Publications*

in American Archaeology, Anthropology, and Ethnology
(UCPAAE), which he helped to found and to edit, was
a respected professional journal.

35. ALKP: ALK-Putnam, 2/19/08, ALKP: ALK-Sapir,
?/12/18, see also Darnell, 1990a: 27-29. Sapir was
to experience the travails of administration, the
conflicts inherent in making personnel decisions, and
the vagaries of funding when he moved to Ottawa in
1910 to assume the position of Chief of the Division
of Anthropology of the Geological Service of Canada,
a position he held until 1925 (see especially Darnell,
1976/84).

36. ALKP: Sapir-ALK, 3/12/08. See also ALK-Sapir,
12/6/18, and Sapir-ALK, 12/17/18, in which they
revisited this matter in a somewhat forced conciliatory
manner during an exchange on Sapir's poetry, a safety-
valve sideline topic on which they occasionally flared
at each other benignly. See Darnell, 1998: 27-29, 199-
204, and Golla, 1986: 21-24.

37. For example: ALKP: Sapir-ALK, 1/6/13, 1/6?/13,
ALK-Sapir 1/3/13, 1/6/13, 1/21/13, 2/18/13, 3/18/13,
7/9/18.

38. Sapir also eventually moved off on a tangent with
regard to "culture and personality", though in this
he was in multitudinous company, for this research
program tracked the general popularity of Freudian
psychoanalysis as it became the fastest growing trend
in anthropology after World War One. Kroeber had
little use for it, which was surprising in view of his
work in psychoanalysis and his ethnographic method
of interviewing one or a few informants and using
their personalities as indicators of the value of what
they said about their culture. Sapir eventually pursued
it in search of the level at which mind, language, and
culture were linked (Sapir, 1933a). Boas was tolerant of
this program, probably because it would have seemed
a natural outgrowth of his own, and was populated

with his students, and possibly because he would have been viscerally disposed to accept a program of work that encouraged subjects to talk about their cultures, as opposed to programs that observed and compared behaviors. He even once wrote to A.M. Tozzer that culture and personality had been the central point of his own early paper on Salish basketry (Boas, 1897; FBP: Boas-Tozzer, 10/4/30).

39. Sapir found Ishi difficult to work with. We must be grateful for the wording of the telegram (Golla 1984: 59), in which Kroeber announced Ishi's arrival: "Have totally wired southern yana at the museul… do you want to come an work him up…" To judge from the photograph of Ishi taken right after his "capture" – a procedure that would have flashed upon him like a mock execution, he was well and truly wired, and plenty worked up already. Eventually Sapir, the authority on Yana, did go to Berkeley to "work him up". Kroeber gave Ishi refuge in the Department Museum, where he remained until his death five years later of Tuberculosis, possibly contracted from Kroeber's first wife, who was consumptive before Ishi arrived. T.T. Waterman (apparently with little pathogenic sense), felt guilty about letting Sapir "…ride [Ishi] so hard" for vocabulary, and blamed himself (T. Kroeber, 1970: 234).

It is difficult to know what should be made of this episode. It was charitable and high-minded, but also had the ring of specimen collection. Ishi became a kind of living exhibit, though by all accounts he did not mind this, and it is hard to see what else could have been done with him. In effect, he had a janitor's job, though the concept of a job must have been alien to him. For his part, Kroeber occasionally used Ishi as his ticket to, and badge of the "other", sending photographs of himself and Ishi together to old friends in New York (ALKP: J. Rosenberg-ALK, 3/3/14), and occasionally grumping to Sapir when Ishi was not communicative. He once expressed relief that Ishi had been misdiagnosed as tubercular (in fact, he had been correctly diagnosed), saying that "the moral is to get from him what we can instead of trusting that he will last indefinitely" (ALK-Sapir, 4/26/15).

Kroeber was in New York when Ishi died, in March 1916. A legend grew up about how he withstood bloody-minded physical anthropologists and anatomists who wanted to dissect a "stone-age man". He did indeed try, wiring and writing to E.W. Gifford in Berkeley to have Ishi cremated in the manner of his people: "…Tell them science can go to hell. We propose to stand by our friends" (T. Kroeber, 1970: 92; 1971: 234). But Ishi was dissected by his friend, Dr. Saxton Pope, with other friends standing by, before Kroeber's long-distance wishes could prevail, and Kroeber's subsequent behavior was weirdly complicit. He sent Ishi's brain to Ales Hrdlicka at the Smithsonian, who agreed to study it. This exchange, in which Hrdlicka alludes to his crusade to exterminate the Paleo-Indian, did not survive in Kroeber's papers:

> "Your letter of October 27 reached me yesterday on my return from Florida, where I was running down another "ancient man". I need hardly say that we shall be very glad to take care of Ishi's brain, and if a suitable opportunity occurs, to have it properly worked up" (AHP: AH-ALK, 11/8/16).

In 2000, Native American groups succeeded in obtaining the brain for a ceremonial disposal necessarily more political than religious, all direct traces of Ihsi's ideational culture having long since disappeared. This was a happier end than came to Hrdlicka, whose long-suffering second wife unceremoniously deposited his ashes in the Smithsonian department he had tyrannized for two generations. There they languished beneath his portrait until the 1960s, when some irreverent student assistant made off with the urn for purposes unknown.

40. In Darnell's view, Kroeber was recruited because he was not primarily a linguist and might therefore give the group a little leavening. I want to qualify that, at least with regard to Kroeber's self-image. He was known as an ethnologist, to be sure, but in 1912 he probably still considered himself a linguist first and foremost. His substantive publications in the preceding years had shifted from predominantly folklore-related titles to predominantly linguistic ones. In Steward's (1972) Kroeber bibliography, see titles: 31, 44, 47, 53, 54, 68, 75, 77, 78, 81, 83, 84, 85, 86, 87, 88, and 92.

41. This incident drew heavy fire from Kroeber, who was still inclined to over-react to prospective rivals or independent work in California (ALKP: ALK-T.T. Waterman, 1/20/16, 1/27/16). Harrington, whom Kroeber acknowledged to be a first rate linguistic scholar, had been a thorn in his side for some years (FBP: ALK-Boas, 9/11/09), as he had independent fieldwork ideas which he tried to put into effect with the sponsorship of E.L. Hewett. He also sided with Hewitt in a dispute with Boas over the Archaeological Institute of America, which rivaled Boas' international field school in Mexico. He was almost dropped when it was discovered that he was not an AAA member, and therefore ineligible to sit on its committees.

42. My account of Kroeber and Sapir's relationship during 1913 is indebted to Darnell (1990: Ch. 6). My version differs from hers in suggesting that Kroeber did not convert Sapir to a genetic view of languages, but rather it was Sapir who elicited a stronger genetic stance from Kroeber. For all their cooperation, Kroeber and Sapir both wanted priority (Dixon, less certain of the idea, appears to have remained rather relaxed about it). As Kroeber witnessed the superiority of Sapir's work he settled for a tacit agreement that they would share credit, but gradually they came to behave rather like racers for the finish. I take Darnell's point that Kroeber was chiefly interested in California languages,

while Sapir worked on a nearly continental front. But when Kroeber yielded the field to Sapir the California situation was far from being in hand. Indeed only the surface features of the complex linguistic situation there had been mapped.

43. After Sapir's death Kroeber offered a double-edged compliment to his brilliance (Kroeber, 1940d). He outlined two methods available to linguists and ethnologists, the "inspective-comparative" approach used by Powell and Boas (the term "comparative" is somewhat puzzling here, but Kroeber seems to have meant "inductive"), and the "reconstructive", meaning an evolutionary account as adopted by Sapir from Indo-European models. Kroeber suggested that problems arose when anthropologists used Sapir's "gossamer" structure, his "tenuous but brilliant hypotheses" as "given truth."

44. See Golla, 1984: 75. Kroeber's preliminary survey of California languages in 1902 (reported in Dixon and Kroeber, 1903), produced a triple grouping of language families on morphological grounds.

45. Truman Michelson was an Indo-Europeanist who later sided with Boas in opposition to employing the methods of his field in the New World – not on grounds of disbelief regarding language consanguinity, but rather of lack of proper (i.e. written) evidence.

46. See Darnell (1990: 143-50) for an account of Kroeber and Sapir on psychoanalysis providing the context and the jargon of their more personal exchanges. Kroeber practiced psychoanalysis for several years. Sapir dabbled in it, but was more inclined to poetry.

47. Chimariko was declared almost extinct by Kroeber and Dixon in 1903 (only two speakers were believed to have survive, one of them "brutally stupid" and useless, in Kroeber's view). More speakers kept appearing however, and by 1919 a handful of them, almost all elderly, had been traced. By 1927, when

the matter came up again, they were all gone and the chance was lost. Sapir blamed Kroeber for this.

48. See ALKP: ALK-Sapir, 11/24/14, 12/7/14; Sapir-ALK, 12/2/14, 12/14/14; Darnell, 1990a: 91-95; WDSP: WDS-W. Wedel, 4/21/47.

49. FBP: A.M. Tozzer-FB, 1/30/18. The position went to J. Fewkes, of whom Boas said that he was "not very kindly disposed to linguistics" (FBP: FB-ALK, 9/23/18).

50. As the U.S. had entered World War One against Germany American public opinion rapidly become strongly anti-German to a degree that must have shocked and frightened German-Americans, who had always considered themselves the most assimilated and law-abiding of immigrants, as well as the core of America's scientific community. All this prompted Boas to what Kroeber believed were politically unwise statements and actions. He had responded to one of them in a hasty note from a seaside hotel only six days before:

> "I sincerely hope that you will not speak out, or if so, that you are denied the opportunity. Your complaint is not a national one, and you would have the same grounds [prejudice against aliens from hostile nations] in England or Germany. War is coercion, which must strike in as well as out. You would only be swimming against an impossible torrent, with no good to yourself or anyone else. It will run out of itself soon. It's not a question of "detachment" but of fighting or taking the inevitable." (FBP: ALK-FB, 8/2/17)

> To this Boas replied, belatedly but firmly, "you cannot change me." (FBP: FB-ALK, 9/7/17)

51. Ironically, Sapir had championed Radin's cause repeatedly over the years before this incident, trying to find work for him and maintaining that the ill

opinions of others about him were unfounded (FBP: ALK-Boas, 1/25/17). Kroeber considered Radin, whose lifestyle was bohemian and who subsequently spent much of his life between jobs, to be "scatty" and unreliable (ALKP: ALK-H.M. Lydenberg 10/3/45; ALK-Sapir, 11/15/18). Later, in the depths of the Depression, with no onward position in the offing, Radin abruptly resigned a job at Berkeley, where he had been working on the Patwin language and culture. On that occasion he wrote an angry letter to Kroeber (ALKP: Radin-ALK: 11/11/32), accusing him of neurotic incapacity for real kindness and of inflicting "extrinsically superficial emotions" on him. He closed by breaking off all contact. In fact, Kroeber was critical of Radin's work, and had gossiped about his character to Sapir. They finally re-established cordial contact in 1957, when Kroeber helped him to place an essay on the history of anthropology (ALKP: ALK-Radin, 10/19/57).

52. Interestingly, Kroeber's review of historical linguistics in America, entitled *On Taxonomy of Languages and Cultures* (reprinted in Hymes' 1964 book *Language in Culture and Society*), contained a latter-day attribution of the main genetic idea to Radin (p, 657) along with an implication that Sapir's students followed up Radin's insight. He recollected then that Radin had been "laughed or shrugged off."

53. By 1920 Sapir thought that Uto-Aztecan was probably connected to Kiowan and perhaps to Zuni (Golla, 1984: Appendix II). Kroeber did not agree. Ultimately, in his 1929 classification Sapir lumped Nahuatl, Pima, Shosonean, Tanoan, Kiowa, and Zuni together with Uto-Aztecan into Aztec-Tanoan (Darnell, 1998: 223). Kroeber would not have gone so far, and his letter revealed how their "feel" for a language could direct their judgment. The degrees of similarity Kroeber referred to were measured in lexical cognates. Grammatical homologies would have been

more decisive, but he offered none, suggesting that he had not transcended what Sapir saw as one of his methodological failings.

54. "Polysynthesis", a term in use in European philology since the early nineteenth century, had come to refer to the most heavily synthesized end of the spectrum of languages, with analytic languages at the other end. Synthesis referred to the morpheme-to-word ratio. In synthetic languages compound words became something like concise sentences. In contrast, an analytic language did not combine words into single concepts (as in Chinese), or did so "economically" (French or English). Much of the sense of an utterance in an analytic language was therefore manifest at the level of the sentence, something Boas held to be the case for most American languages. A synthetic language (Latin, Finnish) did the opposite, elaborating individual words to give different meanings. A polysynthetic language (Turkish, Eskimo, Nootka) did this to an extreme degree. Sapir, who saw psychology at work in phonemes and morphemes, felt likewise about the long, complex words in the lexicon of a polysynthetic language (Sapir, 1921b: 130, 134-36).

55. In his elaboration of drift, Sapir (1921a: 160-66) had postulated a linguistic evolutionary process that mirrored Darwin's re-interpretation of the static Linnaean classifications in mobile, evolutionary terms, and had introduced the idea of drift in rather Darwinian terms, apparently to counter the objection that potentially useful variants would be "swamped" by the sea of language around them.

56. Late in life Kroeber tended to downplay his linguistic work (ALKP: ALK-Shryock, 4/10/47), presumably because he knew how unfavorably it compared with Sapir's (ALKP: ALK-Sapir, 11/18/11, 11/15/18). He once claimed that his interest in linguistics faded in the teens of the century, but mentioned that he had stayed active on the Committee on Native American

Languages because he wanted to hold it together at a time when Boas and Sapir were feuding (ALKP: ALK-ACLS, 4/10/47). This was true, but it retrospectively telescoped events. The ACLS clash between Boas and Sapir that began in 1927 was not as serious as a later rift between them in the mid-1930s, when the ACLS monies were nearly exhausted and Kroeber, too, was estranged from Boas. It is possible that Kroeber merely meant that the clash between Boas' more purely descriptive approach and Sapir's more genetic and broadly theoretical Indo-European style was clear to the combatants long before it became an issue in print.

57. Steward (1972) made a glancing reference to Kroeber's hatred for de Angulo as an inside joke for those among his readers who knew Kroeber in those years, musing innocently that for some reason he was never to be seen at any of de Angulo's "North Berkeley Gang" bootleg gin parties. In fact, Kroeber and de Angulo were not always estranged, though it is doubtful that Kroeber ever more than barely tolerated his flippant attitude and bohemian lifestyle. Brightman (2004), has given a full account of this highly charged and vitriolic relationship, and of de Angulo's fey and self-destructive personality.

58. Yuki was an isolated speech family with no obvious connection to any of the other three great families of languages in California (Athabascan, Hokan, and Penutian, by Dixon and Kroeber's analysis). Kroeber (1913) suggested that the situation paralleled that of Basque in Europe, and claimed that its speakers likewise had a different physique than their neighbors. He maintained that it was possible that Yuki was closest to the autochthonous speech of Californians, overlain by successive influxes of other groups (somewhat counter to his usual resistance to migrations as explanations for languages patterns on maps). Yuki divided into Yuki

proper, Huchnom, Coastal Yuki (which he studied in detail), and Wappo.

59. Laying claim to the ethnographic study of the Yokuts was a good strategy. They were a truly tribal people (of which there were not many in California), with about fifty distinct tribes and a collective population of some 20,000 persons, widely flung in two geographic areas, particularly the San Joaquin Valley. In staking out Yokuts Kroeber claimed about thirty percent of the native population of California, and also the most centrally located group. Kroeber later classed Yokuts as the southernmost branch of the Penutian Language Family.

60. These were two sub-divisions of a language super-family known as Lutuamian, scattered throughout the vicinity of the Klamath River Valley, including lower Oregon. Kroeber (1923: 318) suggested that their territory constituted a "natural topographic area, but called their culture "a pallid, simplified copy of the Yurok and Karok". The Modoc handed the US Army one of its few defeats in the Indian wars.

61. Kroeber described the Karok as upstream neighbors of the Yurok and virtually indistinguishable from them in patterns of custom, social structure, and material culture. Yet they spoke utterly unrelated languages. Yurok was "an offshoot of the great Algonquian Family", while Karok was "the northernmost member of the scattered Hokan group. This was a good candidate for a case study of Boasian doctrines of the separation of language and culture (Kroeber, 1903, 1923: 98-108).

62. Kroeber contrasted the broken dialect maps of the mountains and foothills with the "monotonous" uniformity of most valley speech over long distances (Kroeber, 1923: 569). The Washo, a small group living mostly along the Truckee and Carson Rivers, close to the Nevada frontier, were a little-studied group,

perhaps because of their extreme poverty. They had been defeated and marginalized by the Northern Paiute in post-contact times. Their language was of the Hokan stock, but so distinctive as to be mis-classified by Dixon and Kroeber (1903, 1913a and b).

63. Wintun was a Penutian language. Some speakers survived, but several of its dialects were gone and could not be accurately classified. These sub-tribal groups occupied the central part of Northern California, especially in the western side of the Sacramento Valley (Kroeber, 1925:351-55).

64. There were three groups of Miwok-speakers, called by Kroeber and Dixon the "Coast", "Lake", and "Interior" Miwok. These were sub-tribal people, interspersed with the many other language families represented in North-Central California, especially the Yokuts, who crowded them out of the central valley and into more marginal areas. Those living in the foothills of the Sierra Nevada were dialectically distinct.

65. The Shoshonean family of languages was the largest in East-central and Southeast California, into which it intruded from even larger fields to the East and South (Panama to Montana). Many of its speakers were tribal peoples. The Shoshonean-speakers in California were mostly desert-dwellers with the simplest material culture inventory; a far cry from their distant linguistic cousins, the Aztecs of Mexico. Here, too, was grist for Boas' mill.

66. Luiseno was spoken by a quite small group of peri-coastal dwellers of Southern California (also possibly Catalina Island in pre-contact times).

67. Serrano was believed to be one of four dialects of a Shoshonean language. Called "mountaineers" by the Spanish, the Serrano ranged in the San Bernardino and San Gabriel Chain.

68. Northern Paiute, the language on which Sapir made much of his reputation, was spoken by a tribal people

of many (Uto-Aztecan) dialects, located mostly in Northeastern California. They had some cultural affinities with the Plains cultures.

69. Kroeber (1925: 109) described the Chimariko as "one of the smallest distinct tribes in one of the smallest countries in America" (about a twenty-mile segment of the Trinity River). This poor tribe spoke a dialect of one of the Hokan stocks sufficiently unique and primal for Kroeber to call it "as near their original form as any Hokan language." Chimariko was declared almost extinct by Kroeber and Dixon in 1903, though in fact a few speakers survived into the nineteen-twenties. Esselan was a Hokan language spoken by a very small group living near the mouth of the Carmel River. They were so linguistically distinctive that Kroeber concluded that they were a remnant of a much larger group that once ranged over far wider territories. The Chumash (pp. 550-52), also a coastal group, were the first California Indians to make contact with Europeans. The result of this was a population crash, bizarrely caused as much by abortion as by disease; an instance of assisted ethnic suicide. There was a dialect at each of the five missions established among them (an indirect tribute to the linguistic savvy of some Spanish friars), but details were scanty beyond suggestions of lexical affinity with Yokuts. The Salinan speakers were down to about forty surviving individuals in 1910, with almost no children speaking the language. Early Spanish records indicated that between two and three thousand people spoke the language in the seventeenth century. Salinan was not related to Yokuts, to which it was adjacent geographically, but rather distantly with Esselan and Chumash. The sketch of linguistic diversity in California given in Kroeber's *Handbook* (which did not otherwise deal with languages), was a sorry one of language extinctions just as anthropological inquiry was beginning.

70. Kroeber was sensible of his "debt" to the Mohave, Yurok and Yuki, incurred by delaying publication of old linguistic notes for so long (ALKP: Alk-Fejos, 1/21/57). It was never paid in full. Late in life he received funding from Wenner-Gren to write a *Luiseno* grammar and worked up his materials on the other three languages as best he could. Two small pieces resulted (Kroeber 1959, 1960), along with several on more distantly related languages, in the several years before his death.

71. It is in intriguing question whether Boas was aware of impending moves in government-influenced funding circles toward greater cultural involvement in Latin America. As war loomed this funding flowed together with U.S. Government needs for influence and intelligence there; an ironic way for Boas to go, wittingly or not, after his experiences in World War One, even considering the wholly different character of the Nazi regime.

72. Kidder had some prior knowledge in this affair. He sat on the Advisory Section of the ACLS, and approached Boas in November of 1934 with some "specific complaints" about Boas' handling of the Linguistic Committee's work. These complaints, which could only have come from Sapir, caused Boas to write to all the committee members to protest this irregular proceeding, an action that in turn angered Kidder and caused him to resign his advisory position. Boas described this to A.M. Tozzer as "always the same stupid thing, that matters are taken personally which should be treated from a purely objective point of view." (FBP: FB-Tozzer, 11/26/34)

73. Neither of these things was likely to happen, but the fact that Kroeber acknowledged this so freely indicates that it was an open secret that Sapir was maneuvering to slay the Father. It is worth reflecting upon the state of Boas' mind at that time. He was under considerable strain (his greatest clash with Kroeber also followed

hard on this nasty argument with Sapir). He was old, ill, and facing attempts from several quarters to wrest what remained of his control of American anthropology from him. A.R. Radcliffe-Brown's growing reputation among students troubled him. Earlier he had written to A.M. Tozzer of Radcliffe-Brown's messiah complex and his alarming attempts to ingratiate himself with the Rockefeller Foundation, a primary source of funding for anthropology (FBP: Boas-Tozzer, 12/1/32, 12/2/32). Most of all, events in Germany angered and depressed him, though they also were to give him his last (anti-Nazi) mission in life.

74. Each page of the draft of this letter was carefully numbered and labeled by content, indicating that Kroeber re-wrote it several times. There is only one surviving example of him being more wary of a correspondent than he was of Bidney here, or as tentative of claiming knowledge and authority – he was almost equally wary of Sapir, and more wary of White. Bidney and White were also almost the only correspondents to whom Kroeber ever underlined words for emphasis.

75. See for example, ALKP: ALK-D. Aberle, 9/16/53, 11/5/53; ALK-Bagby, 9/8/52; ALK-Bidney, 3/26/45, 8/1/46, 9/17/46, 12/18/46, 1/24/47, 2/12/47, 9/15/53, 6/3/54; ALK-P. Fejos; 5/5/53; ALK-Guggenheim Foundation, 2/3/50, 3/9/51.

Index

A

Aleut 44

Algonkin 68, 81, 82, 83, 84, 85, 86, 91, 91–92, 92, 94, 104, 169

Algonquian 42, 57, 79, 86, 168, 196

Alsean 94

American Anthropological Association (AAA) xiv, 16, 25, 33, 41, 43, 56, 60, 61, 62, 84, 100, 101, 122, 123, 125, 127, 129, 130, 131, 151, 157, 162, 163, 164, 171, 175, 190

American Anthropologist (AA) 64, 76, 84, 102, 152, 157, 158–171, 171

American Association for the Advancement of Science (AAAS) 101, 106, 157

American Council of Learned Societies (ACLS) 110, 110–113, 120, 123, 130, 131, 132, 157, 195, 199

American Museum of Natural History 53, 54, 127, 157

Anthropology x, xi, xii, xiii, xiv, xv, xvi, 4, 5, 10, 12, 13, 15, 16, 23, 24, 26, 29, 30, 32, 34, 35, 41, 43, 44, 52, 54, 55, 56, 57, 61, 108, 109, 110, 112, 118, 124, 128, 131, 136, 137, 147, 149, 155, 175, 179, 184, 185, 186, 187, 193, 200

Anthropos 90, 165

A Preliminary Sketch of the Mohave Indians 50, 164

Arapaho 32, 80, 82, 91, 92, 165

Archaeology 4, 9, 15, 26, 29, 31, 32, 38, 45, 49, 52, 108, 109, 110, 160, 172, 177, 185, 187

Archaeopteryx 22

Aztec 78, 193

B

BAE 23, 25, 40, 41, 51, 61, 88, 101, 111, 122, 157, 159, 161, 166, 168, 170

Bancroft Library xv, 11

Beothuk 91, 104

Berkeley xv, 9, 11, 13, 27, 30, 32, 41, 49, 50, 52, 53, 54, 79, 87, 88, 98, 100, 107, 112, 113, 114, 116, 118, 120, 121, 124, 159, 160, 161, 162, 166, 167, 168, 181, 186, 188, 189, 193, 195

Bidney, D. xvi, 4, 133, 135, 136, 137, 138, 140, 141, 142, 143, 144, 146, 147, 148, 149, 151, 152, 153, 156, 158, 177, 178, 200

Bloomfield, L. xv, 7, 11, 29, 115, 123, 125, 126, 128, 130, 159, 174

Board of Education, California State 115, 120

Boasian Ascendancy x, xv, 4, 23, 35, 56, 135, 149, 156

Boasians x, xi, xii, xiii, xv, 4, 6, 7, 11, 12, 13, 14, 15, 17, 18, 23, 24, 27, 31, 33, 34, 35, 37, 38, 40, 41, 42, 44, 51, 55, 56, 57, 58, 60, 61, 64, 80, 84, 85, 103, 110, 120, 135, 136, 137, 139, 144, 146, 149, 150, 151, 156, 160, 171, 176, 183, 184, 196

Boas Plan 24, 58, 111, 122, 171, 172

Bopp, F. 34

Breal, M. 35

C

California languages 18, 30, 39, 40, 42, 50, 57, 75, 90, 94, 102, 118, 190, 191

Chardin, T. 20

Cheyenne 92

Chimariko 65, 66, 67, 68, 87, 89, 120, 161, 177, 191, 198

Chinese 25, 105, 107, 120, 194

Chinook 27, 91, 95, 96, 105, 159

Chinookian 94

Chontal 39, 87, 89, 165

Chumash 39, 97, 98, 117, 120, 165, 198

Civilization xii, 14, 15, 16, 166, 178, 179

Columbia University 27, 169, 171

Committee on American Indian Linguistics 110, 122

Configurations of Culture Growth 12, 17, 21, 136, 140, 151, 166, 172

Coos 91, 94, 95, 96, 97

Costanoan 10, 65, 66, 72, 90, 165

Cultural anthropology xvi, 26, 29, 43, 108, 147

Cultural evolution ix, x, 4, 6, 9, 16, 17, 18, 19, 21, 28, 34, 36, 37, 38, 43, 47, 135, 136, 149

Culture x, xi, xiii, xv, xvi, 4, 6, 9, 13, 14, 15, 18, 19, 20, 21, 22, 23, 25, 28, 34, 36, 37, 38, 40, 43, 45, 46, 47, 88, 105, 109, 124, 135, 136, 137, 138, 139, 140, 141, 142, 143, 144, 147, 148, 149, 150, 152, 153, 156, 163, 167, 169, 178, 179, 180, 182, 186, 187, 188, 189, 193, 196, 197

Culturology 136

D

Dangberg, G. 117, 119
Darnell, R. xv, xvi, 4, 8, 10, 23, 27, 29, 40, 41, 43, 51, 56, 57, 59, 60, 61, 62, 64, 87, 88, 101, 111, 160, 171, 173, 175, 176, 177, 184, 187, 190, 191, 192, 193
Darwin, C. x, 17, 18, 19, 21, 22, 28, 35, 146, 167, 179, 186, 194
Darwinian Centennial 146
de Angulo, J. 113, 114, 115, 116, 119, 121, 159, 161, 195
Diffusion 13, 21, 31, 35, 36, 38, 41, 45, 46, 68, 78, 89, 90, 105, 149, 150, 155, 159, 166, 172, 179, 180, 182
Dixon, R.B. 10, 18, 25, 31, 36, 38, 39, 40, 41, 42, 44, 50, 57, 58, 64, 65, 66, 69, 70, 72, 73, 80, 83, 84, 86, 87, 90, 91, 98, 100, 101, 102, 117, 119, 137, 161, 177, 180, 182, 190, 191, 195, 197, 198
Dolores, J. 120
Drift xiii, 7, 105, 106, 108, 173, 175, 194

E

Eighteen Professions 84, 88, 165
Emergent complex systems ix
Emergent levels 16, 19, 143, 144, 149
Emic 7, 89
Ethnography xiv, 4, 24, 27, 33, 49, 52, 63, 79, 109, 172, 181
Etic 7, 89

Evolution ix, x, xi, xiii, xiv, 4, 6, 7, 8, 9, 16, 17, 18, 19, 20, 21, 22, 26, 28, 34, 35, 36, 37, 38, 39, 40, 43, 45, 47, 69, 105, 135, 136, 137, 138, 139, 146, 147, 149, 150, 153, 154, 155, 156, 159, 162, 166, 167, 169, 171, 172, 174, 175, 176, 178, 179
Evolutionism 149, 155, 171, 172
Evolution or Diffusion 45, 159

F

Frachtenberg, L. 91, 94, 96
Freud, S. 17

G

Galapagos 18, 144, 165
General Anthropology 46, 159
Germany 38, 93, 127, 192, 200
Gifford, E.W. 16, 32, 162, 189
Glottochronology 38
Goddard, P.E. 52, 53, 54, 61, 63, 79, 95, 100, 102, 103, 106, 117, 162, 176, 186
Golla, V. xiii, 5, 8, 9, 10, 44, 45, 49, 52, 53, 54, 56, 60, 61, 74, 79, 80, 81, 82, 84, 91, 94, 97, 98, 106, 162, 176, 187, 188, 191, 193
Grammar 13, 23, 27, 36, 37, 38, 39, 41, 46, 47, 51, 56, 59, 65, 66, 68, 71, 79, 89, 90, 100, 106, 117, 177, 182, 199
Grimm, J. 35

H

Handbook of American Indian Languages 25, 27, 45, 109, 159, 161, 170

Handler, R. xv, 10, 159, 161, 163, 176

Harrington, J.P. 10, 36, 61, 62, 63, 97, 116, 117, 119, 121, 181, 190

Harris, M. 4, 5, 136, 150, 163, 175, 176

Harvard University 41, 127

Hearst, P.A. 49, 53

Hewett, E.L. 63

Historical linguistics xi, xiii, 6, 31, 37, 40, 42, 44, 63, 66, 112, 180, 183, 193

Historical Particularism xii, 55, 182

Hodge, F.W. 40, 83, 84

Hokan 49, 51, 57, 67, 74, 87, 89, 91, 94, 98, 100, 103, 104, 118, 119, 165, 170, 195, 196, 197, 198

Hoopa 120, 121

Hrdlicka, H. 24, 157, 189

Hupa 79, 120, 132, 170, 181

Hymes, D. 4, 5, 15, 25, 26, 28, 29, 30, 31, 32, 33, 34, 37, 38, 44, 101, 163, 167, 171, 183, 184, 193

I

ICOA 62

India 64, 65

Indo-European xi, xiii, 6, 15, 20, 28, 34, 35, 36, 37, 39, 42, 45, 46, 56, 60, 68, 69, 70, 83, 90, 95, 101, 102, 111, 112, 166, 175, 176, 177, 181, 185, 191, 195

International Congress of Americanists 59, 61, 62

Ishi 60, 61, 65, 188, 189

J

Jacobs, M. 115, 163, 175

Jones, W. 34

Journal of American Linguistics 88

K

Kalapuyan 91, 94

Kato 79

Kidder, A.V. 122, 123, 124, 127, 128, 131, 132, 199

Kinship 12, 18

Klamath River 33, 196

Kluckhohn, C. 135, 143, 149

Koerner, K. xv, 7, 158, 160, 161, 163, 164, 167, 170, 172, 173, 176, 181, 182

Kymograph 120

L

Language: An Introduction to the Study of Speech 11, 170, 174

Leland, W.G. 123, 125, 126, 127, 128, 130, 132

Linguistic phylogeny 14

Linguistics ix, xi, xii, xiii, xv, xvi, 1, 3, 4, 6, 8, 9, 10, 14, 15, 23, 24, 25, 26, 27, 28, 29, 30, 31, 32, 35, 37, 38, 40, 42, 44, 45, 48, 49, 50, 51, 52, 54, 55, 56, 58, 59, 60, 61, 62, 63, 66, 67, 68, 69, 70, 77, 80, 84,

87, 88, 90, 91, 93, 94, 97, 99, 101, 105, 106, 107, 108, 109, 110, 111, 112, 114, 115, 116, 118, 120, 122, 125, 127, 128, 131, 144, 160, 161, 163, 164, 166, 170, 171, 172, 173, 175, 176, 177, 180, 181, 183, 184, 192, 193, 194
Linguistic Society of America 9, 29, 162
Lowie, R. 12, 13, 21, 51, 56, 58, 85, 88, 114, 121, 141, 157, 158, 167, 174, 175

M

Maidu 39, 66, 67, 68, 69, 72, 73, 89, 95, 119, 161, 177
Maiduan 10, 90
Mason, J.A. 117, 120, 177
Materialism 16
Maya-Tsimshian 39
Merriam, C. 52, 186
Michelson, T. 37, 80, 85, 86, 92, 93, 101, 111, 112, 128, 168, 169, 191
Mitochondrial DNA 38
Miwok 65, 66, 72, 90, 95, 117, 118, 119, 197
Mohave 33, 50, 51, 119, 164, 167, 181, 199
Morgan, L.H. xiv, 136
Morpho-phonemics 25
Muskogean 94

N

Na Dene 7, 44, 74, 75, 87, 93, 169
Nahuatl 60, 169, 193

National Anthropological Archives xv
National Research Council (NRC) 122
Near East 13
Nelson, N. 16, 168
New synthesis 95
North American languages 23, 80, 105
Northwest Coast 20, 21, 32, 159

O

Oceanic cultures 13
Old World xi, xiii, 6, 13, 15, 21, 28, 31, 34, 35, 37, 42, 44, 56, 81, 87, 173
Oregon 33, 78, 90, 94, 95, 96, 115, 170, 196
Orthogenic evolution 7
Orthography Committee 25, 60, 61, 73, 87
Ostwald, W. 151

P

Paiute 56, 59, 60, 78, 89, 117, 119, 169, 197
Paleontology 18, 20, 70, 185
Paleo-species 15
Papago 78, 117, 120, 132
Penutian 10, 42, 44, 49, 57, 67, 87, 89, 90, 91, 94, 95, 96, 97, 100, 103, 104, 170, 195, 196, 197
Peru 4, 160
Philippines 13, 166
Philology 32, 162, 163
Phoneme 7
Phylogeny 14, 36, 45, 70, 82

Physical anthropology 24, 26, 29, 184
Piman 60
Pinner, B. 11, 121, 186
Pomo 42, 66, 67, 68, 117, 119
Powell, J.W. 23, 24, 25, 60, 61, 62, 64, 75, 76, 80, 160, 168, 191
Psychoanalysis 10, 17, 87, 109, 110, 187, 191
Putnam, F.W. 28, 49, 50, 52, 53, 79, 186, 187

R

Radcliffe-Brown, A.R. 146, 200
Radin, P. 36, 60, 74, 80, 81, 100, 101, 102, 103, 105, 106, 117, 118, 119, 168, 192, 193
Rask, E. 34
Reichard, G. 115
Relationship of the Indian Languages of California 64, 161, 177
Richardson, J. 12, 166
Ripley, W. 40
Ritwan 67
Rivers, W. 12, 18, 163, 169, 196

S

Salish 74, 76, 77, 78, 96, 184, 188
Saltation 69
San Joaquin Valley 33, 196
Schleicher, A. 35
Seri 39, 74, 87, 89, 165
Shasta 65, 66, 67, 69, 71, 117, 119, 177

Shoshonean 48, 60, 67, 103, 119, 165, 197
Siouan 93, 103, 104, 118, 119
Siuslaw 91, 94, 96
Smithsonian Institution 63, 122, 162, 189
Spencer, H. x, xiv, 138, 147
Steward, J 4, 5, 11, 16, 17, 29, 30, 33, 136, 171, 183, 186, 190, 195
Stimulus Diffusion 21, 166
Stratigraphy 47
Style 5, 8, 14, 20, 33, 195
Superorganic xvi, 4, 12, 16, 19, 20, 34, 56, 84, 85, 88, 90, 98, 99, 133, 135, 136, 137, 138, 139, 142, 143, 147, 148, 149, 151, 154, 156, 165, 169
Swadesh, M. 38, 62, 123, 125, 128, 172, 173, 182, 184
Swanton 10
Swanton, J.R. 10
SWJA 149

T

Takelma 59, 78, 90, 91, 94, 96, 170
Taxonomy 193
The Ancient Oikoumene as an Historic Culture Aggregate 13, 166
The Determination of Linguistic Relationship 64, 165, 177
Tlingit 74, 81, 93, 162
Tones 25, 120, 121
Tozzer, A.M. 125, 126, 127, 128, 129, 130, 131, 132, 188, 192, 199, 200
Tsimshian 39, 77, 95, 96

Tylor, E. xiv, 173

U

UCPAAE 78, 100, 101, 157, 161, 162, 164, 165, 168, 170, 171, 187
Uhle, M. 52, 107
Uniformitarian 46
University of California 27, 32, 100, 157, 162, 165, 186
University of Pennsylvania 51, 117
Utian 90
Uto-Aztecan 59, 60, 68, 75, 76, 77, 94, 104, 169, 193, 198
Uto-Aztekan-Algonkan 39

V

Vera causa 17
Vocabulary xii, 23, 33, 36, 37, 39, 41, 46, 47, 49, 51, 59, 65, 81, 100, 140, 188
Voegelin, C.F. 45, 58, 172, 183

W

Washo 97, 98, 117, 119, 165, 170, 196
Waterman, T.T. 75, 76, 77, 80, 87, 88, 181, 188, 190
White, L. xiii, xvi, 16, 133, 135, 136, 137, 140, 142, 143, 144, 146, 147, 148, 149, 150, 151, 153, 154, 155, 156, 158, 167, 172, 175, 177, 200
Whorf, B. 14, 172, 178
Wintun 66, 72, 95, 96, 117, 119, 197
Wissler, C. 125, 127

Wiyot 7, 57, 79, 80, 81, 82, 83, 84, 85, 86, 118, 169
World War Two xii, 16, 34, 44, 135

Y

Yana 48, 51, 53, 59, 60, 64, 65, 66, 67, 68, 69, 71, 72, 73, 74, 78, 79, 100, 167, 170, 188
Yokuts 33, 66, 72, 89, 95, 96, 117, 118, 164, 196, 197, 198
Yuki 33, 97, 98, 103, 117, 118, 120, 121, 122, 164, 167, 195, 196, 199
Yuman 33, 39, 74, 117, 119, 165
Yurok 7, 33, 39, 42, 57, 74, 75, 76, 77, 78, 79, 80, 81, 82, 83, 84, 85, 86, 114, 117, 118, 120, 169, 196, 199

Z

Zuni 93, 104, 165, 193